THIRD WORLD COOPERATION

To My Parents

THIRD WORLD COOPERATION

The Group of 77 in UNCTAD

MARC WILLIAMS

Pinter Publishers, London
St. Martins Press, New York

© Marc Williams, 1991

First published in Great Britain in 1991 by
Pinter Publishers Limited
25 Floral Street, London WC2E 9DS

British Library Cataloguing in Publication Data

A CIP catalogue record for this book is available from
the British Library.

ISBN 0 86187 154 5

First published in the United States of America in 1991

ISBN 0-312-05725-3

Library of Congress Cataloging-in-Publication Data

Williams, Marc.
    Third World cooperation : the group of 77 in UNCTAD / Marc Williams.
        p. cm.
    Based on the author's thesis (Ph. D.) — University of London, 1986.
    Includes bibliographical references and index.
    ISBN 0-312-05725-3
    1. International economic relations — Developing countries.
    2. Developing countries — Commercial policy. 3. Group of 77.
    4. United Nations Conference on Trade and Development. 5. General Agreement on Tariffs and
    Trade (Organization) I. Title.
    HF1413.W54 1991
337'.09172'4 — dc20   90-22680
                                                                                 CIP

Typeset by The Castlefield Press Ltd, Wellingborough, Northants in Ehrhardt 10/12 pt.
Printed and bound in Great Britain by Biddles Ltd, Guildford and Kings Lynn

Contents

List of tables

Acknowledgements

This study could not have been completed without the support and assistance of a large number of individuals. I am indebted to the many diplomats in Geneva who gave so freely of their time. I am also very grateful to the various UNCTAD officials who not only answered my questions but also assisted in the collection of documentary material. I am especially grateful to James Mayall, who provided guidance and encouragement at a crucial stage in the evolution of this work. Carlos Fortin, Andrew Williams, Michelle Weldon. Geoffrey Goodwin, Michael Donelan, Rosemary Taylor, Clarence de Gama Pinto, Rosemary Foot, Tim Kennedy and Roderick Ogley at various stages read and commented on all or part of the manuscript.

This book is an abridged and updated version of a doctoral dissertation presented to the University of London in 1986.

Financial support was provided by the Economic and Social Research Council and the University of Sussex. I would also like to express my appreciation to Sue Dunkley, Carroll Brown and Ellice Begbie who typed earlier versions of this manuscript.

Marc Williams

List of abbreviations

AASM	Association of African and Malagasy States
ASEAN	Association of South East Asian Nations
BTN	Brussels Tariff Nomenclature
CACM	Central American Common Market
CARICOM	Caribbean Community and Common Market
CCP	Committee on Commodity Problems
CECLA	Special Committee on Latin American Co-ordination
CECON	Inter-American Special Committee for Consultations and Negotiations
CF	Common Fund
CIAP	Inter-American Committee of the Alliance for Progress
CIEC	Conference on International Economic Cooperation
DIC	Developing Island Country
ECA	Economic Commission for Africa
ECAFE	Economic Commission for Asia and the Far East
ECDC	Economic Cooperation Among Developing Countries
ECLA	Economic Commission for Latin America
ECOSOC	Economic and Social Council
EEC	European Economic Community
ESCAP	Economic and Social Commission for Asia and the Pacific
FAO	Food and Agriculture Organisation
G75	Group of Seventy-five
G77	Group of Seventy-seven
GATT	General Agreement on Tariffs and Trade
GSP	Generalised System of Preferences
IAEA	International Atomic Energy Agency
IBRD	International Bank for Reconstruction and Development
ICA	International Commodity Agreement (Arrangement)
ICCICA	Interim Co-ordinating Committee for International Commodity Agreements
IMF	International Monetary Fund
IPC	Integrated Programme for Commodities
IRB	International Resources Bank
ITO	International Trade Organisation
LAFTA	Latin American Free Trade Area

LDC	Less Developed Country
LDDC	Least Developed Developing Country
LLC	Land-locked Country
MFN	Most Favoured Nation
MSA	Most Seriously Affected (country)
MTN	Multilateral Trade Negotiations
NAM	Non-Aligned Movement
NIC	Newly Industrialising Country
NIEO	New International Economic Order
OAS	Organisation of American States
OAU	Organisation of African Unity
OECD	Organisation for Economic Cooperation and Development
OPEC	Organisation of Petroleum Exporting Countries
SCP	Special Committee on Preferences
SELA	Latin American Economic System
SITC	Standard International Trade Classification
TDB	Trade and Development Board
UK	United Kingdom
UN	United Nations
UNCTAD	United Nations Conference on Trade and Development
UNGA	United Nations General Assembly
US	United States of America

1 Introduction

The focus of the study

The Third World's attempt to reform the international economic order sprang to prominence in the 1970s with the onset of the New International Economic Order (NIEO) negotiations. The demise of the NIEO, global recession and debt crises in the 1980s have pushed global economic reform initiated by Third World states to the back of the contemporary international agenda. Nevertheless, in the face of Western indifference and hostility and increased economic differentiation and disparity, the Third World coalition has remained in existence. The Group of 77 (G77) is the central instrument through which the developing countries have attempted to transform international regimes in trade and payments.[1] The G77 not only articulates and aggregates the interests of over 100 countries, it also functions as the principal collective negotiating instrument of the developing world in international development diplomacy.

A central purpose of this book is to explain the creation and maintenance of this Third World coalition. The importance of the G77 to its membership lies in its ability to transform international economic relations. A survey of the Third World's challenge to the liberal international economic order reveals limited overall success and for specific members of the coalition the gains may be even more modest. This study attempts to explore the reasons why, despite the wide-ranging diversity of its membership, the absence of a permanent institutional framework and the uneven impact of global capitalism on its membership, the G77 remains in existence. A second aim is to assess the ways in which the cleavages in the G77 affect its bargaining behaviour. This book tries to show the impact of cleavages on the creation of a common G77 position and the influence of these cleavages in the ensuing negotiations with other groups. A final purpose of the book is to explore the importance of organisational characteristics on development diplomacy. It attempts to assess the importance of institutional venue, socialisation and organisational dynamics in structuring outcomes in development diplomacy.

From its creation in 1964 the United Nations Conference on Trade and Development (UNCTAD) assumed the key institutional role in the campaign by the developing countries to reform the international economic order. This book examines the G77 within the specific organisational context' of UNCTAD. UNCTAD's organisational activities can be divided into three distinct phases. I term the first period (1968–73) 'the formative phase'. In this period the organisation slowly expanded its competence and politics moved from a confrontational to a mildly constructive dialogue. The second period (1974–80) can be termed 'the militant phase'. This period coincided with the Third World's campaign for the NIEO. And although almost all NIEO demands had been voiced in the preceding period, the increased politicisation served to heighten the profile of the organisation.[2] This was UNCTAD's most active period and politics in the organisation rarely shifted from the confrontational mode. I term the third period (1981–present) 'the retreat phase'. It began in a mood of confrontation, but after UNCTAD VI in 1983 a more pragmatic approach has been taken. UNCTAD has retreated from its high profile partly as a result of attacks on its mandate by the United States, partly as a consequence of its failure to produce concrete results during its second phase and partly because it has been marginalised by the changing international political economy. In a sense, UNCTAD has been fighting for its survival during this period; apart from warding off attacks from the developed countries it has had to prove that it is still relevant to the needs of its most active constituency. UNCTAD, of course, cannot be abstracted from the international political economy. In what follows the effect of changes in the international political economy on UNCTAD's capacity to effect regime change and on the state of the North–South dialogue will be an important consideration. From the creation of UNCTAD to the present a five-fold periodisation is discernible in international development diplomacy: namely, 1964–68, 1968–74, 1974–76, 1976–80, 1980–present. It was only during the first of these periods that the international climate was at all propitious for the negotiation of the type of regime change sought by the Third World. Although the long wave of capitalist expansion after World War II did not end until about 1972, the series of monetary crises from 1968 onwards made the industrialised states turn inward. The outward-looking policy which had ushered in the first development decade in 1961 was effectively buried by 1969. During the 1974–76 period the power of the oil weapon gave the Third World its best chance of increasing its influence in global negotiations. The waning of the leverage of the oil weapon led to the resumption of old patterns. The period 1976–80 was a period of residual oil power but the second 'oil shock' in 1979, the subsequent global recession and the increasingly unlikely prospect of wide-ranging Third World commodity power effectively ended any hopes that the new poor power could bring meaningful change. In the 1980s the North–South dialogue has been shelved as a result of the debt crises, increased economic differentiation in the Third World, the negative response of the leading industrialised countries to Third World demands and the primacy accorded to market solutions. A history of the G77 would entail an examination of its activities in all the international fora in which it is an active participant.

This book is not a historical account of the G77 and therefore does not document the behaviour of the group in various international organisations. A central assumption of this study is that an investigation confined to the G77 in UNCTAD will provide an adequate explanation of the nature and behaviour of the wider coalition. Thus, although the empirical data is drawn solely from the UNCTAD context, the conclusions can be generalised to cover the G77 in other organisational contexts.

Plan of the book

The division of the book into three sections reflects certain underlying assumptions. Three characteristics are held to be important in the search for an explanation of coalition formation and maintenance. The first is a historical perspective.[3] The pattern of interactions in the past and the particular processes of transformation experienced serve to structure the existing set of relations in the present. To understand and to explain the current role of the coalition it is necessary to investigate the origins of the coalition and to trace its historical development. Chapters 2 and 3 provide detailed historical analysis of the origins of Third World cooperation on economic issues at the global level. The mass aggregation of Third World demands could only have taken place within the framework of international organisation. The weak bargaining position of the developing countries in international trade and finance and the lacunae in international institutions dealing with trade and development issues led these countries to increase their demands on the UN system. We therefore investigate the growth of Third World solidarity within the context of the UN and also the General Agreement on Tariffs and Trade (GATT), the major postwar organisation responsible for trading issues. It was at UNCTAD I that the G77 first emerged as a significant force in world politics and therefore the immediate origins of the group are to be found in a consideration of events at this conference. Chapter 2 traces the development of cooperation in the UN system and Chapter 3 analyses intra-G77 relationships at UNCTAD I. A deficiency of most North–South studies and indeed of studies on the Southern coalition is the absence of a historical perspective. In tracing the origins of the coalition prior to its creation in 1964 this book hopes to provide a useful corrective to prevailing interpretations. Studies which focus on the G77 only from the 1970s are apt to see the intense political climate of the NIEO dialogue as essential to Third World unity. In looking at events before the onset of the NIEO discussions we provide a focus which allows explanation of the G77's behaviour to be situated in a wider historical context.

Secondly, explanation must come to terms with the reciprocal interactions between organisational identity and the roles played by members of the organisation. The G77 is not independent of nor autonomous from an organisational basis; and the modalities of organisational behaviour are affected by the demands, needs and interventions of the member states. Chapters 4 and 5 investigate the organisational framework and assess the importance of structural and process variables. Realist, state-centric analyses of international organisation tend to reduce the activities of the organisation to the characteristics of its members.[4] The approach adopted here explicitly rejects this form of reductionism and posits the existence of a subtle and continuous interactive process of influence between states and international organisations. The behaviour of the G77 cannot be reduced to the attributes of its member states. Stable, regularised patterns of activity, as Sewell, noted have significant effects on outcomes.[5] Chapter 4 analyses the importance of UNCTAD as an environmental framework for the G77. Attention is paid to impact of organisational structure and the political process on decisional outcomes. Chapter 5 analyses the organisational structure and political process of the G77. As an informal coalition with no written constitution, the development of standard operating procedures are crucial to the maintenance of orderly relations among the member states. The rules and modalities of group interaction are explored with a view to assessing the effect of the institutionalisation of group procedure on group cohesion. Organisational structure and process cannot, by itself, reveal the totality of group dynamics. Only a form of reductionism could infer behaviour solely from institutional features. The analysis therefore continues with an investigation of the structure of influence, decision-making and the nature and source of conflict within the group.

Thirdly, recognition must be given to the fact that bargaining over the most important issue areas among the G77's many concerns will highlight and reveal more about the parameters of conflict and cooperation within the group than investigation of issue areas of secondary importance. Accordingly, in Chapters 6 and 7 two detailed case-studies are undertaken of the most salient issues in North–South relations within the UNCTAD forum during its twenty-five year history. The focus is not on the G77's bargaining strategy but rather on intra-G77 relations. The influence of ascriptive, attitudinal and behavioural cleavages on the unity of the G77 and the effect of these cleavages on the final outcomes are assessed. Chapter 6 analyses the negotiations leading to the creation of the Generalised System of Preferences (GSP). Chapter 7 is concerned with the negotiations on the Integrated Programme for Commodities (IPC).

Theoretical considerations

Theoretical concepts pertaining to (i) conference diplomacy and international negotiations, (ii) conflict theory, (iii) the study of political cleavages and (iv) coalition theory provide us with the theoretical frame of reference for this study.

Conflict and cooperation can be conceived as being the two separate ends of a continuum spanning inter-governmental relations. Pure conflict and pure cooperation are ideal states within any model of international relations. Inter-state relations, in other words, exhibit both conflictual and cooperative characteristics. In pursuance of their various aims and objectives, states may either find themselves in conflict with other states or may discover that they share similar or compatible goals and decide to cooperate in order to maximise individual gains. Within international organisations, this paradigmatic state of international relations is conditioned by the prevailing institutional rules and norms. State behaviour within an international organisation is constrained by the agenda, rules of procedure, various elements of the decisional process (such as voting provisions, time available to arrive at decisions, type of decision permitted) and the size of the organisation (number of members, budgetary provisions). The size and importance of the plenary and the structure of decision-making influences the political process within the organisation. The larger the assembly, the more likely it is that states will form caucusing groups or blocs. Within the United Nations system the phenomenon of bloc politics developed early in its history.[6] The development of bloc politics in UNCTAD was thus influenced from the outset by the political practices of the UN system.

UNCTAD's decision-making competence, i.e. whether the organisation is primarily deliberative or legislative is a contested issue.[7] The developing countries have argued from the outset that UNCTAD is a negotiating forum but the developed countries have insisted that it is merely a deliberative body. The unwieldy nature of the Conference agenda, the large number of countries involved and the 3–4 weeks time span of the proceedings provide definite parameters within which intra-group relations must be understood. The development diplomacy practised at UNCTAD conferences is similar to parliamentary diplomacy in that it involves public debates followed by votes on resolutions.[8] These public debates are a visible aspect of an extremely complex negotiating process. A large part of the negotiations is conducted outside the formal framework in contact groups and bilateral discussions. This private face of conference diplomacy, 'the fine art of corridor sitting' in Marya Mannes' striking phrase is not subject to scrutiny by the researcher. The researcher must be aware of and show sensitivity to this process in the evaluation of public documents but cannot have access to this aspect of the decision-making process.[9] The close face-to-face contact characteristic of conference diplomacy not only increases the ability and range of inter-governmental communication but also changes the quantity and mode of inter-state contact.[10] Moreover, this type of diplomatic exchange increases the amount and type of presssure that can be brought to bear on individual governments: for example, given the social importance of groups strong pressure can be used in order to ensure group cohesion.[11]

The type of negotiations which takes place within this general framework provide important clues to understanding the nature of intra-group relations. In so far as the G77 acts as a pressure group there are two sets of negotiations which occur in the organisational framework. First, negotiations within the group to arrive at a common negotiating strategy and, secondly, negotiations between the G77 and Group B and Group D.[12] Three distinct analytical modes of bargaining can be identified:[13]

(i)   distributive bargaining — the process in which the parties attempt to maximise their share of a fixed 'cake';
(ii) integrative bargaining — the process in which the parties attempt to increase the share of the joint gain;

(iii) Mixed bargaining — the process in which the parties attempt to increase joint gain and decide how to allocate the shares of the 'cake'.

Most bargaining situations are mixed and intra-G77 bargaining corresponds to the mixed bargaining mode. Negotiations between the G77 and Group B and Group D, however, most closely correspond to the distributive bargaining mode. In this respect, moving along Midgaard's continuum from strictly cooperative negotiation to pure bargaining, relations within the G77 are closer to the strictly cooperative negotiating end and G77 relations with other groups closer to the pure bargaining end of the continuum.[14] Outcomes are conditioned by the relevant bargaining mode and the method for arriving at collective decisions. Five ways of arriving at collective decisions, four of which are pertinent to intra-G77 relations, can be identified.[15] These are:

(i)   coercion — the attempt at injuring or threatening to injure the other party;
(ii)   persuasion — the attempt to persuade the other party by appeals to shared values or showing them where their real advantage lies;
(iii) adjudication — the use of third parties to make an award;
(iv)   bargaining — trading off different goals;
(v)   institutionalisation — the influence of persisting, stable patterns of conduct sustained by norms and sanctions, for example use of selected offices.

The first method is not relevant to G77 politics but as the study will show elements of the remaining four methods are continually used within the political process of the group.[16]

The bargaining situation, which can be defined as the interrelationship between the bargaining mode and the bargaining method, is dependent on the specific conflict strategy. March and Simon distinguish two types of conflict strategies — bargaining and analytical processes. They argue that bargaining approaches are important when disagreement over goals is taken as fixed, whereas analytical processes require an assumption that objectives are shared or 'that disagreement over sub-goals can be mediated by reference to common goals'.[17] Within the context of UNCTAD's organisational framework both types of conflict strategies have been evident. Intra-G77 relations have more closely corresponded to the latter strategy whilst relations between the developed and developing countries vary depending upon the issue-area and time frame. In the early years of the organisation when North–South relations were distinctly confrontational a bargaining process obtained across the spectrum but as the organisation matured the conflict strategy varied with the particular issue. Ernst Haas distinguishes three modes of decision-making — minimum common denominator, splitting the difference and upgrading the common interest — in international organisation.[18] As this study shows the latter two modes were most frequently employed by the G77 in order to arrive at group consensus.

Central to this study is the concept of conflict and it is therefore necessary to proffer a working definition at the outset. Conflict can usefully be broken down into the following components: (i) a conflict situation; (ii) conflict behaviour; (iii) conflict attitudes and perceptions.[19] Behavioural scientists enmeshed in a positivist methodology tend to define conflict situations in terms of goal incompatibility.[20] In other words, for a conflict situation to exist the parties must perceive that they possess mutually incompatible goals. This I term 'observed' or 'actual' conflict and distinguish it from latent conflict, where the existence of an incompatibility of interest between parties may be perceived by an external observer but is not seen as such by the participants. Thus, in this study conflict is defined as the existence of an incompatibility of interest between two or more parties.[21] Although this study is mainly concerned with actual conflict situations the analysis of ascriptive cleavages reveals the existence, in certain cases, of latent conflict. Moreover, it should be stressed that a conflict situation may arise from a similarity or from a dissimilarity of objectives. In other words, conflict is not confined to the pursuit of different goals but may arise from the pursuit of common goals.

In order to analyse the conflictual process within the G77 the concept of cleavage will be employed.[22] The G77 is a heterogeneous grouping and the political analysis of cleavages, with its focus on the effect of attribute and behavioural differences on outcomes, is a relevant analytical tool. Three types of cleavage can be identified: (i) ascriptive (trait); (ii) attitudinal; and (iii) behavioural. With regard to the G77 ascriptive cleavages would include levels of development, patterns of alignment and the structure of domestic economies. Attitudinal cleavages refer, for example, to a government's analysis of the political economy of trade and development, ideological orientations and perceptions of the benefits to be gained from the proposed measures. Behavioural cleavages result from trait and attitudinal cleavages and refer, for example, to organisational membership and voting behaviour. The existence of cleavages does not determine the political dynamics of group behaviour. It is the intensity of the relevant cleavage, i.e. the strength of the actor's beliefs, which determine the homogeneity or heterogeneity of the group (ascriptive cleavage), the existence of consensus or dissensus (attitudinal cleavage), and cohesion or fractionalisation (behavioural cleavage). The intensity of a cleavage is dependent for ascriptive cleavages on the political importance attached to a trait; for attitudinal cleavages on the strength with which a particular conviction is held; and for behavioural cleavages on the significance attached to the relevant actors' actions. The use of cleavage analysis is particularly helpful when attempting to assess the extent of division (fragmentation); the similarity (commonality) of interests; and the existence of cross-cutting conflicts and the existence of overlapping interests within the G77.

The G77 is clearly an organisation of developing countries with an institutional structure but without any formal centralised machinery, i.e. a secretariat which coordinates positions both before and during international conferences on a wide variety of issues. At these conferences the G77 attempts to bargain and to vote as one group, for example at the Law of the Sea Conferences, the 1972 Conference on the Environment and the 1974 World Food Conference. As well as this coordination and voting function at *ad hoc* conferences, the G77 meets regularly and performs these same functions within the continuing machinery of permanent multilateral bodies, such as the International Monetary Fund (IMF), Food and Agriculture Organisation (FAO), United Nations General Assembly (UNGA) and UNCTAD. Thus in purely organisational terms the G77 would fulfil the conditions for two and possibly three of the six types of groups which Hovet identified in the context of the General Assembly.[23] The identification of the G77 as a bloc, caucussing group or even a common interest group, however, does not contribute significantly to an analysis of its political process: it merely describes one of its behavioural characteristics.

The concepts of 'alliance', 'coalition' and 'pressure group' provide alternative starting points for the study of group behaviour. In the international relations literature the first two terms tend to be used synonymously or interchangeably to mean a collective organisation of states pursuing a common goal or set of goals. The terminological confusion within the literature can be overcome if coalition is seen as a generic term referring to a grouping of two or more actors (states) who have decided to pool certain resources for the pursuance of a common goal[24]. If coalitions refer to any partnership then partnerships with specific features can be seen as special cases of coalitions, that is, if all groups are coalitions, then particular characteristics will define and distinguish different types of coalitions. Thus alliances and pressure groups can be seen as specific types of coalitions. The central feature of an alliance is the contemplation of military engagement and the specification of certain enemies. Whether offensive or defensive, alliances commit the members to the armed defense of their common territory.[25] Whilst alliances have been a constant feature of international relations, pressure groups are relatively new.[26] A pressure group can be thought of as a collection of states (individuals etc.) applying pressure as a political device to secure a change (or the maintenace of the status quo) on a particular set of issues. In this respect the G77 is a pressure group exerting pressure for the reform of the international economic system, the creation of new international regimes and the transfer of resources from rich states to poor ones. As a coalition the G77 represents a temporary conjoining of interests between more than one hundred states who can increase their bargaining power through joint action.

The G77 as a coalition is by definition engaged in the pursuit of collective goods for its members. A collective good has two distinguishing characteristics. First, if the common goal is achieved all who share the goal automatically benefit; and, secondly, if the good is made available to any one member of the group it can be made available to others at little or no marginal cost.[27] But the membership of coalitions may be such (and this is more true of large than small coalitions) that in order to pursue the collective good non-collective goods must be provided for some of the membership either as incentives to join or as incentives to remain in the coalition. This is because members of a coalition have individual as well as joint interests and although individual interests are usually left to individual action it is often impossible for the organisation to serve purely common interests.

Within the context of the international political economy the members of the G77 feel that they have certain interests which are not only shared with other members of the coalition but which by their very nature could not be pursued on an individual state basis. Thus, although the mass level of aggregation at which the G77 operates is held to be a sham and essentially a non-productive exercise, it is precisely the central element of commonality. In other words, from its inception the G77 has been seeking changes in the rules which govern international economic relations and, where it has not been seeking such changes, it has been campaigning for the introduction of new norms and new policies related to economic development. Regime change can only be pursued through concerted multilateral pressure because existing instruments and modalities are multilateral in nature. It is, of course, possible for a single powerful state to to effect regime change, for example President Truman's declaration (1947) on the Continental Shelf, but this course of action is not available to the weak states which comprise the G77. Conjointly with these general demands and shared interests, the member states of the G77 have different interests and needs arising from their specific levels of development, the structure of their economies, their political and social systems and their political and social philosophies. Hence they have specific interests which often conflict and within the wide area of agreement there is divergence concerning the application or interpretation of any proposed change.

Given the occasional non-coincidence or non-congruence between individual interests and common interests, the coalition had to devise procedures whereby the common interest could be determined and in which the conflicting interests of various members could be reconciled. In the pursuit of their national interests states will not retain membership in a coalition if there is a continued divergence between the national interest and the collective interest. Neither will states continue to retain membership in a coalition if the costs of membership begin to outweigh the benefits. Thus there must be a striving of a conscious political nature to equilibrate the gains. The foregoing stipulations relate not to any objective criteria but to a perceptual process. We cannot stipulate certain divergencies between the national interest and the collective interest nor quantify the costs and benefits of membership of the G77 in numerical terms because any division is essentially a political one. The costs of membership will vary from state to state and although it is possible to categorise them as economic, political, strategic, etc., a cost is not one until it is perceived as such by a relevant decision maker. Hence it is both naive and bad scholarship to condemn states for remaining in the G77 when it can be shown that according to certain statistical evidence they would be better off outside the coalition.[28] One of the main faults with this type of analysis is its unidimensional nature.

We are not arguing that it is impossible to know in advance the likely outcome of the strains and stresses on any coalition. Rather the point is that there is a need for extreme caution in making predictive statements. Furthermore, analysis needs to go beyond objective quantifiable criteria and must examine the perceptual and psychological processes involved. It is also important to recognise the relevance of the institutional context. Institutional arrangements can either encourage or discourage conflict. The relative decentralisation of decision-making in the G77 and the necessity for unanimity, although it introduces elements of rigidity and also means that much time is expended in the search for consensus, is also valuable in curbing the level of conflict. This, coupled with bureaucratic inertia and ignorance of what is being discussed in Geneva in many Third World countries, combines to make conflicts in the G77 less dangerous from the perspective of coalition maintenance than it would otherwise be.

The existence of other possible coalitions and the question of side payments are important influences on coalition maintenance. Within UNCTAD there are two other coalitions — Group B (the developed Western nations) — and Group D (the socialist states of Eastern Europe). Membership in an UNCTAD group is largely based on ascriptive characteristics. Membership of Group D is not a viable option for most members of the G77; even those G77 members with centrally planned economies are unlikely to join. Romania defected from Group D, Yugoslavia was a founder member of the G77 and the other developing countries of a socialist orientation lack the geographical and institutional features which the Group D countries have in common. Membership of Group B would be a viable option for the most economically advanced G77 members, but to do so would require a brave decision. Membership of Group B would signal that the country no longer wished to be considered as part of the developing world. Any benefits which were currently accruing as a result of membership of the G77 would have to be abandoned.

Side payments can be understood in this context to operate in two distinct ways. The first occurs when the developed countries attempt through bilateral and multilateral arrangements outside the UNCTAD structure to provide a developing country or a group of developing countries with certain benefits that will either lead to direct conflict in the G77, such as preferential trading arrangements, or will make the country concerned lessen its support for a common position, for example the conclusion of a commodity agreement. The second type of side payment occurs directly in UNCTAD when a developed country makes an offer to some members of the G77 designed to reduce those countries support for a common position, for example at UNCTAD V Australia made certain concessions on air transport to the Philippines, Malaysia and Indonesia, which caused them to withdraw their prior support for a Singapore sponsored resolution sharply critical of Australian air transport policies.[29] These disintegrative tendencies operate in the context of positive and reinforcing bonds. The precise nature of the common interests of the G77 can best be garnered from the various declarations and collective statements issued by the G77 at the ministerial meetings held since 1967. These documents argue that the prevailing order works inequitably and is biased against the interests of the developing countries. Apart from this commonality of interest, support for the G77 also arises from the calculation that membership of the G77 provides indirect benefits. The concerted pressure of the G77 in one organisation has a spillover effect on other organisations. Thus some of the more advanced countries in the G77 can use group pressure as a bargaining lever in their negotiations with the developed countries. A Brazilian delegate observed that if Brazil were to speak on its own in GATT it would be by-passed by the developed countries: but with the weight of the G77 behind it, although the G77 is not formally constituted in GATT it would be listened to. Thus although a concrete multilateral agreement might not result from G77 pressure in UNCTAD, individual states may perceive political and economic gains in other fora to be a result of G77 pressure.

We have identified the G77 as a coalition engaged in the pursuit of collective goods. The major source of power possessed by the coalition comes from its aggregation of over a hundred states in a multilateral bargaining context. The power of the coalition within any bargaining context will be affected by the integrative and disintegrative tendencies in the coalition.[29] Members share certain common interests which can only be pursued through the pressure group. Nevertheless, the membership is diverse and this heterogeneity makes the coalition subject to splintering since members may defect to other winning coaltions or accept side payments. The stability of the group is therefore dependent on the development of procedures which negate or contain the conflictual tendencies and also provide a basis of accommodation satisfactory to the entire membership.

Notes

1. The concept of international regime is used to refer to the 'principles, norms, rules and decision-making procedures' which exist in specific issue-areas in international relations. Although a great deal of imprecision exists in the literature concerning the causal status of regimes and their relation to power resources and bargaining the concept is nevertheless useful as a description of the regulatory arrangements which exist in specific contexts. In so far as the G77's *raison d'être* is to change existing principles, norms, rules and decision-making procedures in the international political economy, the concept of regime seems an appropriate one for this study. For a discussion of regimes and regime theory see S. D. Krasner (ed.), *International Regimes* (Ithaca, N.Y.: Cornell University Press 1983).
2. In using the term 'politicisation', I do not intend to imply that these were technical issues which were suddenly injected with inappropriate political considerations. In the first place, UNCTAD is a political organisation and, secondly, such an assumption makes an untenable separation between politics and economics. Politicisation here refers to the political importance attached to the issue by the participants and the nature of the discussions which took place.
3. For a methodologically different approach see D. C. Smyth, 'The Global Economy and the Third World: Coalition or Cleavage?' *World Politics* (July 1977)' pp.584–610; and K.Iida, 'Third World Solidarity: The Group of 77 in the UN General Assembly', *International Organization* (Spring 1988), pp.375–95.
4. See F. Kratochwil & J. G. Ruggie, 'International Organization: A State of the Art on the Art of the State' *International Organization* (Autumn 1986), pp.753–75.
5. J. P. Sewell, *UNESCO and World Politics* (Princeton N. J.: Princeton University Press, 1975).

6. Various authors have identified different numbers of groups operating in the UN, for example: T. Hovet (eight), H. G. Nicholas (seven) R. O. Keohane (six), G. L. Goodwin (five) and P. Willetts (five).
7. See J. Kaufmann, *Conference Diplomacy* (Leyden: A. W. Sitjhoff, 1968) for a discussion of this and other aspects of conference diplomacy.
8. See C. F. Alger, 'Personal Contact in Intergovernmental Organizations' in R. W. Gregg & M. Barkun (eds), *The United Nations System and its Functions* (New York: Van Nostrand 1968), p.106.
9. See J. G. Hadwen & J. Kaufmann, *How United Nations Decisions Are Made* (Leyden: A. W. Sitjhoff, 1960), pp.49–54 for an account by two UN diplomats of this aspect of the negotiating process.
10. See Alger, op.cit, pp.108–13.
11. 'A group is a social system rather than a mere collection of individuals', Peter Warr, *Psychology and Collective Bargaining* (London: Hutchinson, 1973), p.13.
12. The UNCTAD political process is based on a division of its membership into groups. Group B refers to the developed Western nations and Group D to the socialist states of Eastern Europe. See Chapter 4 for an extended discussion.
13. See R. E. Walton & R. B. McKersie, *A Behavioral Theory of Labor Negotiations* (New York: McGraw-Hill, 1965), p.13, and Warr, op.cit, pp.118–21.
14. See K. Midgaard, 'Co-operative Negotiations and Bargaining: Some Notes on Power and Powerlessness' in B. Barry (ed.), *Power and Political Theory* (London: John Wiley, 1976), pp.118–21.
15. See L. Kriesberg, 'International Decision-Making' in M. Haas (ed.), *International Systems: A Behavioral Approach* (New York: Chandler Publishing Co., 1974), pp.234–7.
16. An alternative categorisation might give three modes of conflict resolution — reconciliation, compromise and award.
17. J. G. March & H. A. Simon, quoted in J. M. Thomas & W. G. Bennis, *Management of Change and Conflict* (Harmondsworth, Middx.: Penguin Books, 1972), p.21.
18. E. B. Haas, *Beyond The Nation-State* (Stanford: Stanford University Press, 1964), pp.103–13.
19. C. R. Mitchell, *The Structure of International Conflict* (London: Macmillan, 1981), pp.15–46.
20. See M. Nicholson, *Conflict Analysis* (London: The English Universities Press, 1968).
21. See S. Lukes, *Power: A Radical View* (London: Macmillan 1974), pp.34–35.
22. My use of the concept is based on D. W. Rae & M. Taylor, *The Analysis of Political Cleavages* (New Haven: Yale University Press, 1970).
23. See T. Hovet, *Bloc Politics in the United Nations* (Cambridge, Mass.: Harvard University Press,) pp.30–46.
24. For a definition along similar lines see W. Riker, *The Theory of Political Coalitions* (New Haven, Conn.: Yale University Press, 1962), p.21.
25. See J. R. Friedman, 'Alliance in International Politics' in J. R. Friedman, C. Bladen & S. Rosen (eds), *Alliance in International Politics* (Boston, Mass.: Allyn & Bacon, 1970), pp.4–5.
26. See Carol Lancaster, 'The Politics of the Powerless' (doctoral dissertation, University of London, 1972) for an application of the pressure group concept to development diplomacy.
27. See M. Olson, *The Logic of Collective Action* (New York: Schoken Books, 1968), pp.14–15; M. Olson & R. Zeckhauser, 'An Economic Theory of Alliances', *Review of Economics and Statistics* (August 1966), pp.266–79; J. G. Head, 'Public Goods and

Public Policy', *Public Finance* (1962), pp.197–219 for definitions of a collective good.

28. See R. D. Hansen, *Beyond the North–South Stalemate* (New York: McGraw-Hill, 1979), pp.87–125 for a critical treatment of the G77's strategy; also S. Krasner, 'Third World Vulnerabilities and Global Negotiations', *Review of International Studies* (October 1983), pp.235–49.

29. For a formal demonstration of the relationship between coalition cohesion and coalition power see Anatol Rapoport, *N-Person Game Theory* (Ann Arbor: The University of Michigan Press, 1970), pp.234–53.

Part I
Constructing the coalition

2   The origins of cooperation: the Third World and global reform, 1945–63

A key feature of contemporary world politics is the diplomatic solidarity of the developing countries, most effectively portrayed at multilateral conferences. This solidarity is not organic and neither was its growth inevitable. Rather it was the result of political processes within the United Nations and elsewhere. The aim of this chapter is to discuss and explain the origins of this cooperation in the period prior to the establishment of the G77. The Third World coalition is the result of a historical process. A close examination of this process will show not only how and why the G77 came into existence, but enable us to understand its longevity. The most significant political factors in the formative period were the developing countries' disillusionment with their economic position in the postwar period, their frustration with the efforts of existing international economic organisations to remedy their perceived problems and the manner in which international organisational processes structured developed and developing countries into distinct groupings and helped LDCs aggregate their interests. This, coupled with the emergence of the Afro-Asian and non-aligned movements within the context of global cold war, accentuated the self-identification of a Third World. Two important consequences for action developed as a result of these political perceptions: first, the realisation of a certain commonality of interests; the developing countries increasingly became aware of common problems arising from the underdeveloped nature of their economies and their peripheral location in the global economy;[1] secondly, the awareness that regime change could only be brought about by the use of concerted pressure.[2] These integrative tendencies were balanced by disintegrative ones from the outset. A variety of political loyalties cross-cut this bloc interest and ascriptive and attitudinal cleavages existed from the outset. Moreover, the responses of the West and the Communist states and the climate of international political relations were also salient factors affecting the process of coalition formation.

   This chapter therefore traces the origins of developing countries' cooperation on economic issues in the UN system through (i) an examination of the developing countries and the international economic order and (ii) an investigation of their diplomatic activity in the United Nations. In our examination of each of these issue-areas, close attention will be given to the development of the coalition. In other words, the analysis aims to show that the solidarity was the result of a historical process and not an already existent reality in 1945.[3]

The developing countries and the international economic order

The restructuring of the international economic system

The origins of solidarity can be found in the dissatisfaction of the developing countries with the liberal economic order instituted at the end of World War II. During World War II, American and British negotiators began making plans for the restructuring of international economic relations once the war terminated.[4] These discussions were initiated by the United States and progressed from the Atlantic Charter (1941) through the Mutual Aid Agreement (1942) to the discussion based around the plans of John Maynard Keynes and Harry Dexter White (1943), culminating in the meeting at Bretton Woods, New Hampshire, in July 1944, which resulted in the creation of the IMF and International Bank for Reconstruction and Development (IBRD). This latter conference, although a multilateral affair, was dominated by the United States and the United Kingdom. The plans which delegates agreed to had largely been decided upon in advance by the United States and to a minor extent the United Kingdom.

Given this background to the conference it obviously reflected the interests and concerns of the United States, the hegemonic power in postwar international economic relations. It was American political and economic power which played the decisive role in shaping the postwar liberal international economic order. The Bretton Woods system failed to take adequate account of the interests of the developing countries although these countries were in the numerical majority at the Bretton Woods conference. Of the forty-four allied and associated countries which took part in the conferences leading to the establishment of the IMF and IBRD, twenty-eight can firmly be classified as being underdeveloped. These countries failed to have a significant impact on the shaping of the postwar international economic order for a variety of reasons. First, the United States was the most powerful country economically and politically and it almost singlehandedly dictated the shape of the postwar institutions.[5] Secondly, the problems of economic growth and development, as they subsequently unfolded, did not exercise the consciousness of either politicians or general public in the developed countries.[6] Thirdly, the intellectual leap necessary to recognise the special problems facing underdeveloped countries had not been taken.[7]Finally, the planners of the postwar economic and political order did not envisage the dramatic increase in the number of sovereign states which subsequently occurred, thus providing both the necessity for the problem of world poverty to be placed on the international agenda and the means by which it could be accomplished. The developing countries in 1944 were still mainly colonies and hence the concern for their development rested with the metropolitan countries in which colonial development was viewed as dependent on the health of the metropole's economy. Moreover, many colonies had earned considerable sums by selling primary commodities during the war and at its close had healthy balances of payments, for example India's sterling balance amounted to some $5bn. In Latin America industrialisation had been given a fillip since domestic producers had been shut off from their competitors during the war. Furthermore, immediately after the war, there was a heavy demand for primary commodities, thus improving the terms of trade of the poor countries. The predominant emphasis on the problems of the developed market economies was based not on numerical superiority but on the prevailing distribution of political and economic power and the influence of a liberal philosophy of international economic relations.

Postwar planning stemmed from both economic and political considerations. Developments in global capitalism necessitated the coordination and harmonisation of national economic policies. An international economy had begun to emerge during the nineteenth century, the result of the spread of industrialisation, changes in the technological base of societies, the development of communication networks, the massive export of long-term capital and the high levels of European migration.[8] The inter-war period demonstrated the imperative of economic cooperation in the face of increased economic interdependence. National economic prosperity depended on the creation of a favourable international climate. Moreover, it was believed by many that a link existed between economic and political instability and war.[9] A foremost exponent of this view was Cordell Hull, the US Secretary of State.[10] There was thus on the one hand a recognition of the interdependence of national economies and the existence of an international economy, which needed global management if prosperity was to ensue for all, and on the other a clear and explicit connection between the political settlement and the economic one. This appreciation of the problems facing the world community could have remained solely at the theoretical level if it had not coincided with the interests of the dominant state within the system.[11] A liberal international economic order benefiting all countries was perceived by the decision makers in the US government to be coincidental with their own interests. The United States stood astride the postwar world like a colossus. It had expanded its industrial production whilst other countries had shrunk. A clear priority was the necessity of finding export markets for surplus production estimated to be between $10 and $14 bn.[12] Standing in the way of US exporters were the various discriminatory and protectionist schemes of their main competitors.

Two particular areas of concern were the British Imperial Preference System which governed trade between the United Kingdom, dominions and colonies and the systems of protection which had arisen in many underdeveloped (mainly Latin American) countries during the war to boost home production. At this time the American administration still felt that the British would pose a serious threat to American interests in the postwar period. The full extent of Britain's economic decline was not visible and the United States extracted concessions of 'good behaviour' in exchange for loans. The underdeveloped world represented vast untapped reservoirs where the United States could supplant the economically weak colonial powers, but needed access to these markets to be retained through the prohibition of nationalist economic policies. American hegemony was therefore in favour of the creation of a non-discriminatory, multilateral system of trade and payments. In technical terms this meant the institution of the most-favoured-nation principle, international supervision of tariff policy and the outlawing of quantitative restrictions in international trade and the imposition of fixed exchange rates and freely convertible currencies in monetary relations.

The tasks of reconstruction were conceived to be an essential prerequisite to the satisfactory working of such a system. Hence attention was focused on those war-damaged economies which had previously enjoyed a high standard of living and needed outside assistance to regain a high level of effective demand; in other words, to provide markets for American goods once again. There was also a strong political motive behind reconstruction. Healthy European economies would provide the base against which the spread of communism would be halted. Further, the European governments themselves acquiesced in these priorities since economic revival was important not solely for the sake of their countries but also for the political future of the elites. The Cold War was an added systemic consideration to those who remembered the chaos in European financial markets at the end of World War I. All concerned were determined not to repeat the mistakes of the settlement that followed World War I. It is also important to remember that Europe included important members of the states system — Britain and France — whose participation was vital for an orderly return to peace. In this context there was a justified fear concerning the possibility of recession in the developed world. The developing countries, as a consequence, were hardly awarded any priority. This lack of urgency in finding solutions to the problems of the LDCs was further accentuated by the relatively favourable terms of trade enjoyed by primary commodity exporters in the immediate postwar years.

Although the major motivation of the postwar planners was to mitigate the effects of the war, and not to eliminate poverty, the major preoccupation of the LDCs, we can still note the minor influence exerted by these states at Bretton Woods. At this conference the viewpoint of the underdeveloped countries was especially represented by the Latin American countries who were concerned about the priorities to be attached to the proposed World Bank. Afraid that the allocation of resources would be biased in favour of reconstruction, thus leaving meagre resources for developmental purposes, they proposed that the Bank should annually allocate equal amounts for reconstruction and development. Limited success was achieved by having the word 'development' added to the name of the Bank and the including in its Articles provisions that equal emphasis should be given to reconstruction and development.[13] The inclusion of development functions was a concession granted by the United States in order that Latin American countries would be willing to join the IMF, access to the Bank's lending being tied to membership of the Fund.[14]

The institutional structure of world trade, 1945–63

The developing countries played a minimal role in the monetary and financial negotiations but took a more active part in the discussions on reform of the trading system. Central to the vision of the creation of a managed system of international economic relations was the idea of a global trade organisation. The Havana Charter for an International Trade Organisation, which comprised an outline for an International Trade Organisation (ITO) and a Code of Conduct for ITO members in respect of international trade, was the outcome of the deliberations of a preparatory committee[15] and the United Nations Conference on Trade and Employment, held at Havana, Cuba, from 21 November 1947 to 24 March 1948 and attended by fifty-three states.

It is possible to identify the developing countries as a specific interest group during these negotiations.[16] From the very first meeting of the preparatory committee, the LDCs espoused a different view from the developed countries, arguing that the thrust of the developed countries' proposals was negative, in prohibiting restraints on trade rather than seeking to stimulate it.[17] They wanted the developed countries to take a more positive attitude towards trade promotion, including the exchange of technical skills, producer goods and credits and the provision of non-remunerative funds.[18] The LDCs put forward several arguments and proposals to support a claim for special treatment within the new institutions. They argued that a relaxation of the proposed trade rules would enable governments to promote industrialisation through the use of protectionist measures such as import quotas; and that the inclusion of a Charter on Economic Development would permit the underdeveloped countries to impose restrictions on trade in order to aid their infant industries. Although defeated on most of these issues the LDCs were able to secure the inclusion of eight articles covering development issues and an entire chapter (Chapter VI) devoted to international commodity agreements in the Final Act. The general tenor of the Final Act, however, was one of free trade; it was against preferential arrangements, restrictions on trade and subsidies. In respect of international commodity agreements (ICAs), it was agreed that in their efforts to help producers no measures should be taken which were likely to worsen the equilibrium situation and also that producers and consumers should be given equal weight in the negotiated ICA.[19] This left the developing countries dissatisfied,[20] although it has been argued that their economic analysis was erroneous[21] and therefore the claimed benefits, from an agreement partial to LDC demands, largely illusory. This is a somewhat moot point because the Havana Charter was never ratified and its provisions, including the ITO, died an abortive death. President Truman's decision in 1950 not to submit the Charter for Congressional ratification signalled the demise of the ITO.[22] Without US approval the ITO would have proved unworkable and other governments would not join an ITO which did not include the United States. Indeed, prior to the United States decision, only Australia and Liberia had formally ratified the treaty. With the demise of the ITO, an institutional vacuum was created in world trade, the effects of which were partly responsible for the development of the Third World coalition. The efforts to fill the gap left by the ITO and the dissatisfaction with the workings of its erstwhile successor, the General Agreement on Tariffs and Trade (GATT), provided the developing countries with a focus of common interest and a stimulus toward collective action.

The organisation that was left holding the centre of the stage was one that in many respects was ill-equipped to deal with the spotlight. GATT has been termed 'a slender reed on which to base progress toward a multilateral regime . . . [which was] permeated by an atmosphere of impermanence'[23] and in the context of the ITO, Eugene Black (the former President of the World Bank), reflected that it was 'a sad monument to our unwillingness in the late 1940s to adhere to the still-born International Trade Organisation.'[24] GATT was a direct result of the negotiations leading to the Havana Charter. In March 1947, when the prospects for the successful conclusion of the ITO were favourable, twenty-three nations met in Geneva to negotiate the tariff concessions envisaged in Article 17 of the Havana Charter. In January 1948, in the same hopeful atmosphere, these provisions were put into effect. The major aspect of this trade agreement incorporating reciprocal tariff concessions between the contracting parties was the existence of the most-favoured-nation clause. It was envisaged that with the establishment of the ITO the GATT would cease to exist. GATT is different from all existing international organisations in that it is not a standing organisation but a contractual agreement among its members. It has never been ratified by its members and exists through a 'protocol of provisional application.' But it has acquired new organisational features during its existence and has an independent secretariat[25] and various tribunals concerned with dispute settlement. The main principle governing GATT's activities is the most-favoured-nation (MFN) principle. This means that any concession granted to one Contracting Party must be extended to all others — hence the basis for a liberal, multilateral, non-discriminatory system is established. The GATT authorities favoured the use of tariffs as the only permitted protectionist device. The original General Agreement consisted of three parts. Part I contained the MFN clause and the tariff schedules of the contracting parties; Part II the commercial policy regulations; and Part III, *inter alia*, the provisions on territorial applications and regional arrangements.

From the standpoint of the developing countries the original agreement was notable for its omissions, rather than its inclusions. It excluded the development provisions and commodity framework of the Havana Charter. The LDCs' dissatisfaction with the scope of the agreement was reflected by the fact that the exclusion of the eight articles on development issues, the limitations on the use of quantitative restrictions, subsidies and preferential agreements, and the omission of Chapter VI of the Havana Charter concerning commodity agreements led only three Latin American countries (Brazil, Chile and Cuba) to sign the original General Agreement, whereas seventeen had signed the Havana Charter.[26] The specific provision of primary interest to the developing countries in the original agreement was Article XVIII entitled 'Adjustment in Connection with Economic Development'. This article permitted countries to apply restrictions to trade under certain conditions. Paragraph C therein sanctioned the use of quantitative restrictions for the purposes of economic development. Nevertheless, this could only be done to promote an indigenous primary industry and not a secondary one, or one which had developed under war-time conditions and the consent of the Contracting Parties was needed before such action could be taken.

In practice, this article was hardly ever used. Between 1948 and its revision in 1954 only four countries availed themselves of its use — Ceylon, Cuba, Haiti and India — getting the consent of the Contracting Parties to impose quantitative restictions on thirty-two commodity groups. The non-automaticity of Article XVII inhibited many developing countries from invoking it and they turned instead to Article XII which permitted the imposition of import restrictions for balance of payments purposes.

The disgruntlement at the limited applicability of Article XVIII provided one of the first unifying elements among the developing countries in the GATT. Moreover, the developing countries resented having to go 'cap in hand' to the richer Contracting Parties asking for permission to impose restrictions when the richer GATT members were unilaterally imposing restrictions to protect their own high-cost agriculture.[27] Six further complaints concerning the operation of the GATT in the 1950s tended to unite the developing countries. First, many felt that the price of entry was too high. On entry a country had to make certain tariff concessions in equivalence for tariff reductions already made by existing members of the agreement.[28] Secondly, many found that the rates at which they 'bound' their tariffs on entering GATT were too low when their infant industries began to develop. It proved very difficult to renegotiate these rates. Thirdly, the mode of negotiation in GATT favoured the more developed states, marginalising the weaker ones. The combination of the twin principles of reciprocity[29] and non-discrimination worked in favour of the more competitive economies. Bargaining focused on commodities of special interest to the more powerful negotiating countries, hence indirectly discriminating against third parties. Furthermore, the spillover of the benefits of tariff concessions to third parties resulting from MFN treatment proved limited.[30] Thus LDC participation in the five completed 'rounds' — Geneva (1947), Annecy (1949), Torquay (1950–1), Geneva (1956), Geneva 'Dillon Round' (1960–1) — was minimal. Only Chile, Haiti, India, Israel, Nigeria, Pakistan and Peru of the twenty LDC GATT Contracting Parties participated in the Dillon Round. Of some 4,400 tariff concessions only 160 bindings or reductions of duties were on items of interest to the LDCs.[31] Fourthly, the developing countries had little means of exerting pressure on the developed states; for example agricultural protectionism in the developed countries discriminated against LDC exports. Fifthly, although permitting the development of the European Community, GATT was held to be inflexible towards regional groupings among developing countries.[32] A final grievance concerned the unsatisfactory implementation of GATT reports.[33]

The identification of special interests and special needs was the beginning of a process that would lead Third World countries to cooperate in seeking institutional change. The shortcomings of the GATT and the efforts to reform the organisation led to increased solidarity among the developing countries. A key feature of this process was increased LDC membership of the GATT (see Table 2.1).

Table 2.1   *Growth in LDC membership of GATT, 1952–64**

1952	1953	1955	1957–58	1960	1961	1962	1964 (Feb.)	1964 (Nov.)
13(33)	14(34)	14(35)	16(37)	18(39)	20(43)	35(59)	38(62)	40(64)

*Total number of GATT members shown in parentheses.
Sources: GATT, *Trends in International Trade* (Annual), 1952–65.

There was no conscious attempt to construct a coalition but certain features of the organisational process tended to create the conditions necessary for the formation of the coalition. These were: (i) the overall satisfaction of the rich countries with the workings of the GATT and their resistance to changes in the rules governing world trade; (ii) the growing polarisation of opinion and the increasing stridency of the developing countries; (iii) the clearer definition of a developing country; (iv) the piecemeal attempts at reform which instead of quelling resistance only served to increase demands.

Two major reform initiatives were undertaken in this period. The 1954/55 review of the General Agreement was intended to make the GATT provisions even more stringent. For the developing countries the major significance of the revision was the implementation of a new Article XVIII entitled 'Governmental Assistance to Economic Development'.[34] Apart from liberalising the conditions under which poor countries could resort to trade restrictions, the new article was an important step in the self-identification of developing countries. It was made clear that the provisions contained in the four sections of the article would only apply to a country, 'the economy of which can only support low standards of living and is in the early stages of development'.[35] This served to exclude certain states — South Africa, Israel, Yugoslavia, Australia and New Zealand, which were sometimes classified as LDCs from this category. Nevertheless, some of these countries continued to be treated as underdeveloped. A further distinction was made in paragraph 4 between Contracting Parties with the type of economy referred to above and those in the process of development but capable of supporting a higher standard of living.

The concern expressed by delegates to the 12th session of the Contracting Parties in 1957 concerning the slow growth rates experienced by the developing countries led to the convening of a panel of experts to examine trends in international trade with particular reference to 'the failure of the trade of less developed countries to develop as rapidly as that of industrialised countries, excessive short-term fluctuations in prices of primary products and widespread resort to agricultural protection.'[36] In 1958 the results were published as *Trends in International Trade: Report by a Panel of Experts*,[37] and this ushered in a process of consultation and discussion concerning LDC trade problems which culminated in the addition of a new section (Part IV) to the GATT in 1965. As a direct consequence of the report the Contracting Parties decided in November 1958 to formulate a *Programme of Action Directed Towards an Expansion of International Trade*. To assist in this task three committees were established. Committee I was supposed to encourage general tariff reductions. Commitee II was entrusted with the task of examining the problems of international trade arising from the agricultural protectionist policies of the rich countries. Committee III's task was to examine other restrictive practices impeding the flow of exports of primary products and manufactured goods from LDCs to the developed countries. As a consequence of these studies the developing countries began to organise as a pressure group in GATT. A note submitted in May 1959 by Brazil, Cambodia, Chile, Cuba, the Federation of Malaya, the Federation of Rhodesia and Nyasaland, Ghana, Greece, India, Indonesia, Pakistan, Peru and Uruguay was the first joint action by these countries in GATT and the outcome of their first meetings as a distinct group in this forum.[38] This note pointed out the limited capacity of the developing countries to participate in tariff negotiations, noted the importance of tariffs in development policy and asked the industrialised countries to make unilateral concessions in this area. Above all the LDCs stressed the urgency of finding a solution to the problems of increased export earnings and the early provision of tangible results.[39] This marked the beginning of increasing cooperation by the developing countries in the framework of the discussions on reform. The slow pace of the negotiations and the lack of any tangible results led to an increasing stridency in LDC demands. At the 19th session of the Contracting Parties in November 1959, nineteen developing countries submitted a note to the Ministers calling for a programme of action to help their export prospects. A separate note by Nigeria called for the immediate elimination of tariffs on tropical products. The continuing gap between intention and performance continued to draw the LDCs together and in 1962 twenty-one LDCs submitted a seven-point programme of action (later increased to eight, following a speech by an IBRD representative to Committee III on 1 April 1963). The programme called for:

(a)   a standstill on new tariffs and non-tariff barriers,
(b)   the elimination of quantitative restrictions within a year (at the latest, by the end of 1965),
(c)   duty-free entry for tropical products by 31 December 1963,
(d)   elimination of tariffs on primary products,
(e)   reduction and elimination of tariff barriers on semi-processed and processed products from LDCs on a scheduled basis providing for a reduction of at least 5 per cent of present duties over the next three years,
(f)   reduction of internal fiscal charges and revenue duties on products wholly or mainly produced in LDCs (completely eliminated by 31 December 1963),
(g)   reporting procedures to help insure implementation of the action programme,
(h)   other measures facilitating diversification and expansion of export capacity and foreign exchange earnings of the economies of the LDCs.[40]

This eight-point Programme of action was discussed at the GATT Ministerial Meeting 16–21 May 1963. Many reservations were expressed (mainly by the

EEC) concerning the scope and speed of implementation. It was decided not to take specific action but to set up an action committee to clarify and elaborate the programme in more concrete and consistent terms. The Action Committee which began work in September 1963 was submerged by other developments within the GATT. First, the guidelines for the Kennedy Round were agreed upon and, secondly, the Contracting Parties began to take measures to alter the GATT in order to take account of the special problems of the developing countries.[41] This was in response to the convening of UNCTAD. The GATT secretariat and the major developed countries wanted to preserve GATT's role in the trading system and to increase its relevance to the developing countries. Hence, immediately prior to UNCTAD I in spring 1964, the Contracting Parties drafted Part IV of the General Agreement, a new chapter on Trade and Development, which was added to the General Agreement in February 1965. Another new development was the opening of the GATT International Trade Centre in Geneva in 1964 to provide market information for LDCs and a liaison system to facilitate communication among governments.

The increased LDC membership of GATT and the recognition of their special problems — weak bargaining position attributable to small market shares and low tariff structures; desire to protect infant industries and accumulate capital quickly; the ability of the developed countries to use 'waivers' which affected LDC export prospects; and the unequal results of the MFN principle — led to studies of these problems by GATT and this in turn stimulated the developing countries to press for even greater reform. The success of LDC pressure in GATT fostered the belief that collective action was necessary in order to obtain a favourable response to LDC demands from the developed countries. A recognisable caucus of developing countries emerged within the organisation and was an important forerunner of the wider coalition which would soon be formed. These developments were taking place simultaneously with the growth of collective Third World pressure on economic issues in the United Nations General Assembly (UNGA).

GATT was the most important institutional venue in the trading system in this period but developments elsewhere in this network contributed to the growth of Third World solidarity. In 1963 a study listed forty-three international organisations concerned with trade and commodity problems.[42] This was more than five times the number of such organisations existing in 1945. The mushrooming of international organisations in this field contributed to the growth of Third World solidarity in two distinct ways. First, the absence of a central organisation and the haphazard manner in which bodies were created, sometimes duplicating each other's efforts but never seeming to fill the existing vacuum, provided the basis of a common grievance and a rallying point for efforts to reform the system with the creation of a central institution. The central organs dealing with trade and related problems were the UNGA, the Second Committee (Economic and Financial) of the UNGA, the Economic and Social Council (ECOSOC), the Commission on International Commodity Trade (CICT), the Committee on Commodity Problems(CCP), GATT and the Interim Coordinating Committee for International Commodity Agreements (ICCICA). From the perspective of the developing countries these organisations were deficient and incapable of filling the gap left by the demise of the ITO. The Second Committee of the UNGA and ECOSOC had overcrowded agendas and the eighteen-nation ECOSOC was also held to be unrepresentative, hence the LDCs launched a campaign to increase its membership to twenty-four. The ICCICA, CCP and CICT were merely consultative organisations and hence of limited usefulness in attaining the goals sought by the developing countries.

Secondly, one type of organisation, the regional economic commissions — the Economic Commission for Africa (ECA), the Economic Commission for Asia and the Far East (ECAFE) and the Economic Commission for Latin America (ECLA) — were important centres where developing countries could exchange information and coordinate policy. The regional economic commissions served as intellectual centres for the development of ideas. Here detailed research was undertaken and statistics computed to embellish and support the Third World's claims for greater justice in the global economic system. The later importance of the regional economic commissions in the group politics of the G77 and the regional organisation of the G77 are direct outgrowths of this early involvement in the formation of the coalition. The supreme example of this interest aggregation and articulation function is provided by ECLA and the doctrines of Raul Prebisch.[43] Furthermore, the desire of the LDCs to play an increasingly important role in the economic activities of their regions led to a *de facto* situation where the regional economic commissions were performing functions that were questionable from a *de jure* approach. This tension between competing interpretations and the asymmetry between intent and performance came to a head at the end of the 1950s and the meetings of the three regional commissions in 1960 produced a situation where it was no longer possible to ignore their status.[44] The attempt to remedy this discrepancy and to increase the power of the regional bodies was made in the General Assembly. The result was GA Resolution 1518(XV) entitled 'Decentralization of the United Nations' economic and social activities and the strengthening of the regional economic commissions', which provided for an expanded role for the regional economic commissions.

The institutional deficiencies in the global economic system became more noticeable as the LDCs found themselves in a disadvantageous position as a result of the operation of market forces during this period. The institutional issue increased in saliency when individual efforts at problem solving proved ineffectual. Therefore it is to an examination of the (common) trade and payments problems of these countries that we now turn.

The developing countries in the international economy, 1945–63

The definition or identification of a developing country is one that is fraught with controversy.[45] For our purposes, a procedural definition will be followed. A developing country is one which considers itself as such and is generally included in this category by international economic organisations. Thus there is both an element of self-selection and independent validation for this status. Moreover, since membership, of any international coalition is both voluntary and dependent on the approval of existing members, membership of a developing country coalition will be taken as evidence of developing country status. Accepting a political definition does not imply that economic criteria are irrelevant, merely that they are insufficient as a distinguishing characteristic.

The uneven development of capital on the global scale creates a range of disparities between countries. Although for purposes of analysis the developing countries can be treated as a single group the disparities in income and wealth to be found in this category means that analysis must also be sensitive to these differences. Cognisance of the economic heterogeneity among developing countries is crucial for the subsequent analysis. The distinction between developed and developing countries, however, became the key division in the global economy. Various economic indices can be used to categorise states in the global economy. Per capita GNP, level of industrialisation, rate of infant mortality, percentage of doctors per 1,000 of population, the ratio of manufactured goods to primary commodity exports, the ratio of exports to national income, the incidence of malnutrition and disease are all indices which can be used to reveal the existence of international inequality and a stratified international society with poles of wealth and poverty reflecting the unevenness of economic development.

Two major problems — the remuneration received by developing countries as exporters of raw materials and their receipts of external financial assistance — form the background to their attempts to reform the international trade regime during the 1950s. The LDC trading pattern can be divided into three areas, namely, primary commodities, manufactures and invisibles. Trends in these three areas provided the environmental context in which economic development policies were formulated. The slow pace of economic development coupled with balance of payments problems led to a growing dissatisfaction with the existing trading system. The trading environment was a vital contributory factor in the growth of Third World cooperation. The declining share of the developing countries in world trade, the slow growth of their export earnings and declining terms of trade were three crucial problems highlighted during this period. In examining the statistical evidence presented below two important qualifications need to be borne in mind. The Korean War boom had a distorting effect on raw material prices. Hence the base-year calculations may be abnormally high thus exacerbating the subsequent decline in export earnings. Secondly, in discussing aggregate figures it is instructive to remember that these give an overall picture and may not correspond to the experience of many of the countries covered in the sample.

As a group the developing countries' share of world trade declined steadily during this period. Between 1953 and 1961 it fell by 22 per cent, the most marked increase coming after 1955 when the inflationary aspects of the Korean War boom had played itself out (see Table 2.2).

Table 2.2   *World trade: percentage shares of exporting country groups in value of exports, 1953, 1955, 1960 and 1961*

Region	1953	1955	1960	1961
Developed market economies	59	64	63	67
Developing market economies	27	26	22	21
Centrally planned economies	10	10	12	12

Source: 'International Trade and its Significance for International Development', *Proceedings* (1964), vol. VI.

An examination of the commodity composition of trade shows that in four commodity groups, agricultural raw materials and ores, base metals and manufactures the developing countries' share of world exports fell between 1955 and 1961. Only in fuels where their share rose from 57 per cent to 60 per cent did an increase take place.[46]. The export earnings of the developing countries grew slowly. Between 1950 and 1962 the developing countries experienced a 3.4 per cent annual rate of export growth to all destinations. The rate of growth of exports was slowest at 1.8 per cent to the developing country importing group. Exports to the centrally planned economies at 8.5 per cent was the only area which showed significant expansion but this was slower than both the expansion of intra-communist trade and developed countries' exports to the socialist bloc.

With 70–90 per cent of their export proceeds coming from primary commodities the developing countries were concerned at the trends in the price and volume of these products. Price and demand instability led to calls for some kind of stabilisation scheme. During this period manufactured products accounted for between 50–60 per cent of the developing countries' import bill. The movement in the relative prices of raw materials and manufactures gave rise to concern about the declining terms of trade of the developing countries.[47]

The flow of international aid increased steadily in this period mainly as a result of developing country pressure but was insufficient to meet the demand for increased capital transfers. The campaign in the UNGA to create SUNFED was a result of LDC dissatisfaction with the flow of economic aid. Table 2.3 shows the net disbursements of the international aid agencies in the period 1951 to 1962.

The economic problems experienced by the developing countries created a growing sense of injustice concerning the workings of the international economic system.[48] The pressures for remedial action to remedy these perceived ills were mounted in the GATT and the United Nations. Having discussed developments in the GATT above we now turn to an examination of LDC reform efforts in the UN and its importance in the creation of the coalition.

Table 2.3   *Net disbursement by international financial agencies to developing countries, 1951–62 ($m.)*

Organisation	Cumulative total 1951–62	Annual average			
		1951–5	1956–9	1960–1	1962
IBRD	2,301	124	243	220	269
IFC	47		3	11	15
IDA	57				57
IBD	53			2	49
EDF	63			10	53
Total	2,521	124	246	243	443

Source: Bureau of General Economic Research and Policies of the UN Dept. of Economic and Social Affairs, *Finance in International Trade (1964)*.

The developing countries in the United Nations: diplomatic cooperation on economic issues, 1945–63

Diplomatic cooperation among developing countries during this period was affected by a variety of institutional, political and economic factors. A combination of events internal to the UN and those arising from the wider network of international political relationships helped to shape a developing coalition. The grouping which successfully created a new international organisation at the end of this period was the outcome of recognisable developments. The changing perceptions of the developing countries were accompanied by changes in the fabric of world politics which affected the structure and functioning of the United Nations. Foremost among these were the effects of the process of decolonisation, which increased the representation of the Third World in the UN system; the formation of the Non-Aligned Movement (NAM); and the changes in the East–West conflict with the ushering in of a phase of 'competitive co-existence'.

Three of the six principal organs of the UN — the General Assembly, ECOSOC and the Secretariat — are concerned with development diplomacy. The General Assembly and ECOSOC provided organisational contexts within which the unity was forged and the secretariat contributed towards increased awareness and solidarity through its investigation of development problems. In both the General Assembly, specifically the Second Committee (Economic and Financial), and ECOSOC detailed consideration was given to international development policy. The secretariat in a series of reports from the mid-1950s focused attention on LDC trade problems and showed the limitations of import-substitution policies.[49]

In the attempt to translate political independence into economic independence the United Nations emerged as a relevant forum for pressure. The weak bargaining position of individual LDCs prevented the success of reform efforts in bilateral contexts. The aggregation of states in a multilateral forum provided developing countries with potentially greater leverage. However, the development of solidarity and the articulation of demands for change were conditioned by the dependent nature of their economies and their foreign policy orientations. For much of the 1950s any common interests on economic issues were obscured by the East–West conflict. Cold war alignments were frequently incorporated into economic conflicts, thus dividing the LDCs into non-aligned (after 1955), pro-West and pro-Socialist groups.[50]

Despite the existence of these divisions there were examples of concerted pressure during this period. The developing countries were united in their attempt to create a Special United Nations Fund for Economic Development (SUNFED) and the creation of the CICT in 1955 against the wishes of the United States and the United Kingdom was the first time the LDCs had been able to erect an institution opposed by the major trading states. This pressure began to be channelled more effectively after 1955 as a result of the increase in UN membership and the emergence of the NAM. Between 1955 and 1959 twenty-three new members were admitted to the UN, among them twelve Afro-Asian countries and four Eastern European states. The increase in membership sparked off a battle between the United States and the Soviet Union for leadership in the General Assembly during the period of competitive co-existence. The Soviet Union attempted to seize the initiative by making various proposals from 1956 onward for the convening of an international trade conference.[51] The developing countries dependent on the West for aid and knowing that the West opposed such a move refused to support the Soviet bid. Soviet moves also spurred the LDCs to reassert the primacy of development objectives in the face of the the wider Soviet campaign. The Afro-Asian conference at Bandung, Indonesia, 18–24 April 1955, had important repercussions for the emerging coalition. The Final Act of the conference urged participants to make greater use of international organisations, to join those to which they did not currently belong and to work together in international organisations to promote their mutual interests.[52] The policy of non-alignment gave the LDCs a common basis for political cooperation and proved attractive to newly independent countries. Non-alignment provided the opportunity for developing countries to put pressure on economic development issues without making any concessions on security matters.[53] This was still in many respects a nascent development because at this juncture security issues still dominated the agenda of the NAM. Further changes in the political, economic and institutional environments produced both an intensification of pressure for negotiated change and the evolution of Third World cooperation into a distinct negotiating group.

The year 1961 marked a new phase in the development of the coalition. The 16th session of the General Assembly, which centred on trade and development issues, was convened in September 1961 and marked the onset of a struggle to create a new institutional mechanism concerned with international trade. It was not a simple question of the LDCs combining to use their numerical majority against developed country opposition to form a new trade organisation. Rather it was a process in which the radical African and Asian states, who pressed the institutional issue, and the more conservative Latin American states, who wanted a discussion of development problems but were against the creation of a new organisation, began to find a common position. Once the conference was decided upon they pooled their efforts in order to secure maximum benefits from the forthcoming event. The organisational context provided both the opportunity and the necessity for pressure-group politics.

Certain background features influenced the discussion at the 16th Session of the General Assembly. First, the entry of eighteen new states to the General Assembly in 1960 gave the developing countries a majority in that body. Secondly, both GATT and the UN were taking a greater interest in trade and development issues. In GATT the discussions ushered in by the Haberler Report were continuing. Earlier in 1961 the Group of Experts established through UNGA Resolution 1423(XIV) published a report entitled, 'International Compensation for Fluctuations in Commodity Trade' (Posthuma Plan), which called for the creation of a Development Insurance Fund in order to counteract the 'adverse effects of instability in commodity trade, particularly in the less developed of the primary producing countries', and also urged the creation of compensatory financing schemes to protect the LDCs against 'setbacks in their development caused by instability in the world commodity markets'.[54] Thirdly the Final Act of the Belgrade Conference of Non-Aligned Nations, held 1–6 September 1961 called for the convening of an international trade conference to discuss the trade problems of the developing countries. During the debates of the Second Commitee, the Posthuma Plan and the Belgrade Declaration were constantly mentioned by spokesmen from the developing countries.[55]

The absence of unity among the developing countries was evident in the debate on international trade in the Second Committee. Although there was widespread agreement concerning the urgency of trade and development problems, fierce disagreement existed concerning the advisability of convening a world trade conference. Rival draft resolutions were introduced by six Latin American countries,[56] sixteen African states and Indonesia.[57] The seventeen-power draft resolution, which included the demand for a world trade conference, was withdrawn because of lack of support. Proponents of a world trade conference managed to attach an amendment to the Latin American draft resolution which requested the UN Secretary-General to 'consult the Governments of Member States concerning the advisability of holding an international conference.'[58] But this still proved too radical for many LDCs and the amendment although adopted by 45 votes to 36 with 10 abstentions highlighted the disunity of the developing countries. All the Latin American countries, with the exception of Cuba (at best a marginal member of the Latin American group), voted against and Cyprus, Ethiopia, Iran, the Philippines and Thailand abstained. New Zealand, an original member of the Group of 75 also voted against. The Latin American draft resolution was then adopted by 81 votes to 0 with 11 abstentions.[59] This resolution, amended in the General Assembly to placate those who did not want a conference,[60] became UNGA Resolution 1707(XVI) — 'International trade as a primary instrument for economic development'.[61]

As significant as the debates in the Second Committee was the the adoption by the General Assembly of Resolution 1710(XVI) on 19 December 1961 which inaugurated the (first) Development Decade.[62] This resolution did much to bring economic development to the forefront of UN concern and consequently, to affect the process of diplomatic cooperation among the LDCs. The existence of the concept of an international development decade did much to focus attention on substantive issues. To some extent it put the developed countries on the defensive in their defence of the existing global economic system and encouraged the developing countries to be more assertive in their quest for change.

The year 1962 was crucial both for the development of solidarity among developing countries and in the drive towards an international trade conference. The Conference on the Problems of Economic Development held in Cairo, 9–18 July 1962, was an event of paramount importance in the shaping of Third World solidarity on economic issues. Attended by thirty-six countries from Africa, Asia and Latin America it was significant for two reasons. It was the first time that the Latin American countries had attended such a conference, hence extending the Afro-Asian base to a genuinely Third World one.[63] The conference was a first stage crystallisation of a belief held by many developing countries and succinctly expressed by a Brazilian delegate at the previous session of the General Assembly,

The world is not divided merely into East and West. This ideological cleavage makes us forget the existence of yet another division, not ideological, but economic and social — that between the Northern and Southern hemispheres.[64]

Secondly, the Cairo Declaration of Developing Countries which constituted the Final Act of the conference outlined a strategy to be adopted in pursuance of international economic reform, called for common action by developing countries in the UN and GATT and strongly supported the demand for a world trade conference.[65]

The decision to convene the conference was finally taken at the 34th session of ECOSOC (July–August 1962).[66] In the face of the solidarity shown by the developing countries after the Cairo conference and the favourable response of governments to the Secretary-General's letter on the desirability of holding a conference,[67] the West gave up its opposition.[68] Further differences on the institutional issue emerged in the autumn of 1962 during the meetings of the Second Committee. Whilst the majority of developing countries were now in favour of the creation of a new international trade organisation some leading members of the grouping, such as Yugoslavia, India, Argentina, Ururguay and Tunisia, were opposed. Another issue which caused division among the developing countries was the proposed date of the conference. Although the

Third World states voted as a bloc in favour of calling the conference in 1963, the Francophone African states supported the Western view that the conference should be held in 1964. They felt that the earlier date was an implicit criticism of their association with the EEC, since one of the reasons for the proposed early date was an attempt to conclude the conference before the proposed British entry into the EEC. The Francophone African states produced another note of dissension when they abstained *en bloc* over the inclusion of the Cairo Declaration on the agenda of the committee. Since they had not been invited to the Cairo Conference they argued that the Cairo Declaration was unrepresentative of Third World views.[69] These political differences evident in the immediate period before the formation of the coalition were not dissolved but merely papered over when the G77 came into existence.

These divisions should not obscure, however, the continued cooperation on other issues. The developing countries used their numerical superiority to make their resolution the centre of the debate in the Second Committee. They displayed an impressive solidarity in the debates on trade and development and unanimity in voting. When the resolution calling for a trade conference was finally passed by the UNGA the Francophone states had dropped their opposition mainly because the prevailing mood pointed toward LDC consensus.[70] An amendment jointly sponsored by Canada and Peru ensured that effectively the conference would begin in 1964, thus removing the objections on timing of various developed and developing countries.[71]

The desire to ensure some positive results from the forthcoming conference and the convergence of interests of the LDCs participating in the Preparatory Committee provided a basis for interest aggregation thus ensuring that the fragile solidarity recently discovered did not evaporate. At the end of the second session of the Preparatory Committee (21 May–29 June 1963) the 'Joint Statement by Representatives of Developing Countries' was issued in order to stress the importance with which they viewed the forthcoming conference and also as a comment on the clear polarisation of views which existed between developed and developing countries.[72] Included in the report of the Preparatory Committee (E/3799) the statement stressed the importance of the conference for the economies of the developing countries and for the world economy as a whole. It urged the conference to adopt concrete measures to achieve, *inter alia*, the improvement of institutional arrangements including, if necessary, the establishment of new machinery and methods of implementing the decisions of the conference.

The momentum given by the representatives to the Preparatory Committee was maintained by the delegates to the General Assembly when the seventy-five developing countries issued a 'Joint Declaration of the Developing Countries' at its 18th session.[73] This document contained the demands and aspirations of the developing countries. It criticised the world trading structure, stressed the need for concrete decisions to be taken at the forthcoming conference and demanded effective implementation of decisions made.[74] This marked the first appearance of a united group of developing countries. The appearance of the Group of 75 did not lead automatically to the Group of 77. The following chapter, therefore, analyses the process whereby this result was achieved.

Conclusions

Several factors were responsible for the growth of Third World solidarity in the period 1945–63. Cooperation among the developing countries was based on a perception of common needs and shared interests. Distinct LDC demands were formulated when the liberal international economic regime was constructed. Within the existing structure of international production and reproduction the developed and developing countries occupied different places, thus giving rise to different interests. Developments in global capitalism in the 1950s heightened the disparities between the two groups of countries. The LDCs' share of world output and trade fell; their export earnings tended to fluctuate and international capital failed to migrate in sufficient quantity to their economies.

In response to these developments there were many ad hoc alliances during the 1950s in order to press a particular demand in international organisations. The burgeoning of studies addressed to the participation of the LDCs in the world economy demonstrated to these countries that their problems had to be tackled in a systematic rather than a disjointed manner, resulting in an increase in pressure over a wide range of subjects. The existing international organisations provided fora within which pressure for change could be exerted. Here the UN was of paramount importance and the modalities of the political process within that organisation, with its emphasis on caucuses, determined the creation of large blocs for voting purposes.[75] The creation of the NAM gave the Third World a distinct voice in international politics and afforded the beginning of a separation of economic from security issues. The success of cooperation in one forum spilled over into others and the attempt to safeguard minimal gains was a spur to increased solidarity. Thus a systematic examination of trade problems resulted in a demand for an international conference to discuss these issues, which in turn led to an attempt to achieve concrete results from such an enterprise. The political process dictated that only through the use of their numerical majority could the LDCs exert pressure on the major trading nations. This did not, of course, guarantee success but it was a widely held view, although some diplomats evinced scepticism.[76]

Notes

1. The introduction of the Expanded Program of Technical Assistance (EPTA) in 1949 was the first recognition of the need for special measures for poor countries.
2. The stress on solidarity has remained constant in the ensuing period.
3. Both B. Gosovic, *UNCTAD: Conflict and Compromise* (Leyden: A. W. Sitjhoff, 1972) and A. K. Koul, *The Legal Framework of UNCTAD in World Trade Law* (Bombay: N. M. Tripathi, 1977) produce ahistorical analyses of Third World unity.
4. An excellent account of these negotiations is contained in R. N. Gardner, *Sterling–Dollar Diplomacy* (London: Oxford University Press, 1958).
5. At the end of the war the United States accounted for roughly one-third of the world's total output and by 1948 controlled three-quarters of the world's monetary gold. See

L. Anell & B. Nygren, *The Developing Countries and the World Economic Order* (London: Frances Pinter, 1980) pp.35–7.

6. A reflection of this was that even the economic functions of the UN were originally conceived as an agent of 'Northern interests' in contradiction to Article 55 of the UN Charter. See John Pincus, *Trade, Aid and Development* (New York: McGraw-Hill, 1967), p.373.

7. This does not imply the absence of a distinction in economic analysis between rich and poor countries. Nor does it imply the failure of representatives from LDCs to argue the case for special treatment.

8. See A. G. Kenwood & A. L. Lougheed, *The Growth of the International Economy 1820–1960* (London: George Allen & Unwin 1971).

9. See M. Howard, *War and the Liberal Conscience* (London: Maurice Temple Smith, 1978) for a succinct discussion of the history of such ideas.

10. See D. P. Calleo & B. M. Rowland, *America and the World Political Economy* (Bloomington: Indiana University Press, 1973), pp. 35–7.

11. 'We should assume this leadership, and the responsibility that goes with it, primarily for reasons of pure national self-interest.' Cordell Hull quoted in G. Kolko, *The Politics of War* (New York: Vintage Books, 1970), p.251.

12. Kolko, ibid., pp.252–3.

13. Article III, section (a).

14. U. Kirdar, *The Structure of United Nations Economic Aid to Under-developed Countries* (The Hague: Martinus Nijhoff, 1966), p. 103. Gardner, op.cit. p. 85.

15. The nineteen nation Preparatory Committee held two sessions: 15 October–22 November 1946 in London and 4 April–22 August 1947 in Geneva.

16. Australia, Canada and New Zealand were active in support of the underdeveloped nations at this time.

17. Koul, op.cit., p.21

18. Gosovic, op.cit., p.10; C. Wilcox, *A Charter for World Trade* (New York: Macmillan, 1949), pp.142–3.

19. See Wilcox, ibid.; E. D. Wilgress, *A New Attempt at Internationalism: The International Trade Conferences and the Charter, A Study of Ends and Means* (Paris: Société d'édition d'enseignment superieur, 1949); and J. E. C. Fawcett, 'International Trade Organisation', *British Yearbook of International Law*, 24 (1947), pp.376–82, for accounts of the Havana Conference, the Charter and the ITO.

20. Gosovic, op.cit., p.10.

21. G. Curzon, *Multilateral Commercial Diplomacy* (London: Michael Joseph, 1965), p.211.

22. For a discussion of the reasons behind the failure of the United States to ratify the Havana Charter see W. A. Brown Jnr., *The United States and the Restoration of World Trade* (Washington, D.C.: Brookings Institution, 1950), op.cit. pp.362–75.

23. Gardner, op.cit., pp. 349 and 379–80.

24. E. Black, *The Diplomacy of Economic Development* (Cambridge, Mass.: Harvard University Press, 1960), p.141.

25. See K. W. Dam, *The GATT: Law and International Economic Organization* (Chicago: University of Chicago Press, 1970).

26. Burma, Ceylon, China, India, Lebanon, Pakistan, (Southern Rhodesia) and Syria were other developing countries adhering to GATT at its inception. China, Lebanon and Syria subsequently withdrew their membership. See UNCTAD Secretariat (temporary), 'The Developing Countries in GATT' *Proceedings of the United Nations*

Conference on Trade and Development, First Session, Geneva 1964, vol.V, p.444; See ECLA,Study of Inter-Latin American Trade (1956), *UN Sales No.1956 II.G.3*, for an account of why by 1954 seven Latin American states had acceded to the GATT and the reasons why the non-signatories had taken that position.

27. S. Wells, 'The Developing Countries, GATT and UNCTAD', *International Affairs* (January 1969), p.64.
28. This did not apply to those ex-colonies which, on becoming independent benefited from the arrangements previously made on their behalf by the colonial power.
29. On the concept of reciprocity see R. O. Keohane, 'Reciprocity in International Relations', *International Organization* (Winter 1986), pp.1–27.
30. See H. G. Johnson, *Economic Policies Toward Less Developed Countries* (London: George Allen & Unwin, 1967), pp.14–15; K. Kock, *International Trade Policy and the GATT 1947–67* (Stockholm: Almquist & Wicksell, 1969), pp. 232–3.
31. 'The Developing Countries in GATT', op.cit., p.449.
32. Gosovic, op.cit., p.14; Kock, op.cit., p.449.
33. See GATT Secretariat, 'The Role of GATT in Relation to Trade and Development', *Proceedings 1964*, vol.V, and 'The Developing Countries in GATT', op.cit., for differing accounts of the relationship between GATT and the LDCs.
34. Came into force in October 1957.
35. Article XVIII, paragraph 1.
36. GATT Press Release, 30 November 1957.
37. Commonly called the Haberler Report after its Chairman, Gottfried Haberler (GATT, Geneva, 1958).
38. See Curzon, op.cit., p.231.
39. Curzon, op.cit., pp.231–2.
40. *Proceedings 1964*, vol.III, pp.30–1.
41. At the May Ministerial Meeting a Committee on Legal and Institutional Framework was established to consider the 'need for an adequate legal and institutional framework to enable the Contracting Parties to discharge their responsibilities especially in connection with the work of less developed countries.'
42. 'Commodity and Trade Problems of Developing Countries', Report of the Group of Experts Appointed Under ECOSOC Resolution 919(XXIV), *Proceedings 1964*, vol.V, pp.377–423.
43. A brilliant economist, effective public speaker and skilled negotiator, Prebisch was Executive Secretary of ECLA frp, 1949 to 1962.
44. See 'Report of the Economic and Social Council, 1 August 1959–5 August 1960', *General Assembly Official Records (GAOR)*, 15th Session Supplement No.3 (A/4415), pp.38–9 paras 353–87; E/3340 part III, Resolution 31(XVI).
45. The term 'underdeveloped' was first coined in a report to the UN. See 'Measures for the Economic Development of Underdeveloped Countries', E/1986/ST/ECA/10 (3 May 1951).
46. *Proceedings 1964*, vol.VI, p.79.
47. One observer claimed that 'The immediate cause of organising UNCTAD was the worsening terms of trade between primary products and manufactures.' T. Balogh, 'Notes on the United Nations Conference on Trade and Development', *Bulletin Oxford University Institute of Economics and Statistics* (February 1964), p.21.
48. I. Frank, 'Aid, Trade and Economic Development: Issues Before the UN Conference', *Foreign Affairs* (January 1964), p.212.

49. C. L. Robertson, 'The Creation of UNCTAD' in R. W. Cox (ed.), *International Organisation: World Politics* (London: Macmillan, 1969), p.263.

50. The NAM was not formally constituted until 1961 but after the Bandung Conference a bloc of countries espousing a non-alignment ideology can be discerned in international politics.

51. For Soviet views on these issues see M. Lavichenkov & I. Ornatsky, 'Barometer of Interstate Relations', *International Affairs* (Moscow, January 1964), pp.62–8; B. Pinegin, 'Unsolved Problems of World Trade', ibid., pp.69–73.

52. A. S. Friedeberg, *The United Nations Conference on Trade and Development of 1964* (Universitaire Pers, Rotterdam, 1968) p.7, calls this the first sign of the development which would result in the formation of the Group of 75.

53. See Carol Lancaster, *The Politics of the Powerless*, op.cit., pp.44–5.

54. See E/3447.

55. See *GAOR*, 16th Session Supplement. Report of the Second Committee A/C.2/SR., pp.716–793.

56. A/C.2/L.550/Rev.1 and Corr.1.

57. A/C.2/L.556/Add.1/Rev.1.

58. A/C.2/L.559/Rev.1.

59. See A/5056.

60. A/L.379, submitted by Colombia, Liberia, Mauretania, Panama, Philippines and Thailand, requested the Secretary-General to consult member states on the desirability of a conference and its possible agenda.

61. 19 December 1961.

62. President Kennedy in an address to the UNGA proposed that the decade 1960–70 should be designated as the UN Development Decade. See A/PV.1013 (29 September 1961).

63. Apart from Cuba, a maverick in the Latin American system, Bolivia and Mexico attended as full participants and Chile, Ecuador, Uruguay and Venezuela attended as observers.

64. Mr Franco, A/PV.1011 para 13, GAOR 16th Session.

65. A/5162. The Cairo Declaration was circulated in the UN with this document number.

66. ECOSOC Resolution 917(XXIV), 3 August 1962.

67. See E/6331 and Add.4 for the replies of governments. The only developing countries to give negative responses were Colombia and Nicaragua.

68. It has been suggested that Adlai Stevenson persuaded the Kennedy administration to drop its objections. See Robertson, op.cit., p.268.

69. See A/C.2/SR.832.

70. UNGA Resolution 1785 (XVII), 'United Nations Conference on Trade and Development', 8 December 1962.

71. See A/L. 408.

72. El Salvador and Uruguay, which were members of the committee but non-signatories, declared at the 36th session of ECOSOC that they too adhered to the 'Joint Statement' and had failed to join the original signatories because their representatives had been absent. See E/3817.

73. Cuba and the Ivory Coast did not co-sponsor the Joint Declaration but New Zealand, a major exporter of primary products, did.

74. UNGA Resolution 1897(XVIII), Annex, 11 November 1963.

75. 'Had there been no United Nations the formation of a political bloc of under-

developed countries might have been deferred.' Robert Asher, 'Problems of the Underdeveloped Countries' in R. E. Asher *et al.*, *The United Nations and Promotion of the General Welfare* (Washington, D C: The Brookings Institution, 1957), p.639.
76. Robertson, op.cit., p.270, quotes a spokesman from the Third World as saying, '75 is too many. They think that votes equal power.'

3 The creation of the coalition: UNCTAD I, 1964

The transition from the diplomatic solidarity manifested in the 'Joint Declaration of the Developing Countries'[1] issued in November 1963 during the eighteenth session of the General Assembly to the permanent unity envisaged by the 'Joint Declaration of the Seventy-Seven Developing Countries'[2] made at the conclusion of the Geneva conference was neither inevitable nor unproblematic. It was during the course of the conference that this 'event of historic significance' was actualised. The aim of this chapter, therefore, is to examine the events of the Geneva conference in order to assess the pertinent factors surounding the creation of the G77. But before the conference opened in March 1963 intense diplomatic negotiations in the intervening four-month period helped to shape the emerging coalition.

The transitional phase

Between November 1962 and March 1963 definite attempts were made to develop the new-found solidarity. In New York, Yugoslavia was instrumental in organising the Group of 75 around a common programme. At these meetings strategy and tactics were never fully discussed lest the new-found unity disappeared. Nevertheless, an impressive measure of discipline was attained.[3] The preparatory groundwork for the creation of the coalition was prepared in a series of meetings in the three regional centres of the developing world. The African, Asian and Latin American states all met at the regional level to discuss the forthcoming conference and to coordinate their respective strategies. In this process the influence of the regional economic commissions was paramount.

Latin America had the most highly developed degree of institutionalisation of the three developing regions. Several regional economic organisations existed in which matters pertaining to subsystemic and global economic policy issues could be discussed. Among these institutions it was ECLA which took the lead in the planning of a coordinated Latin American response to the issues confronting the conference. ECLA's predominance arose from its possession of a coherent organisational ideology concerning the causes of underdevelopment in Latin America. This ideology stressed the relationship between the global economy and Latin American poverty. The ECLA secretariat in consultation with eight eminent economists produced a report, *Latin America and the United Nations*

Conference on Trade and Development[4] which was extremely influential in setting the framework within which regional discussions subsequently took place. The five chapters of the report covered: foreign trade and economic development of Latin America; the main obstacles to an expansion of Latin America's foreign trade; future prospects and lines of action; principal background data on the process of establishing a new world trade order; and the requisites for a new structure of international trade and ways of achieving such structures. In the light of subsequent developments its most important agenda setting role was the proposal for the creation of a specialised organisation in the UN system to supervise all international economic relations. Recognising the difficulty of establishing such an agency immediately, the report suggested that in the interim UNCTAD could act as the focus of a new international trade organisation.

The ECLA proposal for the creation of a new international trade organisation was endorsed at two separate meetings in January 1964. The Extraordinary Session of the Central American Trade Sub-Committee, held in Mexico City, 6–11 January, and the conference of Latin American Government Experts held in Brasilia, 20–25 January both supported the ECLA recommendations. Thus by the time the Organisation of American States (OAS) met in Alta Gracia, Argentina, in February–March 1964 in order to establish the general lines of a uniform policy for development, a broad consensus based on the ECLA report already existed in the region.

The Latin American position for the Geneva conference was contained in the Charter of Alta Gracia. The most striking aspect of the Charter is the attitude taken towards Third World solidarity. It maintained that the decisions taken at Alta Gracia also applied to the other developing regions. The Charter stressed that,

Latin America is convinced that an essential element for the success of this Conference lies in the common denominators that can sustain a concerted action with the developing countries in other areas of the world. Consistent with this objective, *we have proposed to establish a mechanism of coordination, not only to ensure a common Latin American front, but also to achieve unified action in the benefit of all developing countries.*[5]

Coordination of policy in Latin America with the aim of increasing Latin American solidarity and forging links with other Third World states was pursued vigorously in various regional organisations. An outcome of this process was the creation of the Special Committee on Latin American Coordination (CECLA) established by the Inter-American Economic Council of the OAS in 1963. CECLA became a permanent institution in December 1964 and became the main forum for the coordination of Latin American positions in UNCTAD until it was superseded in 1975 by the Latin American Economic System (SELA).

The Economic Commission for Africa (ECA) and the Organisation of African Unity (OAU) were both instrumental in the attempt to coordinate the foreign policies of the independent African states for the forthcoming conference. The creation of the OAU in August 1963 had ended a period of diplomatic conflict between African states. This new spirit of compromise proved helpful in the attempt to achieve solidarity. The major potential source of conflict in the group was confronted directly and a formula found which protected the interests of the opposing factions. The signatories of the Yaoundé Convention, which created a selective preference system between the Francophone countries and the European Economic Community (EEC), were determined to maintain the recently concluded agreement, whereas the other African states argued for the replacement of selective preferences by a comprehensive scheme. The ECA secretariat supported the majority position and argued that 'it would be in the long-range interest of the region as a whole to see such (selective) preferences abolished.'[6] The debates in both ECA and the OAU recognised that vertical preferences could not be abolished without the provision of compensation to the recipients of preferences. The resultant decision upgraded the common interest in that it supported both vertical preferences and a comprehensive scheme of preferences.

The sixth session of ECA held in Addis Ababa in February 1964 pursuant to a decision of its fifth session attempted to formulate a joint strategy before the Geneva conference. The agenda for the discussion was set by a report of the ECA secretariat.[7] On the institutional issue the report urged the creation of a new international trade organisation but recognised that this might prove difficult. As a second best solution it proposed that UNCTAD be created as a permanent organisation and be merged with GATT and existng organisations. The meeting failed to agree on a broad-ranging common programme but did conclude with a resolution which among other things called on African governments to establish a committee to coordinate the positions of African countries among themselves and with other developing countries.[8]

Discussions in the more political OAU took a firmer stand on the question of unity. At its first session held in Niamey, Niger, 9–13 December 1963 the Economic and Social Commission of the OAU passed a resolution calling on member states to pursue jointly common positions concerning international trade and development issues. The Niamey resolution outlined eleven areas of possible joint action.[9] It was this resolution which became the common programme of the African group at the Geneva conference.

Meeting after both the Latin American and African groups had forged common regional platforms, the Asian group had little choice but to respond in a similar fashion. The political process was developing along bloc lines and states seeking influence would be unlikely to be successful outside the regional context. It was at the twentieth session of the Economic Commission for Asia and the Far East (ECAFE) in March 1964 that the forthcoming conference was discussed at the regional level. The diverse nature of the Asian group in contrast to the African and Latin American groups was evident from the outset. Three topics not given consideration by the other two developing regions figured prominently in the discussions. The transit trade of landlocked countries; trade with centrally planned economies; and shipping and ocean freight rates reflected the concerns of interested states.

The Teheran resolution, which was adopted at the end of the meeting, reflected a conservative attitude to the institutional issue. Although the existing machinery was held to be inadequate the only innovation desired was the periodic convening of UNCTAD every two years. Moreover great stress was placed on the continued use of existing international organisations. On the other hand it supported the drive for increased cooperation among the developing countries arguing that such cooperation was vital not only for 'the immediate success of the Conference but also for their long-term interests.'[10]

Before UNCTAD I most states had been involved in some form of collective decision-making with the aim of arriving at the conference with a group consensus.[11] In the African, Asian and Latin American regions some preliminary steps had been undertaken to promote regional solidarity and to present a common front at the Geneva Conference. Furthermore, the three regional groups had all stressed the necessity for coordinated action by all developing countries. At the conclusion of this process, therefore, the developing countries came to Geneva with the readiness to cooperate, initially at the regional level, but ultimately looking beyond that to a broader coalition of all developing countries.

UNCTAD I

The United Nations Conference on Trade and Development held in Geneva fom 23 March to 16 June 1964 and attended by over 2,000 delegates from 120 countries was the first major conference on international economic relations held within the framework of the UN since the UN Conference on Trade and Employment of 1948.[12] It was the first international conference at which the North–South divide appeared as a salient feature in world politics, obscuring and relegating the East–West conflict to a secondary position. It was in this setting that the coalition was constructed. In studying the role played by Dr Raul Prebisch, the Secretary-General of the conference, and the negotiating process, we can identify key features in the process of coalition formation.

The role of the secretary-general of the Conference

Prebisch played an important role in fostering and nurturing the Third World solidarity which culminated in the Joint Declaration of the Seventy-Seven Developing Countries. In his capacity as the Secretary-General of the Conference he produced a report, *Towards a New Trade Policy for Development*, which exercised an enormous degree of influence over the conference proceedings.[13] The report largely determined the agenda of the conference and the structure of the five main committees and it also became the manifesto of the developing countries. The report's influence in agenda setting enabled it to affect the resolution of conflicting interests through compromise formulae contained in its pages. Prebisch's conference report was elevated to the status of a manifesto by the developing countries for a number of reasons. In a clear and penetrating manner Prebisch provided a searching critique of Western trade and aid policies and argued, forcefully, for reforms of the international trading system which would benefit the developing countries. In both analysis and prescription, although the report exhibited a marked bias towards the interests of the more advanced among the developing countries, it did contain sufficient points of merit to make it acceptable to all members of the emerging coalition. The report provided a common conceptual framework through which the developing countries, could first, reach agreement among themselves and, secondly, provide the bases of the arguments for bargaining with the developed countries. Key concepts and phrases, such as the deteriorating terms of trade, and the trade gap together with a concentration on the external obstacles to development with little corresponding analysis of the internal obstacles increased its appeal to the developing countries.[14] Moreover, among a plethora of varied documentation the report stood out for its brevity, clarity and forcefulness, making it the major discussion document of the conference.

The underlying analysis and arguments of the Prebisch report were not new.[15] What the report did was to produce the argument in an intelligent, closely argued and accessible manner. Moreover, the neutral air surrounding the report of the conference's Secretary-General gave these ideas greater legitimacy than they had hitherto enjoyed.

Prebisch presented a structural analysis of the causes of underdevelopment. He argued that the global capitalist economy tended to produce disparities beteen the centre (developed countries) and the periphery (developing countries). The processes of economic exchange between the two groups, unequal bargaining power and the structural obstacles arising from the nature of underdevelopment impeded the development prospects of the Third World. He further argued that the GATT was an insufficiently dynamic organisation to satisfactorily address the needs of the developing countries. He therefore proposed the creation of a new international trade organisation. Prebisch's argument that there is a secular tendency for the terms of trade of primary products to fall came in for severe criticism on theoretical and empirical grounds.[16] His estimation of a $20 billion trade gap by 1970 was refuted by studies using more sophisticated techniques.[17] Critics also argued that GATT could respond effectively to the needs of the developing countries. The criticisms of the report in Western academic and governmental circles and the positive support for his arguments among developing countries created a situation in which the report became a political issue.

Apart from the influence he exercised through his report Prebisch's control of the secretariat increased his stature and his efforts at mediation and exhortation. At the conference, members of the secretariat under his direction cooperated openly with the G75. They helped them to draft resolutions and to present their arguments. On one hand this reflected Prebisch's belief in a biased (in the interests of justice) but objective secretariat[18] and on the other it mirrored the self-interest of the UN officials who stood to gain if a new organisation was created. This close cooperation between international officials and national delegations, whilst perhaps inappropriate in such a setting, was not unknown in international organisations.[19] However, the openly political role adopted did not please the Western nations.[20] Prebisch was in constant touch with officials of the G75 and he was very instrumental in mediating between conflicting interests within the group. The institutional issue which proved the most contentious issue at the conference and which also provided the spur to greater LDC unity was largely solved due to Prebisch's intervention. It was he who pleaded with the radicals in the G75 to accept the compromise with the West worked out by the contact group. At a private dinner attended by the leaders of the key delegations 48 hours before the conference threatened to collapse in disarray, he pleaded with the assembled delegates to accept a compromise.[21]

Prior to the conference Prebisch had toured Africa and Asia attempting to get support for increased Third World solidarity. At Geneva he provided both intellectual and material input in attempting to construct the coalition. Possibly without him the diverging interests would have been too great and the fragile unity would have collapsed.[22] Together with trusted secretariat officials, Prebisch tried to devise a common strategy for the G75 and assisted their internal deliberations by intervening in the process whereby interests were reconciled.

The negotiations

Negotiations at the conference were conditioned by two structural features. The formal structure composed of the officers of the conference and the main committees was supplemented by the development of an informal structure which arose because of the inappropriate nature of the formal process. Informal groups became increasingly important as the conference progressed. The unwieldy nature of the conference proceedings and the antagonisms generated by conflicting views led to the increasing resort to informal meetings. The Conciliation Group, consisting of representatives from five developed countries and eleven developing countries, chaired by Prebisch was important in the search for compromise solutions.

The major substantive issues facing the conference had been the subject of intensive discussion prior to Geneva in the Preparatory Committee[23] and by the Group of Experts appointed by ECOSOC.[24] Discussion centred around (i) commodities; (ii) manufactures; (iii) capital flows; (iv) invisibles; (v) institutional arrangements. Mixed bargaining over commodity policy, preferences and institutional arrangements provided the immediate framework within which the nascent coalition emerged.

In the negotiations on commodity policy the developing countries were united in seeking measures to correct perceived problems arising from their reliance on primary commodity exports. They attempted to persuade the developed countries to implement measures which would remove obstacles to primary commodity exports, stabilise primary commodity markets and provide compensation for fluctuations in export earnings. The developed countries were reluctant to agree to any proposal which would lead to direct action. Most of the negotiations on commodity policy presented the developing countries with the opportunity to coalesce around a common position. Nevertheless, the issue of preferential arrangements between developed and developing countries although of minor concern in respect of commodity trade produced a heated and bitter argument between the Francophone Africans and the other developing countries.

An initial draft resolution submitted by thirty-nine developing countries proposed the elimination of preferential arrangements between developed and developing countries.[25] The Francophone African states refused to accept such a formulation since it meant the loss of the preferences they enjoyed under the Yaoundé Convention. The developing countries sought some form of compromise which would include all members of the G75 and meet the objections of the Francophone Africans. This was found by a formula which split the difference between the two groups. Support was maintained for the abolition of selective preferences with the proviso that compensation would be provided for those countries whose preferential market access would be phased out.[26] For the G75 the preference issue presented an exercise in distributive bargaining but the other, more important, aspects of the commodity negotiations corresponded to integrative bargaining.

Conflict over preferential schemes proved more divisive in the negotiations on manufactured products.[27] The ascriptive cleavage between preference receivers, e.g. EEC Associates and Commonwealth countries, and countries not enjoying such preferences, e.g. Latin American states, produced dissensus among the developing countries. In the negotiations in the Second Committee the developing countries attempted to reconcile their differences since in the absence of LDC unity no conference decision would be possible. Agreement on the preference issue was further complicated by the divisions among the developed countries. The United States was adamantly opposed to any preferential scheme arguing that it would have an insignificant impact on the promotion of manufactured exports from LDCs, would promote inefficiency, and would be administratively costly. The other major developed countries supported the idea in principle but differed on its application. The United Kingdom, Germany, the Netherlands and Denmark argued in favour of a single preferential scheme granted by all developed countries to all developing countries. Belgium and France supported a scheme first proposed by Maurice Brasseur, the Belgian Minister for External Trade in GATT in 1963 and revived by France at the conference.[28] The Brasseur Plan envisaged a system of limited scope and duration negotiated on a bilateral basis between individual preference givers and preference receivers.

The developing countries were divided over the purpose (to increase export proceeds or support infant industries); duration (permanent or for a definite period of development); coverage (equally to all LDCs or differentiated according to the stage of development); existing preferences (to be retained or to be sacrificed in favour of general preferences). This division was reflected in four draft resolutions submitted to the Committee[29] and the arguments among the developing countries. The most intense conflict occurred between the Latin American group, which refused to accept the continuation of selective preferences, and the African Associates who supported the Brasseur Plan and argued that the abolition of selective preferences could not be contemplated until their economies were fully integrated into the world economy. The Prebisch proposals formed the basis on which compromise was reached. This compromise resolution[30] fudged all the main difficulties. The African Associates agreed to support a generalised system and the Latin American countries agreed that compensation would be given to existing preference holders. The agreement reached in the G75 represented a temporary tactical retreat by the Francophone Africans. The eventual G75 position emerged and unity was attained because of the operation of a number of factors. First, the Francophone Africans were in a minority and had already lost the argument in the African group. Secondly, they were assured that the EEC would never implement any scheme detrimental to their interests. Thirdly, Prebisch and the secretariat supported a generalised scheme and lobbied tirelessly on behalf of the proposition. Fourthly, the Francophone states lacked the diplomatic skill of larger developing countries, who supported the abolition of vertical preferences. Finally, as one of the poorest constituent groups of the emerging coalition, the Francophone states needed the support of the majority for measures, for example on commodity trade, of direct relevance to their economic development.

It was the institutional issue in the UN which had been the original impetus behind the increasing solidarity of the developing countries. And it was this issue at the conference which was mainly responsible for the creation of a permanent grouping. Two major reasons accounted for this. First, the developing countries came to believe that in the absence of significant progress on substantive issues at the conference, the campaign for reform would fail to make further progress unless a new organisation was created to push for change. Secondly, the response of the Western countries to the demands for change angered many developing countries.

When the negotiations commenced on the institutional issue four different factions can be identified among the developing countries.[31] Some countries, such as Burma and Ghana, wanted the creation of an international trade organisation. The vast majority of developing countries supported the idea of periodic conferences with a standing committee. Other states, such as the Dominican Republic, India, Liberia and Malaysia, argued that existing institutions coupled with a remodelled GATT would be adequate. There was a small group of states, for example Jamaica, Nepal and Trinidad and Tobago, who could see merit in either creating a new organisation or in expanding GATT's role. The existence of these attitudinal cleavages threatened consensus formation. No attempt was made at the outset to reach agreement among the different factions. It was not until the fourth week of the conference that the issue became such a central one. The immediate cause of the frantic negotiations and acrimonious debates, which were to last until the final day of the conference, came on the 20 April when Burma, Ghana, Indonesia, Nigeria and Syria tabled a joint draft resolution in the

Fourth Committee.[32] This envisaged the Conference becoming a standing organ of the UN. Established under Article 22 of the UN Charter, it would become the highest specialised forum in the UN dealing with trade and development. It would meet periodically every three years and report directly to the General Assembly. It would be composed of a standing committee (the Trade and Development Council), specialised commissions and an independent secretariat. GATT would become a Commission on Tariffs reporting annually to the Trade and Development Council. This resolution was tabled without any prior consultations with other developing countries and the co-sponsors had been instructed by the secretariat to present such a strong resolution as a bargaining tactic in the attempt to get a unified LDC position.[33] As such the resolution was successful in that the Latin American group responded with a draft based on the Charter of Alta Gracia.[34] Milder in tone than the five-power draft, it envisaged a Conference reporting to the General Assembly through ECOSOC and an Executive Council which would be an organ of the General Assembly. The independence of the secretariat was not stressed and no mention was made of GATT. The attempt to reconcile these two conflicting positions was affected by the submission of a Western draft resolution on 6 May.[35] This resolution, although it accepted the idea of a periodic conference and a standing committee, was nevertheless wholly negative in character. The Western countries proposed that the new organisation would be completely subservient to ECOSOC. The role of the Conference was limited to that of a forum for the discussion of trade and development problems. It was envisaged that the secretariat would be an integral part of the UN and GATT would retain its autonomy.

At this stage of the conference the failure to reach agreement on other substantive issues with the developed countries and the dynamic of conference procedure contributed to the quest for compromise on the institutional issue. After intensive negotiations the group of developing countries were able to agree on a joint draft resolution[36]. The Fourth Committee considered this along with a revised resolution submitted by the Eastern European states[37] and a revised Western draft resolution.[38] The debate became polarised between the developed and the developing countries. In the negotiations which ensued the fragile unity of the G75 was severely tested. This paper unity of the G75 was to become a common feature of G77 politics, i.e. agreement on broad principles which hide conflicting interests, perceptions and interpretations.

Disagreement between the developed and developing countries focused on four key issues: the autonomy of the continuing machinery; the size and composition of the standing committee and the principle of equitable geographic distribution; areas in which other bodies should be created; and the voting arrangements. Certain members of the G75 sought to reach a compromise on all these issues while more militant states refused to consider any changes to the draft resolution sponsored by the developing countries. The radical states were successful in forcing through the LDC draft resolution by 83 votes to 20 with 3 abstentions because many developing countries voted for the draft in an outward show of solidarity confident that without Western support and hence funding no new organisation would emerge. The developed states argued that the vote was not definitive and a new phase of negotiations now ensued. Given the unease expressed by developed countries' representatives and perhaps remembering the fate of the CICT, the developing countries agreed to more consultations. Within the G75 there were two contrasting positions on these new negotiations. The maximalists, such as Burma and Ghana, believed that the resolution adopted should be adhered to, whilst the moderates, like India and Brazil, saw it as the basis of a negotiating position.[39] A small compromise group led by Prebisch attempted to reconcile the two sides but the radicals in the G75 refused to support the negotiators, accusing them of a sell-out. The original negotiators then withdrew and their place was taken by the maximalist states. Dissension within the group was at its most severe and at this juncture the group was on the verge of collapse. The uncompromising position adopted by the new negotiators failed to make any headway with the developed countries and, realising the futility of their efforts, the radicals withdrew ensuring the return of the original negotiators who managed to secure a compromise with the developed states.[40] The developing countries had forged a unity on the institutional issue where none existed at the outset and had succeeded in maintaining this unity despite severe strains and conflicting interests. Those who did not want to jeopardise any gains in GATT, such as India, and were prepared to compromise with the West and those who wanted an ITO, for example Burma and Ghana, in the end sank their differences to preserve the fragile unity. Although it had become clear during the negotiations that votes alone were insufficient to force change, the unity of the G75 had attained a symbolic role. In seeking accommodation with the West the importance of unity was paramount. Collective pressure might be no guarantee of success but individual action was even less likely to bring success. Those states seeking to preserve the group highlighted the common interests held by the developing countries. Hence, the tendency toward fractionalisation was curbed through persuasive appeals to shared values.

Group dynamics

The most striking and important feature of the Geneva conference was the display of unity exhibited by the developing countries.[41] As the *Observer* noted at the time, 'The emergence of the 75 as a united front is seen by the Western delegates as perhaps the most important political phenomenon of the last 20 years.'[42] At the outset of the conference the developing countries were not organised as a group.[43] For the first two to three weeks there was little attempt at coordination and the delegations and regional groups worked at cross-purposes. It was only as the conference drew to a close and especially over the institutional issue that the divisions began to disappear and the impressive display of unity so noticeable in the voting on the recommendations and resolutions contained in the Final Act emerged.

Prior to the conference the OECD, Comecon and the developing regions had attempted to establish group positions. The initial atmosphere, therefore, was one which encouraged group negotiations, and the size and complexity of the agenda, the types of issues under discussion and the modalities of UN politics made a group politics approach inevitable. The developed capitalist states had been unable to agree on a coordinated strategy beforehand, and during the conference there were significant splits between the United States on one hand and the EEC (mainly France) and sometimes the United Kingdom on the other. As the conference progressed, the Western states made more strenuous efforts to act as a group. The socialist states had from the outset acted as a group and their marginality to the central issues made this solidarity easier to maintain. The development of a group approach to negotiations accentuated divisions, heightened tension and increased confrontation. This confrontation did not hamper the work of all the committees. In the Third Committee dealing with invisibles and financing there was much constructive dialogue and some draft resolutions were co-sponsored by developed and developing countries.

The developing countries saw unity as a source of strength in that it aided in the articulation of demands and improved their negotiating capacity. The use of bloc voting and log-rolling tactics gave a greater appearance of unity than our investigations have shown. If unity can be conceived as having both positive and negative sources, the unity achieved by the developing countries was founded on negative rather than positive factors. This unity was inspired by the negativism of the developed countries and the realisation that results would only be achieved through concerted pressure. The larger states lacked the means to negotiate change on their own and needed the diplomatic support of the smaller ones. The poorest states were in the weakest position of all and needed to belong to a larger coalition to make any gains. With more sophisticated representatives and larger delegations the more advanced among the developing countries were able to exercise the greatest influence over group deliberations, hence the interests of the least developed tended to be given less weight. The all-inclusive, composite nature of the draft resolution allowed the inclusion of diverse and sometimes competing claims, but the influence of the Prebisch Report with its bias towards the more advanced LDCs resulted in decisions favouring this group. On the other hand, the manner of reaching accommodation within the group, through persuasion and conciliation, meant that all opinions received an equal hearing, hence minorities could play a larger role than their numbers allowed. Two rules of behaviour giving equal weight to all members allowed countries to cooperate while preserving their interests. First, all proposals had to be agreed by the group before they were presented to the developed countries. Secondly, all proposals had to be endorsed by group members. The wide-ranging nature of the coalition and the mutual support for different demands provided a unifying thread. In this sense the existence of cross-cutting cleavages diminished the fragmentation within the group. The method of reaching agreement in the group and the nature of the issues ensured that the unity created was of a rather special kind.[44] It was sufficiently strong to harmonise policies whilst retaining reservations on particular issues. On the issue of preferences, which was essentially one of distributive bargaining, the conflict in the group was the greatest.

It is possible to identify various sub-groups and special interest groups in the G75. A detailed examination of the work of the plenary and main committees shows that, depending on the issue and the relevant ascriptive or attitudinal cleavage, the G75 split into different groups. In other words a division into radicals and moderates is too simplistic.[45] We can distinguish between the more advanced LDCs and the poorer ones, between the countries contemplating an abolition of selective preferences and those favouring their retention, between those pressing for an ITO or at least a strong continuing machinery and those prepared for compromise. The land-locked states also formed an interest group insisting on special treatment. The existence of fluid alliances rather than stable ones prepared the way for the development of a wider consensus. Brazil and India, for example, both led the argument against the retention of selective preferences but took different approaches to the institutional issue. One can, however, identify certain ideological differences of approach. Some states, for example Burma and Ghana, were more willing to blame the international capitalist division of labour for the ills of the LDCs than others. In so far as the institutional issue was the most highly politicised and polarised, it is possible to identify those countries with faith in existing machinery and those who thought that only new machinery could help LDC trade problems. In this respect, a division can be made between radicals, e.g. Burma, Ghana and Indonesia, and moderates, like India, Pakistan and Malaysia.

The influential developing countries at Geneva were generally those which were influential in the general politics of their region. Given the regional organisation of the group this is not surprising. The possession of the attributes and capabilities necessary for exercising influence at the conference did not differ markedly from the influence of resources at the regional level. The major actors, Algeria, Ghana, Nigeria, UAR (African Group); Burma, India, Indonesia, Malaysia, Pakistan, Philippines (Asian Group); Argentina, Brazil, Colombia (Latin American Group); and Yugoslavia can with a few exceptions be identified as major regional actors. Influence depended on the issue under consideration, the interest taken in it by a delegation, their technical expertise and the comprehensiveness of their preparation and the quality of the delegate. Within the group states played leading roles either through initiating programmes or acting as mediators. Another source of influence came from membership of the Steering Committee of the G75 which comprised twelve states, four from each of the three geographical regions. The members were Cameroon, Ethiopia, Nigeria, the UAR, Ceylon, India, Pakistan, Yugoslavia, Argentina, Bolivia, Chile and Mexico. Each member of the Steering Committee represented the group in one of the main committees and acted as spokesman. The Chairman of the Steering Committee was permanently in contact with the Conference President and Prebisch.

The degree of cohesion achieved by the group was certainly remarkable. Analysis of the voting records shows a very high degree of agreement. Using the Lijphart Index of Agreement, we find that the pairing with the greatest measure of disagreement — Thailand and Vietnam — nevertheless have a very high measure of agreement, namely 89 per cent.[46] No developing country voted against any of the fifteen General Principles and the thirteen Special Principles and when all decisions are assessed there were only eighteen abstentions in total from this group. But it should be noted that of the sixty-one Recommendations passed, thirty-two were passed without dissent and of the remaining twenty-nine the roll-call vote is only recorded for fifteen thus making it difficult to give an accurate impression of the solidarity of the developing countries.

Conclusions

This chapter has attempted to describe and account for the transition from the 1963 Joint Declaration of the Developing Countries to the Joint Declaration of the Seventy-Seven Developing Countries issued at the close of UNCTAD I which established the G77 as a permanent group.[47] We have argued that the coalition was the outgrowth of several factors. The importance of the regional groups and regional meetings, the influence of the Prebisch Report as a conceptual framework, the key role played by Prebisch and the secretariat, the lack of progress on substantive issues and the subsequent political significance attached to the institutional issue and the limited bargaining power of the developing countries were important causal factors in this process. The creation of the coalition was the result of the interplay of these factors together with the processes identified in the previous chapter. Underlying the historical survey in these two chapters is an appreciation of the importance of organisational factors to political outcomes. The following two chapters develop the importance of organisational variables through an analysis of UNCTAD and the institutionalisation of the G77.

Notes

1. General Assembly Res.1897(XVII), Annex, 11 November 1963.
2. *Proceedings 1964*, vol.I, pp.66–8.
3. C. L. Robertson, 'The Creation of UNCTAD', op.cit., p.271.
4. Reproduced in *Proceedings 1964*, vol. VII, pp.95–213.
5. 'The Charter of Alta Gracia', in *Proceedings 1964* vol.VI, p.59.
6. ECA Secretariat, 'Activities of the Economic Commission for Africa Related to the United Nations Conference on Trade and Development' in *Proceedings 1964*, vol.VII, p.248.
7. See ibid.
8. ECA Res. 97(VI) 'United Nations Conference on Trade and Development', 28 February 1964.
9. OAU ECOSOC Res. ECOS/12/Res/1 (I), 13 December 1963.
10. ECAFE Res.50 (XX), 'Tehran Resolution on the United Nations Conference on Trade and Development', 12 March 1964.

11. The Western developed nations used the OECD as a forum in which to coordinate policy and the socialist bloc used Comecon.
12. On 27 May 1964 as a result of the formation of the United Republic of Tanganyika and Zanzibar, the delegations of Tanganyika and Zanzibar were reconstituted as a unified delegation.
13. Raul Prebisch, 'Towards A New Trade Policy for Development', Report by the Secretary-General of the UNCTAD (*United Nations*, Sales No: 64 II.B.4,. 1964).
14. Goodwin claims that 'lack of preparation by LDC delegations and general ignorance and lack of skill led to the influence of the Prebisch Report.' G. L. Goodwin, 'The United Nations Conference on Trade and Development. Beginning of a New Era?' *Yearbook of World Affairs 1965*, p.7.
15. See H. W. Singer, 'The Distribution of Gains between Investing and Borrowing Countries', *American Economic Review, Papers and Proceedings* (May 1950), pp.473–85; R. Prebisch, 'The Role of Commercial Policies in Underveloped Countries', *American Economic Review, Papers and Proceedings* (May 1959), pp.215–73.
16. See, e.g. H. G. Johnson, *Economic Policies Towards Less Developed Countries* (London: George Allen & Unwin 1967), pp.249–50; M. June Flanders, 'Prebisch on Protectionism: An Evaluation', *Economic Journal* (June 1964), pp.305–26.
17. See Bela Balassa, *Trade Prospects for Developing Countries* (New York: Richard D. Irwin Inc., 1964) pp.104–5. Balassa calculated that the gap would be between $9.4–$12 bn.
18. Prebisch argued that an international economic organisation if it is to be effective must go through three major stages: (i) outlining and dramatising the problem; (ii) the Secretariat adopts a low profile while the governments confront each other; (iii) the Secretariat acts as a go-between as governments seek compromise. See J. S. Nye, 'UNCTAD: Poor Nations Pressure Group', in R. W. Cox & H. K. Jacobson (eds), *The Anatomy of Influence* (New Haven, Conn.: Yale University Press 1973), p.368.
19. 'such drafting of resolutions with the help of secretariat officials is commonplace in various UN organisations. In all complex multimember organisations the secretariat often leads the delegates since it is a permanent force on the scene.' B. Gosovic, op.cit., p.311 fn.
20. See R. N. Gardner, 'The United Nations Conference on Trade and Development', *International Organization* (Winter 1968), p.106.
21. See Malcolm Subhan, 'How the 75 stuck together', *Far Eastern Economic Review*, 9 July 1964, p.49
22. H. S. Bloch, 'The Challenge of the World Trade Conference', (*School of International Affairs, Columbia University, Occasional Paper, 1964–65*) pp.8–9.
23. See 'Interim Report of the Preparatory Committee (1st, 2nd, and 3rd Sessions)' in *Proceedings 1964*, vol.VIII, pp.3–59.
24. See 'Report of the Group of Experts Appointed Under Economic and Social Council Resolution 919(XXXIV)' — 'Commodity and Trade Problems of Developing Countries: Institutional Arrangements' in *Proceedings 1964* vol.VII, pp.377–423.
25. E/CONF.46/C.1/L.17.
26. E/CONF.46/C.1/L17/Rev.1 and Corr.1 and 2.
27. For a more detailed consideration of this issue see chapter 6 below.
28. See 'Memorandum Concerning Certain Items on the Agenda of the United Nations Conference on Trade and Development', submitted by France, in *Proceedings 1964*, vol.VII, pp.23–5.
29. E/CONF.46/C.2/L.5 submitted by India, Indonesia, Lebanon, Nepal and Saudi Arabia; E/CONF.46/C.2/L.23 submitted by Argentina, Brazil, Bolivia, Chile, Colombia, Costa Rica, Dominican Republic, Ecuador, El Salvador, Guatemala, Haiti,

Honduras, Mexico, Nicaragua, Panama, Paraguay, Peru, Uruguay and Venezuela; E/ CONF.46/C.2/L.27 submitted by Ghana, Kenya, Liberia, Nigeria, Tanganyika and Zanzibar, Sierra Leone, Sudan and Trinidad and Tobago.

30. E/CONF.46/C.2/L.40 and Add. 1–5.
31. Other writers, for example Gardner, Goodwin and Gosovic, who make a neat categorisation of radicals (extremists), moderates and Francophone Africans only see three factions.
32. E/CONF.46/C.4/L.3.
33. Gosovic, op.cit., p.39.
34. E/CONF.46/C.4/L.5.
35. E/CONF.46/C.4/L.9.
36. E/CONF.46/C.4/L.12 and Add. 1 and 2.
37. E/CONF.46/50/Rev.1 and Add. 1 and 2.
38. E/CONF.46/C.4/L.1/Rev.1 and Add. 1.
39. See Robertson, op.cit., pp.271–2.
40. Part of the explanation for this is that many LDC ministers returned near the end of the conference and inserted a very 'political' approach which tended to overlook the nature of international negotiations. They had not followed the issue and were therefore uninformed about events which had taken place before. It has also been alleged that the machinations of the Chinese and some developed countries were behind the militancy of the radicals in an effort to break up the conference; the former to show the futility of cooperating with the capitalist world and the latter to prevent the establishment of the continuing machinery. See Gosovic, op.cit., p.51.
41. With the Joint Declaration issued at the end of the Conference, the Group officially became the Group of 77. New Zealand, a signatory of the 1963 Declaration left the Group, and Kenya, South Korea and South Vietnam joined. There was a possibility that Cuba, Israel and Mongolia would be admitted, but their respective regional groups did not admit them. Yugoslavia, originally a member of the African Group, moved to the Asian Group.
42. *Observer*, 14 June 1964.
43. The claim by HE Mr. João Augusto de Aravja Castro, the Brazilian Minister of State for External Affairs that 'for the first time in the history of economic conferences, the under-developed nations come here as a united front' (24 March 1964), *Proceedings 1964*, vol.II, p.117, was part of an attempt to establish the fledgling unity rather than an accurate expression of the contemporary reality.
44. Sidney Weintraub makes a telling point when he claims that 'The unity of the Seventy-five was too precious for public doubts.' S. Weintraub, 'After the U.N. Trade Conference: Lessons and Portents', *Foreign Affairs* (October 1964), p.47.
45. See Gwyneth Williams, *Third World Political Organisations* (London: Macmillan, 1981); also A. S. Friedeberg, op.cit., who also identifies the Francophone Africans as a separate grouping.
46. See Arend Lijphart, 'The Analysis of Bloc Voting in the General Assembly: A Critique and a Proposal', *American Political Science Review* (December 1963), pp.902–17.
47. It is interesting to note that in introducing the 'Joint Declaration of the Seventy-seven Developing Countries Made at the Conclusion of the United Nations Conference on Trade and Development', Amjad Ali referred to the group as the G75 and said that the term had been retained because of its historic significance. See *Proceedings 1964*, vol.II, p.519. The Declaration itself contained four references to the G75 and none to the G77. See *Proceedings 1964*, vol.I, pp.66–8. By the time UNCTAD convened for the first session as a continuing organisation the present nomenclature had been adopted.

Part II
The organisational framework

4   UNCTAD: Organisational structure and political process

The aim of this chapter is to describe and assess the importance of UNCTAD's instititional mechanism for the growth and development of the G77. The institutional venue for multilateral diplomacy is a vital part of the policy-making process.[1] Conference diplomacy is conducted within the confines of a particular organisation and the legal and political characteristics of the organisation condition policy outcomes. Moreover, international organisations cannot be reduced to the attributes of the member states and therefore to avoid reductionism the organisational context has to be explored. The first part of this chapter examines UNCTAD's institutional framework. Legal, institutional analysis is a valuable starting point for the study of international organisations because development in the competence of an organisation is intricately connected to its constitutional provisions. Furthermore, questions concerning authority and power cannot be addressed adequately without reference to constitutional provisions. The institutional perspective, however, is deficient in its ability to explain change. The orientation of institutional studies is to the static rather than the dynamic aspects of organisational behaviour and therefore key processes of organisational change are omitted.[2] These include redefinitions of goals and tasks, conflictual processes, changes in the scope and level of organisational behaviour and changes in the relevant environments. The second part of this chapter, therefore, analyses the political process in UNCTAD.

Organisational structure

The institutional framework

The compromise reached at UNCTAD I dictated the key features of UNCTAD's constitutive document. The new organisation was created as a permanent organ of the United Nations with the adoption of General Assembly Resolution 1995(XIX).[3] Membership is open to all states that are members of the United Nations or, alternatively, members of the specialised agencies or of the International Atomic Energy Agency (IAEA). UNCTAD's main task was the promotion of international trade as a vehicle for economic development. In order to fulfil this task its main functions were (i) the formulation and implementation of principles and policies on international trade and development; (ii) the negotiation of specific agreements; (iii) to act as a coordinating centre in the UN system in respect of international development policy.

The different perceptions of UNCTAD's role held by the developed and developing countries played an important part in both elaborating the functions and designing the institutional machinery of the organisation. The developing countries wanted an organisation with the ability to implement decisions over a wide range of international economic activity. The developed countries were content with the global management performed by the IBRD, IMF and GATT and sought to restrict UNCTAD's effectiveness.[4] The mandate given to UNCTAD is, thus, contradictory. It asks the organisation to initiate action, to promote international trade and to formulate new principles whilst at the same time exhorting it not to clash with existing international organisations in trade and finance. The principal organs of UNCTAD are the Conference, the Trade and Development Board and the Secretariat. The Conference is the highest organ and is entrusted with the task of carrying out the functions specified by the General Assembly. It can best be thought of as an assembly which is convened periodically. It is open to all member states and is supposed to meet every three years. In practice, apart from UNCTAD V which was convened three years after UNCTAD IV, the Conference has met every four years. To date seven conferences have been held: UNCTAD I in Geneva, 23 March–16 June 1964; UNCTAD II in New Delhi, 1 February–29 March 1968; UNCTAD III in Santiago, 13 April–21 May 1972; UNCTAD IV in Nairobi, 5–31 May 1976; UNCTAD V in Manila, 6–29 May 1979; UNCTAD VI in Belgrade, 6 June–3 July 1983; and UNCTAD VII in Geneva, 9 July–3 August 1987. The conference as the supreme decision-making body of the organisation sets the priorities for future areas of work — consultation, negotiation and research — of the organisation as a whole. It has unlimited power in adopting its rules of procedure, appointment of its Bureau and the creation of sessional bodies. Its work is guided by a President, Vice-President and Rapporteur.

The Trade and Development Board (TDB), ensures continuity between the periodic conferences. The TDB is the key decision-making unit in the intervals between conferences. Membership of the TDB originally restricted to fifty-five states is now open to all members of the Conference.[5] Until 1970 the TDB met biannually in regular session but has since met annually. It also holds special sessions which have been convened annually since the sixth special session in 1975. The TDB performs all the functions of the Conference in the intersessional periods. Moreover, it is charged with keeping under review and taking appropriate action within its competence in respect of the recommendations and other decisions of the Conference. The Board also serves as a preparatory committee for future sessions of the Conference and is therefore responsible for preparing a provisional agenda and the necessary documentation. The TDB's importance is enhanced by its ability to create subsidiary organs 'as may be necessary to the effective discharge of its functions.' Initially the Board had four committees — Commodities, Invisibles and Financing related to Trade, Manufactures and Shipping.[6] Task expansion within the organisation has led to the creation of two new main committees — Transfer of Technology and Economic Cooperation Among Developing Countries. Two further subsidiary committees namely the Special Committee on Preferences and the Committee on Tungsten, have been created. The membership of the committees have been enlarged over time to take cognisance of the increased membership of the organisation. The committees have been entrusted with the task of promoting the decisions of the Conference and the pursuit of integrated policies in their respective areas and the coordination of policies with relevant international institutions. They usually meet twice yearly but special sessions may be convened when necessary.

The Board and its committees establish periodically working groups and other standing committees to assist them in fulfilling their roles. These *ad hoc* bodies have varying life spans depending on the subject under consideration. They are of two types — intergovernmental bodies such as the Intergovernmental Preparatory Group on a Convention of International Intermodal Transport, and groups of experts appointed on the basis of their professional expertise, like the Expert Group on Export Credits as a Means of Promoting Exports from Developing Countries.

The two main functions of the UNCTAD secretariat are the provision of adequate servicing for the Conference, the TDB and its subsidiary organs and the carrying out of research requested by member states. The secretariat comprises professional and general service staff and has expanded with the organisation's growth. It comprises a number of departments, some of an administrative nature and others specifically engaged in research. The UNCTAD secretariat is headed by a Secretary-General who holds the rank of Under-Secretary of the United Nations. This office has been held by Raul Prebisch (1964–8), Manuel Perez-Guerrero (1969–73), Gamani Corea (1974–84) and Kenneth Dadzie (since 1986). The Secretary-General oversees the smooth functioning of the continuing machinery and has a wider role to play in the deliberative process of the organisation. First, he is entitled to attend any meeting and to submit oral and written statements to the deliberative bodies. Secondly, he is involved in drawing up the agenda of the various organs. Thirdly, he can be called upon to use his good offices in relation to UNCTAD's conciliation procedures. Fourthly, he is entrusted with the task of convening commodity conferences within the UN system and is authorised to hold intergovernmental consultations on commodities.

Decision making

The formal decision-making machinery consists of a majoritarian voting procedure and the provision of procedures for conciliation. The Conference, the TDB and all its main committees have been provided with an egalitarian system of decision making. In all organs each state is allotted one vote. At the Conference, substantive decisions require a two-thirds majority of voting representatives present and procedural motions only require a simple majority. All decisions of the TDB and its main committees are taken by simple majority vote of those present and voting, i.e. abstentions are excluded from this definition. Voting at the Conference or the Board is by a show of hands or roll-call if any members request this procedure. The only deviation from these rules concerns elections which take place by secret ballot, unless otherwise decided by the Board.

The process of conciliation envisaged in UNCTAD's constitutive document has never been used. These procedures were adopted because the irreconcilable positions adopted at the Geneva Conference seemed to foreshadow total deadlock in the future. The process of conciliation is supposed to take place before voting and to provide an adequate basis for the adoption of resolutions with regard to proposals of a specific nature which call for action substantially affecting the economic or financial interests of particular countries. Conciliation can take place with regard to proposals before the Conference, the Board or on matters on which the committees have been authorised to submit recommendations without further approval for action. The process of conciliation is only appropriate for substantive economic issues.[7]

The group system is the key feature of the UNCTAD decisional process. For the purpose of election to the Board and its main committees, states were divided into four lists based on geographical and socio-economic criteria (see Table 4.1). List A contains the African and Asian states and Yugoslavia; List B, the developed market-economy countries; List C, the Latin American and Caribbean countries; and List D, the socialist countries of Eastern Europe. The combination of Lists A and C to form the G77 has meant that in practice three rather than four groups have been active in UNCTAD. Apart from various states which are peripheral members of their groups, the group system forms the basis on which UNCTAD works.[8] All deliberations within the organisation take place on the basis of the group system. Before any meetings of the deliberative bodies the group members meet and attempt to coordinate their respective policies. The result of this process is the transformation of UNCTAD into a forum where intra-group consensus becomes as important, if not more important, than inter-group agreement.

Three salient features emerge from this examination of UNCTAD's organisational structure. First, UNCTAD is an inherently contested organisation. Its legal basis arose from a conflict between the developed and the developing countries and its competence and role are subject to competing interpretations. UNCTAD was created by the G77 and they provide its natural constituency. An important element making for consensus in the G77 is the realisation that continued G77 unity is necessary for any increase in UNCTAD's capacity to effect environmental change. Secondly, politics within the organisation is likely to reflect these competing perspectives, with the institutionalisation of the group system perpetuating the fractured nature of the organisation. Moreover, the institutionalisation of the group system with its emphasis on intra-group consensus provides a structural constraint on fractionalisation in the groups. Thirdly, UNCTAD was created as a dynamic organisation but its attempts to initiate regime change bring it into conflict with the established Bretton Woods institutions.

Table 4.1 *The group system in UNCTAD*

List A	
Afghanistan	Jordan
Algeria	Kenya
Angola	Korea, P.D.R.
Bahrain	
Bangladesh	Korea, Rep. of
	Kuwait
Benin	Lao P.D.R.
Bhutan	Lebanon
Botswana	Lesotho
Brunei	
Burkina Faso	Liberia
	Libyan Arab Jamahiriya
Burma	Madagascar
Burundi	Malawi
Cameroon	Malaysia
Cape Verde	
Central African Republic	Maldives
	Mali
Cambodia	Mauritania
Chad	Mauritius
China*	Mongolia
Comoros	
Congo	Morocco
	Mozambique
Democratic Yemen	Namibia‡
Djibouti	Nepal
Egypt	Niger
Equatorial Guinea	
Ethiopia	Nigeria
	Oman
Fiji	Pakistan
Gabon	Papua New Guinea
Gambia	Philippines
Ghana	
Guinea	Qatar
	Rwanda
Guinea-Bissau	Samoa
India	Sao Tomé and Príncipe
Indonesia	Saudi Arabia
Iran, Islamic Republic	
Iraq	Senegal
	Seychelles
Israel	Sierra Leone
Ivory Coast	Singapore

Solomon Islands
Somalia
South Africa*
Sri Lanka
Sudan

Swaziland
Syrian Arab Republic
Thailand
Togo
Tonga

Tunisia

Uganda
United Arab Emirates
United Republic of Tanzania
Vanuatu

Viet Nam
Yemen Arab Republic
Yugoslavia
Zaire
Zambia

Zimbabwe

List B

Australia
Austria
Belgium
Canada
Cyprus†

Denmark
Finland
France
Federal Republic of Germany
Greece

Holy See
Iceland
Ireland
Italy
Japan

Liechtenstein
Luxemburg
Malta†
Monaco
Netherlands

New Zealand
Norway
Portugal
San Marino
Spain

Sweden
Switzerland
Turkey
United Kingdom
United States of America

List C

Antigua and Barbuda
Bahamas
Belize
Brazil
Chile

Colombia
Costa Rica
Cuba
Dominica
Dominican Republic

Ecuador
El Salvador

Grenada
Guatemala
Guyana

Haiti
Honduras
Jamaica
Mexico
Nicaragua

Panama
Paraguay
Peru
St Kitts and Nevis

St Kitts and Nevis	Surinam
St Lucia	Trinidad and Tobago
	Uruguay
St Vincent and the Grenadines	Venezuela

List D

Albania	Hungary
Bulgaria	Poland
Byelorussian SSR	Romania†
Czechoslovakia	Ukranian SSR
German Democratic Republic	Union of Soviet Socialist Republics

* Denotes countries not members of the G77.
† Denotes countries members of the G77.
‡ Namibia became a member of UNCTAD by virtue of UNGA Resolution 34/921 of 12 December 1979.

The political process

UNCTAD's functions

UNCTAD has three major interrelated functions — policy formulation, negotiation and implementation. A fourth function, that of technical assistance, can also be identified. UNCTAD is thus more than a forum; it has aspects of both a service organisation and a negotiating body.[9] A crucial characteristic of UNCTAD's political process is the essentially contested nature of the organisation. Unlike a stable political system in which core values are held in common and bargaining proceeds within a framework of established norms, the UNCTAD political process is inherently unstable and conflictual. The Western countries, the G77 and the socialist bloc all have different conceptions of the role assigned to the organisation. This clash of ideologies reinforces the group system of negotiations on one hand, but restricts the ability of the organisation to achieve significant goals on the other hand.

Policy formulation has involved the elaboration of the agreed principles of the 1964 Conference and the subsequent development of further principles. UNCTAD's avowed aim is the creation of a new trade and development policy for the international community. UNCTAD's reformist goal is constrained not only by the attitudes and actions of member states but by the liberal principles enshrined in post-war international economic regimes.[10] Moreover, although UNCTAD has been given an important role in the elaboration of international development policy,[11] it is nevertheless subject to the higher authority of the General Assembly.[12] Policy formulation has covered a wide range of topics, such as commodity trade, development finance, the transfer of technology, trade in manufactures, the debt problem, monetary reform, the particularly disadvantaged developing countries (the least developed, landlocked and island countries), economic cooperation among developing countries, East–South economic cooperation, shipping and restrictive business practices.[13]

The enunciation of new principles and new concepts is usually the result of initiatives by the G77. Discounting co-sponsored resolutions, G77 members sponsored 91.7 per cent of all the resolutions presented to the TDB between 1965 and 1979.[14] The Third World's attempt to use UNCTAD to rewrite the prevailing rules of the international economic system is a collective exercise which requires group unity.

It is difficult to assess the impact of UNCTAD's decisions on the international environment.[15] One test would be the extent to which UNCTAD's decisions have legal status. However, the extent to which UNCTAD has a legislative or quasi-legislative competence in respect of the creation of international economic law is a debatable point.[16] But in some respects this debate is of limited relevance. Of key importance is the degree of salience attached to the decisions by international and national actors. Even if the resolutions do not possess a quasi-legal character they can be used by the developing countries, international bureaucracies and pressure groups in the developed countries to argue the case for the implementation of programmes sympathetic to the aims of the developing countries. Ansari has detailed the political significance of interest groups in Western democracies to UNCTAD's work. He concluded that for aid, trade in manufactures and commodity trade interest groups do exert an influence on public policy.[17]

Negotiations in UNCTAD are severely constrained by the perceptual foci of the participants. The G77 perceive UNCTAD as a negotiating body with the authority to preside over commodity agreements and a forum in which binding agreements on international economic issues can be taken. The Group B countries see UNCTAD as a communication forum, i.e. one without a negotiating role. In Group B's view UNCTAD can study the basis of multilateral agreements but the actual negotiations must be conducted elsewhere, that is, in organisations in which they control the decision making, like GATT and the IMF. This dispute over UNCTAD's role and the exact meaning of the term negotiation has bedevilled UNCTAD's decision making from its inception. The emergence of the NIEO and the explicit recognition of UNCTAD's competence as a negotiating forum in pursuit of NIEO goals increased the organisation's legitimacy in this area. The case studies discussed in Chapters 6 and 7 reveal for example the crucial importance of this issue in the debate over the Generalised System of Preferences (GSP) and the way in which it played a less salient role in the conflict over the Common Fund (CF) and the Integrated Programme for Commodities (IPC).

The meaning of negotiation within the United Nations context is unclear. Kaufmann provides a useful point of departure when he defines negotiation as 'the sum total of talks and contacts intended to solve conflicts or to work towards the common objectives of a conference.'[18] This definition is broader than that applied by Group B in respect of economic negotiations. They argue that economic negotiations entail a *quid pro quo* bargaining process with an end result of mutual concessions. The UNCTAD process, Group B claim, does not contain this element of reciprocity; instead, it is one of deliberation with an end result of mutual concessions. The UNCTAD process, Group B claim, does not contain this element of reciprocity, instead it is one of deliberation with an end result of a binding resolution. Although there is some recognition in the G77 that negotiation must involve some reciprocal exchange, the prevailing view is that the deliberations in UNCTAD have the status of negotiations.[19] In this view UNCTAD resolutions should commit the parties concerned to specific action.

UNCTAD's competence as a centre for negotiations is a function of both time and issue. A comparison of the two case-studies shows the changing relevance of the negotiation issue. The G77 viewed the deliberations to create the GSP as negotiations[20] but Group B insisted that these talks amounted to no more than discussions of their unilateral offers.[21] Group B refused to concede the point and the G77 eventually accepted that the discussions to be held in the Special Committee on Preferences (SCP) were consultations.[22] In the event *de facto* negotiations took place, as states engaged in complex and hard bargainining over the technical and specialised issues. Resolution 93(IV) adopted at the Nairobi Conference ushered in a series of negotiations on international commodity policy. It would be futile to pretend that the deliberations on the Common Fund were not negotiations. Furthermore, negotiations on the individual commodity agreements under the IPC umbrella took place under UNCTAD auspices. Before the impetus of the IPC tin, sugar, olive oil and wheat agreements had all been concluded under the UNCTAD framework.

The competing perspectives held by Group B and the G77 concerning UNCTAD's organisational competence also affect the organisation's role in the implementation procedure. The developed countries feel that their political and economic interests would be affected by strong implementation procedures whilst the developing countries argue that without effective implementation UNCTAD's resolutions are worthless.[23] The issue of implementation was raised at the very first session of the TDB. The G77 requested the creation of a surveillance system in order to ensure that the provisions of the Final Act of the Geneva Conference were being implemented. The developed countries countered that the lack of unanimity expressed in the decisions taken on the Final Act rendered it non-implementable.[24] Eventually a compromise was arrived at, which provided for a minimal check on the progress of implementation.[25] It was agreed that the Annual Report of the UNCTAD's Secretary-General would review and assess the progress made in implementation of Conference decisions. Sharp criticism by Group B governments of the first such report led to a toning down of the critical comments on the failure of member states to meet their obligations in subsequent reports.

This review function of the secretariat is only one phase of the implementation process. Crucial to this process is the binding nature of resolutions. The obligations conferred by UNCTAD resolutions is dependent on a range of factors. These include, for example, the scope of the resolution; the commitment of the parties in the negotiations; the existence of multilateral or unilateral sanctions; the political atmosphere in which decisions are taken; the existence of a supervisory body to which complaints can be taken; and the perceived equity of the gains to be made.

UNCTAD's resolutions as we have shown fall into two categories: (i) those adopted by majority vote; and (ii) agreed resolutions which express the tacit consent of all states. In cases where resolutions are of the former type little positive action is taken. Although it might appear that resolutions of the latter type would have a reasonable chance of implementation the nature of the consensus method is such that this inference is incorrect. Within an agreed resolution there still exists significant differences on the extent and meaning of implementation. Moreover, although many resolutions and recommendations are adopted without a vote a high proportion of these are severely diluted in the operational context because several important states enter reservations.[26]

Decision making

UNCTAD's decisional process has developed along relatively informal lines using flexible methods of consultation and negotiation. This development has taken place at the general conferences and in the continuing machinery. After the Geneva Conference at which 65 per cent of all decisions were taken by vote, voting has receded into the background.[27] At New Delhi and Santiago approximately one-third of all decisions were voted on but this figure dropped to 12 per cent at Nairobi and 13 per cent at Belgrade (see Table 4.2). Another significant feature of voting at UNCTAD conferences is the low recourse taken to the use of roll-call voting. Roll-calls are the most formal of all voting procedures but as Table 4.3 shows after the Geneva Conference when they reached 48.8 per cent of all decisions taken and were the most important method of arriving at decisions, roll-call votes have not exceeded 14.3 per cent at any of the subsequent conferences except UNCTAD VII. A similar process has occurred in the Trade and Development Board. Moreover, the elaborate conciliation machinery has never been used. On the other hand, the group system has developed from being merely the lists on which states are based for voting purposes into the very cornerstone of UNCTAD politics and decision-making in the organisation. It might have been assumed that with the decline in voting the *raison d'être* for the groups would have disappeared but this has not been the case. Indeed, the existence of the group system has itself curbed the resort to voting.

The group system is an integral part of the UNCTAD decision-making process as it developed over time. These groups, although highlighted within UNCTAD, were not first developed there. The aggregation of states for voting and other purposes is a feature of international organisational activity.[28] In this, international organisations are merely reflecting an irreducible feature of modern politics. It would be virtually impossible to imagine modern political activity and organisational politics in particular without the existence of groups. Where the UNCTAD experience is different in the context of international organisation is that, first, the group system was built into the institutional machinery and,

Table 4.2 *Decision making at UNCTAD Conferences, 1964–87*

Session	Number of decisions taken	Number adopted by vote	Percentage adopted by vote
UNCTAD I 1964	86	56	65
UNCTAD II 1968	35	12	34
UNCTAD III 1972	49	17	35
UNCTAD IV 1976	16	2	12
UNCTAD V 1979	35	9	26
UNCTAD VI 1983	32	4	13
UNCTAD VII 1987	3	1	33

Table 4.3 *Typology of decision making at UNCTAD Conferences, 1964–87*

Session	Number of decisions	Roll-call Number (%)	Show of hands Number (%)	Adopted without objection* Number (%)	Other†
UNCTAD I 1964	86	42(48.8)	14(16.3)	29(33.7)	1
UNCTAD 1968	35	3(8.6)	9(25.7)	20(57.1)	3
UNCTAD III 1972	49‡	7(14.2)	10(20.4)	29(59.2)	2
UNCTAD IV 1976	16§	1(6.3)	1(6.3)	14(87.5)	1
UNCTAD V 1979	35	5(14.3)	4(11.4)	25(71.4)	1
UNCTAD VI 1983	32	4(12.5)	–	27(84.4)	1
UNCTAD VII 1987	3	1(33.3)	–	2(66.6)	–

*The formula 'adopted without objection' is employed in accordance with the editorial instructions of ST/CS/SER/16 of October 1973 to replace 'without dissent', 'by consensus' or 'by unanimity', which appeared in the proceedings of the Conference.
†This category includes 'no action taken', 'by acclamation', 'adopted with reservations from certain delegations' and 'adopted without abstention'.
‡The figures do not add up because Resolution 82 (III) is unrecorded.
§The figures do not add up because the US sponsored draft resolution on an International Resources Bank was defeated.

secondly, all UNCTAD politics revolve around the groups.[29] Furthermore, coordination and cooperation take place on a continuing basis even when a deliberative body is not in session.[30] Coordination within the groups takes place before Conferences, meetings of the TDB, the committees and other subsidiary organs. In other words, groups have an existence independent of specific organisational contexts and the group system has an identity independent of the organisation which first gave it prominence.

The impact of the group system of negotiations on the UNCTAD decision-making process is the subject of competing interpretations. Some analysts argue that the group system contributes effectively to UNCTAD decision making. The group system is seen as facilitating the decision-making process through the provision of the opportunity for regular consultations and the coordination of positions.[31] Decision making, in this view, is simplified when a large group of countries can delegate one spokesman to speak for them. It is further claimed that the group system has been an efficient and practical force in world politics.[32] UNCTAD's failure to reach decisions is blamed not on the group system of negotiations but on the groups themselves and the tendency to meet as groups prior to the Conference.[33] This is a rather perplexing claim since the novel feature of the UNCTAD group system of negotiations is the continuation of group negotiations outside the framework of the organisation.

Critics of the group system argue that the strictures of group discipline limit manoeuvrability by curtailing and inhibiting diplomatic intercourse.[34] Constricting group discipline, it is argued, makes it virtually impossible for states to meet each other on an individual basis, thus inhibiting initiative and the search for compromise. The group system thus leads to both slowness in negotiations and to the failure to achieve meaningful results. Weiss claims that groups have become more important than UNCTAD. He argues that the participants sacrifice agreement with opposing groups in order to maintain group unity.[35]

This debate over the impact of the group system of negotiations on the UNCTAD decisional process has to date been conducted with a set of limiting assumptions. Both supporters and critics assume that the groups primarily represent or ought to represent countries experiencing similar material conditions and hence with common economic interests. The socio-psychological element of group solidarity is omitted from such theories. As forms of analysis such approaches are unaware of the development of group consciousness as opposed to its expression. They fail to see it as behaviour learned within an environmental context. The political impact of group negotiations is derived in such analyses from the analyst's prior assumption concerning the most efficient bargaining techniques. This rational actor, goal-oriented approach fails to take into consideration the contested nature of the organisation. In other words, there is a reciprocal causality between the existence of groups and the development of a group system of negotiations. The group system of negotiations is both a structural and a process feature of UNCTAD's political process. The existence of groups and the group system have been intimately connected from the outset.

UNCTAD did not create groups; it was itself the product of one group and the institutionalisation of the group system reflected the circumstances of its creation. If the prior existence of groups created a group system then the reality of a group system and the centrality of groups in the organisational structure has served to maintain the vitality of the groups. The G77 has, therefore, to be viewed not as an independent actor whose behaviour affects UNCTAD's decision-making process but in relation to the group system itself. The organisation, orientation and the structure of influence in the three groups are key features in the evolution of the political process in UNCTAD. This study is chiefly concerned with the G77 and extensive analysis of this group will appear in Chapter 5. At this point we will consider briefly the political processes operative in Group B and Group D.

The Western countries had a history of consultation on economic matters beginning in the Organisation for European Economic Cooperation (OEEC), which continued when that body was replaced by the Organisation for Economic Cooperation and Development (OECD). The wide-ranging agenda of UNCTAD I and the impetus of the LDCs drive for reform of the international economic order forced the western countries to convene an OECD meeting for the purpose of establishing generally accepted guidelines to govern their response to the developing countries. After the Geneva Conference a special ministerial decision was taken to institutionalise the OECD's role as an organising centre for Group B. Within the OECD's Development Assistance Committee, Trade Committee and Maritime Transport Committee special working groups were created specifically to deal with UNCTAD matters. The OECD secretariat has the task of collecting information, conducting relevant research and analysis and servicing Group B meetings in the OECD and UNCTAD. Although not all members of Group B are full members of the OECD and some are not members of the Development Assistance Committee, the OECD functions as the secretariat of Group B.

The leadership role is shared between the United States, the United Kingdom, the Federal Republic of Germany, France and latterly, Japan. The existence of the European Community (EC) creates problems for decision making in Group B because the EC countries tend to develop a common position outside the group framework and then prove inflexible in negotiating with other group members to arrive at a common position.[36] Another important sub-group in Group B's decisional process is the Nordic group. Initiatives from Group B countries in UNCTAD normally have to go through the complex internal group bargaining system before it is communicated to the wider forum. Agreement among Group B countries is usually reached on the basis of the minimum common denominator, i.e. the group position tends to coalesce around the country or group of countries prepared to make the least generous offer. No conscious trade-off strategy exists but sometimes trade-offs can be sought within an agreed package of topics. A favoured method of reaching agreement is to arrive at a procedural resolution whereby countries are allowed to dissent from the common group position. It is difficult to separate the divisions in the group into neat left, right and centre divisions depending on the degree of sympathy with the aims of the G77. There are many cross-cutting interests but broad alignments can be discerned. The United Kingdom, United States, Germany and Japan on one side have consistently espoused a free market, anti-interventionist philosophy largely unsympathetic to the demands of the G77. The Nordic countries and the Netherlands have been more willing to seek some form of compromise. France has played a floating role. On financial issues the French have sided with the 'conservative' states but on more overtly political issues have tended to side with the 'liberal' European perspective. A large number of Group B countries cannot be identified with either grouping and hold an amorphous middle position. The dominance of the United States in the global political economy gives them a powerful voice in Group B deliberations and it is often said that many countries use the United States as a shield. In so far as US opposition is likely to kill any proposal, some countries can appear to be sympathetic to G77 demands because they know that these demands have little realistic chance of being accepted. The aim of the dominant countries in Group B is to deflect LDC demands, to exploit cleavages in the G77, to minimise the political costs of opposition to G77 demands and to make the minimum possible concessions.[37] Typical Group B tactics include requests for studies and reports in preference to direct action and frequent accusations aimed at the low-level support given by the Eastern bloc countries to development aid and development issues.[38]

The Group D countries also have a long history of cooperation. As socialist countries in the postwar period they have been in the minority in international organisations and until the upsurge in Third World membership of the United Nations in the 1960s were permanently on the losing side of the in-built American majority vote.[39] The socialist countries consistently formed a bloc on procedural as well as substantive issues, as a means of overcoming this isolation. In the economic field the Council for Mutual Economic Assistance (Comecon) acts as an organising forum for the socialist countries. Unlike the G77 and Group B, Group D is rather small and so the problems of coordination are easier. Problems of coordination have also been eased by the fact that until the Manila Conference in 1979 most of the G77 demands have been directed towards the capitalist countries and Group D countries have not been particularly concerned with most of the issues on the agenda. This is not to say that Group D could not have taken a more positive and engaged approach to the demands of the G77. Ritual denunciations of Group B and token support for G77 positions expose the underlying hypocrisy of Group D's position when this is measured against the negligible flows of development assistance flowing from the Eastern bloc and a reluctance to transform the prevailing East–South pattern of international specialisation and exchange. Comecon's coordination is restricted to calling meetings prior to important UNCTAD meetings such as the Conference, the TDB and its committees. Group D has had little difficulty in arriving at a common negotiating position. The main source of dissent within the group was Romania and with its defection to the G77 in 1976 coordination problems became easier for the remaining members. The Soviet Union's hegemony over Eastern Europe gives it the dominant position in Group D.[40]

The existence of the OECD and Comecon gives Groups B and D institutional advantages over the G77. These organisations possess secretariats which conduct research, prepare reports, service meetings and obtain information on other groups. Moreover, the existence of a formal body provides for the possibility of continuous intra-group consultations on a wide range of issues. This combined with a high level of expertise and a long experience in mutual consultations contributes to enhanced bargaining skills. This asymmetry in the group system is not remedied by the efforts of the UNCTAD secretariat on behalf of the G77.

The Peoples Republic of China (PRC) is the major exception to the group system. The PRC acts as an independent party in UNCTAD politics. China invariably supports the G77, occasionally engages in polemics with the Soviet Union but overall adopts a low profile. Chinese participation is hampered by the group structure[41] but also curtailed by a lack of interest. One study of China's behaviour in UNCTAD outlined the following characteristics:

a relatively extensive participation in a wide variety of meetings; a passive and reactive support; an occasional intervention to rebut and reject the Soviet linkage of development with disarmament; an uncharacteristically active participation in any debate relating to tungsten; and a generally modest, diligent and self-effacing behavioural posture.[42]

With the decline in the recourse to voting and the non-use of the conciliation mechanism the group system of negotiations has evolved the consensus method as the key method of arriving at decisions.[43] This approach, more flexible than conciliation in formal terms, means the adoption of a decision without recourse to voting. In institutional terms this means that after a resolution has been debated the presiding officer having consulted with the various groups, informs the meeting that there is no opposition and the resolution is therefore carried. The process of consensus takes place at two different levels. At the first, consultations and negotiations are conducted at the group level. This can be meetings either between groups or within the individual groups. The groups have also developed smaller negotiating bodies, known as contact groups, which meet to explore common areas of agreement and to try to reach agreement on points of dispute. At the second level, the consensus method is reflected in a draft resolution which is submitted to the organ concerned as a result of the deliberation of the contact groups. The proposed text is then adopted if there is no dissent. The work of the contact group is to some extent similar to that envisaged for the conciliation committee. The conciliation process has *de jure* recognition but the consensus method has become the *de facto* method of decision. Quasi-legal recognition has been given to this method by the organisation. The two main organs have both recognised the importance of these developments. The consensus method was welcomed by Conference Resolution 80 (III) which stated that 'full use should be made, wherever is considered desirable, of flexible techniques for inter-group consultations in order to facilitate agreement.'[44]

In a similar vein Board Decision 45 (VII) states: the Board recognised the task of negotiation including consultation and agreement on solutions, is a single process.[45]

Consensus developed in UNCTAD because it is the most effective method of negotiation given the subject matter with which the organisation is concerned, its membership and its power to implement decisions. UNCTAD's redistributivist aims can only be achieved through attitude change, the development of international trade law and the negotiation of new economic agreements. It does not make much sense for the G77 to use its voting majority to pass resolutions calling for regime change when its members lack the effective means to implement these proposed changes. Hence the in-built voting majority enjoyed by the G77 is irrelevant and counter-productive to a decisional process which aims to usher in genuine reform. New methods of decision-making which stressed accommodation had to be developed. The consensus method also has positive appeal to some Group B members. It enables those more sympathetic to G77 demands to use contact groups to press a more accommodating and less confrontational strategy. The consensus method, however, is seriously flawed. So much stress is placed on the texts of resolutions that substantive issues which divide the participants are glossed over. Consensus gives the illusion of progress where none has been achieved.

The secretariat is an important aspect of the political process in UNCTAD. From the perspective of this study the salience of the secretariat will be assessed in Chapter 5. But prior to that discussion some brief observations on the influence of the secretariat on UNCTAD's organisational dynamics will be made. First, the UNCTAD secretariat is an active political grouping interested in structuring outcomes in its own environment.[47] From the outset the secretariat has been the guardian of an organisational ideology with a distinct view of the world economy and the solutions to global poverty. The task of the secretariat has been to create a constituency to support such proposals. The G77 is the effective constituency for the UNCTAD secretariat. Secondly, the close relationship between the secretariat and the G77 further exacerbates the distrust of the organisation held by Group B. Thirdly, the secretariat has been the active source of and generator of ideas — both the GSP and IPC had their origins in the respective Seretaries-General, Prebisch and Corea. The secretariat contributes to the formulation of policy objectives through its servicing role as well as through the preparation of reports and technical studies.[48] The role played by the secretariat is also affected by the rivalries and animosities between various sections and their respective heads.

Conclusions

UNCTAD provides a specific environment for the North–South dialogue. Politics in the organisation reflects fundamental divergencies concerning the competence and the role of the organisation. The political process, although based on the formal procedures has developed decision making in a manner different from that originally envisaged. The most significant features are the group system and the development of a consensus method of decision making. Organisational structure and process place the emphasis on group solidarity and this is enhanced by the conflicting ideologies. There is thus a strong organisational bias in favour of G77 unity. The nature of the deliberative process, the issues discussed and the method of decision making all enhance Southern solidarity. Few gains can be achieved from breaking ranks and the political costs would be high. The G77 is able to maintain unity because the negativism of Group B and the indifference of Group D offer little in the way of positive inducement to defect. Furthermore, UNCTAD's scope of effective decision is so limited that the economic costs of maintaining unity in the face of economic disadvantage are relatively low. UNCTAD's importance as an international organisation affects both the activities of the G77 and its ability to maintain unity. Third World solidarity is necessary in order to promote an expanded role for UNCTAD in multilateral development diplomacy. UNCTAD was created by the G77 and the maintenance of the organisation requires the continued existence of the group. Despite its many shortcomings UNCTAD remains the only organisation which the developing countries can be said to control. This control is of course very limited for although the G77 can set the agenda and the research strategy of the organisation is responsive to their demands they cannot ensure effective implementation of UNCTAD decisions. In other words, decision-making power is not translatable into power over outcomes. Despite this serious shortcoming, to date the coalition has attempted to reconcile the differences of its members in order to maintain UNCTAD in its present form. UNCTAD's importance is thus psychological and symbolic as much as material. Although UNCTAD clearly fails to provide the G77 with tangible economic gains it nevertheless fulfils an important symbolic role. It follows from this analysis that the existence of rival organisations encroaching on UNCTAD's territory strengthens rather than weakens political support unless substantial gains were to accrue from these rival organisations.

The absence of voting not only makes intra-G77 cooperation appear greater, it also contributes towards increasing cohesion and lessening fractionalisation. Persuasion in intra-G77 bargaining is further enhanced because of the existence of shared group norms in contradistinction to Group B. UNCTAD provides a defined pattern of interaction and the negotiating groups and contact groups are a stable and persistent setting for negotiations. After UNCTAD IV the committees became open ended and this removed one sanction (election to office) from group politics but election for officers and nominations to negotiating groups still provide measures through which to enforce discipline.

The conclusion of this chapter is that the UNCTAD framework provides a setting in which the pressures for group conformity and group solidarity act as effective bulwarks against the centrifugal tendencies in the G77. The next chapter analyses the organisation of the G77 in order to assess the extent to which its own organisational dynamics contribute to the resolution of conflictual strains within the coalition.

Notes

1. See R. W. Gregg, 'Negotiating A New International Economic Order: The Issue of Venue' in R. Jütte & A. Grosse-Jütte (eds), *The Future of International Organization* (London: Frances Pinter, 1981), pp.51–69.
2. L. T. Farley, *Change Processes in International Organizations* (Cambridge, Mass.: Schenkman, 1981), p.41.
3. 30 December 1964.
4. See R. C. Ogley, 'Towards a General Theory of International Organisation', *International Relations*, III (1969), pp.599–619, for a theoretical discussion on the effectiveness of international organisations (IO). Ogley argues that the effectiveness of an IO may be measured by its ability to create an institutional structure appropriately sharp/blunt for the effective pooling of national sovereignties for their future limitation.
5. See Conference Resolution 90 (IV) in *Proceedings (1976)*, vol.1. The original limitation on membership of the TDB to fifty-five states had been increased to sixty-eight in 1972 by UN General Assembly Resolution 2904 B (XXVII) on the recommendation of Conference Resolution 80(III). See *Proceedings (1972)*, vol.1.
6. G. A. Resolution 1995 (XIX) para. 23 envisaged three committees but the TDB at its first session created the Committee on Shipping. See *TD/B/SR.10* and *TD/B/SR.13*, *TD/B/L.29* and Board Resolution II (1) Establishment of a Committee on Shipping (13 April 1965).
7. For more detail on the conciliation process see R. Krishnamurti and D. Cordovez, 'Conciliation Procedures in UNCTAD. An Explanatory Note', *Journal of World Trade Law* (July/August 1968), pp.445–66.
8. China does not take part in Group A deliberations and Israel and South Africa are excluded from this group.
9. R. L. Rothstein, *Global Bargaining* (Princeton, N J: Princeton University Press, 1979) treats UNCTAD as merely a deliberative forum.
10. See J. G. Ruggie, 'International regimes, transactions and change: embedded liberalism in the post war economic order', *International Organization* (Winter 1982), pp.379–415.
11. See the various resolutions on the NIEO. The Establishment of a New International Economic Order, G. A. Res. 3201 (S-VI); the Programme of Action on the Establishment of a New International Economic Order, G. A. Res. 3202 (S-VI); the Charter of Economic Rights and Duties of States, G. A. Res 3281 (XXIX); and Development and International Economic Cooperation, G. A. Res. 3362 (S-VII).
12. It is here that the high-level decisions regarding the Second Development Decade, the International Development Strategy and the NIEO were taken.
13. Alan Lamond, 'UNCTAD's Twenty Years of Pioneering Efforts in Trade and Development,' *IDS Bulletin* (July 1984), pp.4–6, provides a brief overview. Also see UNCTAD, *The History of UNCTAD 1964–1984* (UN sales No.E.85.II.D.6).
14. Political and procedural resolutions account for a tiny percentage of the total number of decisions.
15. I have used the term 'decision' here because it seems appropriate. Within the UNCTAD framework, however, the results of the deliberative process have three different titles, namely recommendations, resolutions and decisions. I will use these terms interchangeably in the future since in the opinion of Mr L. H. Sise of the UNCTAD Secretariat Legal Section, no clear-cut division exists between these nomenclatures.

16. See S. D. Metzger, 'Developments in the Law and Institutions of International Economic Relations. UNCTAD', *American Journal of International Law* (July 1967), pp.756–75; P. Berthoud, 'UNCTAD and the Emergence of International Development Law' in M. Zammit Cutajar, *UNCTAD and the South–North Dialogue* (Oxford: Pergamon Press, 1985), pp.71–98.
17. J. A. Ansari, 'UNCTAD: Objectives and Performance, 1964–1976.' (doctoral dissertation, Univertsity of Sussex, 1983), pp.201–28.
18. J. Kaufmann, *Conference Diplomacy* (Leyden: A. W. Sijthoff, 1968), p.23.
19. One dissenting note was echoed by Ambassador Lall of India at the Eighth Special Session of the TDB. He claimed that 'negotiations were dealings between partners with equal bargaining power. There could be no question of refusing to negotiate, but it should be recognised that at present certain negotiations were not possible.' *TD/B/SR.461* (27 April 1977). In voicing this publicly Mr Lall was only saying what has been expressed privately in the G77.
20. The Charter of Algiers had called for negotiations leading to the conclusion of an agreement to be held under UNCTAD auspices.
21. At the OECD meeting in 1967, when they had agreed to preferences in principle they had recognised that this entailed no binding commitment. Group B would be granting unilateral concessions.
22. Conference Resolution 21 (II). See *Proceedings (1968)*, vol.1.
23. Frustration over lack of effective results led to the acronym UNCTAD being held to mean Under No Circumstances Take Any (Effective) Decisions.
24. See *TD/B/SR. 1–24.*
25. Board Decision 19 (II). See *Official Records of the Trade and Development Board, Second Session;* and *TD/B/SR 25–57.*
26. For an optimistic analysis of UNCTAD's growing legitimacy see Gamani Corea, 'UNCTAD: The Changing Scene' in M. Zammit Cutajar (ed.), op.cit., pp.295–302.
27. The retreat from voting was most evident at UNCTAD VII. In what follows decision making at UNCTAD VII will be excluded from the analysis since only two formal resolutions were recorded.
28. Researchers have identified several voting blocs in the UN General Assembly. See, for example, T. Hovet, *Bloc Politics in the United Nations* (Cambridge, Mass.: Harvard University Press, 1960).
29. See T. G. Weiss, *Multilateral Development Diplomacy in UNCTAD* (London: Macmillan, 1986).
30. The mushrooming of UNCTAD groups into other fora contributes to this process. On the operation of the groups during the Law of the Sea negotiations see R. C. Ogley, *Internationalizing the Seabed* (Aldershot: Gower, 1984), pp.81–5.
31. B. Gosovic, 'UNCTAD: North–South Encounter' *International Conciliation* (May 1968), pp.29–30.
32. See, for example, Mahqub ul Haq, *The Poverty Curtain* (New York: Columbia University Press, 1976), p.182 and Koul, op.cit., p.67.
33. Koul, op.cit., p.67.
34. See R. W. Gregg, op.cit., pp.62–3; Rothstein, op.cit., pp.195–203; Gosovic, op.cit., p.29.
35. Weiss, op.cit., pp.43–61.
36. Interviews.
37. For example, Group B supports the LDCs but refuses to recognise the developing island countries as a separate category.
38. For further analysis of Group B's organisation and response to LDC demands see

Geoffrey Goodwin, 'The OECD Industrialised Countries Response' in G. Goodwin & J. Mayall (eds), *A New International Commodity Regime* (London: Croom Helm, 1979).

39. See R. C. Ogley, *The United Nations and East–West Relations 1945–1971* (ISIO Monograph, University of Sussex, 1972).

40. For further analyses of Group D's attitude to UNCTAD see Jan Bielowski, 'The Socialist Countries and the New International Economic Order' in Jutte & Gross-Jutte, op.cit., pp.70–90; C. A. Schwartz, *UNCTAD: Soviet Politics in the North–South Conflict* (Ann Arbor: University of Michigan Press, 1976).

41. Interestingly, however, the PRC was elected as a member of the TDB at UNCTAD III from Group A.

42. Samuel S. Kim, *China, the United Nations and World Order* (Princeton, NJ: Princeton University Press 1979), pp.303–4.

43. The adoption of the consensus procedure in the NIEO negotiations was a clear example of UNCTAD practices spilling over into the UN system.

44. *Proceedings (1972)*, vol.1.

45. 21 September 1968. *Official Records of the Trade and Development Board. Seventh Session. Supp.1.*

46. On the change in the organisation from a confrontationist to an accommodationist strategy see D. Cordovez, 'UNCTAD and Development Diplomacy', *Journal of World Trade Law*, 1972. Weiss, op.cit., sees UNCTAD's history as confrontational.

47. Weiss, op.cit., pp.87–101.

48. For critical, hostile views of the UNCTAD secretariat see Rothstein, op.cit., pp.183–92 and pp.209–16; C. Brown, *The Political And Social Economy of Commodity Control* (London: Macmillan, 1980), pp. 241–71. For a more dispassionate analysis see J. A. Ansari, *The Political Economy of International Economic Organization* (Brighton: Wheatsheaf, 1986), pp. 269–97.

5   The Group of 77: organisational structure and political process

The previous chapter explored one aspect of the organisational framework and its impact on the development and functioning of the G77. This chapter examines the organisational structure and the political process of the G77. It reveals that although the G77 is an informal coalition it nevertheless has evolved a detailed institutional structure. The analysis assesses the impact of the institutionalisation of group procedure on group cohesion. The first part of the chapter examines the organisational structure of the G77 and its development over time. The focus is on the G77 in Geneva, the headquarters of UNCTAD but relevant features from the operation of the G77 in other regional centres are also considered. The second part of the chapter examines the political process of the G77 in UNCTAD. Growth and change in organisational characteristics provide an important dimension for the study of conflict and consensus in the G77. Processes of decision making, the structure of influence and political dynamics provide a more detailed understanding of organisational characteristics and make outcomes more intelligible.

Organisational performance depends upon the initial organisational structure, the political process and changes in these two variables over time. Organisational theorists refer to two specific aspects of structure and process as being of most importance. These are the 'scope' and 'level' of the organisation. Philip Schmitter defined the scope of an international organisation as 'a mixture of two dimensions: the number of social groups or policy sectors potentially involved (in making and elaborating the policy of the international organisation) . . . and the importance of these policy sectors for the attainment of national actor-defined goals.[1] The impact of the organisation on its environment varies in direct proportion to the number of groups involved in policy articulation. The level of an international organisation 'refers to the extent of commitment to mutual decision-making both in terms of continuity i.e. the obligation to meet recurrently and to re-evaluate periodically joint policies, and in terms of techniques i.e. the nature of the policy making process.'[2]. As Ansari notes, 'the greater the commitment to the institutionalization of decision-making processes, subordinating national autonomy in specific issue areas, the greater the likelihood that the organization will transform the environment in accordance with its ideology.'[3]

These concepts cannot be applied to the G77 without some degree of adaptation, nevertheless they are suggestive of further lines of analysis. The continued existence of the G77 and its ability to maintain cohesion can be seen to be dependent upon changes in its scope and level. The unique nature of the G77 — that it is an informal yet highly institutionalised mechanism — suggests a redefinition of scope and level along the following lines. Scope is defined as the number of groups and issue-areas involved in policy making and the importance of these groups and issue areas for national actor-defined goals. Level refers to both the continuity of joint decisions and the decision-making techniques involved. But the less the threat to national autonomy of joint decision-making the greater the potential stability of the organisation. In other words the development of sub-groups in the G77 along relevant issue-areas will enhance rather than disrupt organisational stability provided decision-making protects national autonomy. The accommodation of sub-groups within the organisation will provide certain members with potential benefits not generalisable to all members. This is important because the heterogeneous nature of the coalition ensures that few general policies will benefit all members. This does not mean that the mere proliferation of sub-groups contributes to coalition maintenance. Rather, it is the institutionalisation of sub-groups, provision of gains and access to decision making which is crucial.

Organisational structure

Membership and representation

The G77 expanded from its original membership in 1964 to number 128 in 1988 (see Table 5.1). The Palestine Liberation Organisation (PLO) is the only non-state (and non-UNCTAD) member of the G77. The criteria for membership of the group have never been made explicitly clear. The founder members were those states which signed the Joint Declaration of the Developing Countries at UNCTAD I in 1964. Subsequently, all developing countries joining UNCTAD have joined the Group. The basic requirement for membership is a commitment to support the agreed positions of the G77 in all fora. The acceptance into the G77 of the newly independent states and their willingness to join can be explained in institutional terms by reference to the division of states in UNCTAD into groups based on geographic and socio-economic factors. The existence of the UNCTAD group system and its salience for decision making in the organisation constituted a major reason for the expansion of the G77. Membership of the G77 became a necessary requirement for effective participation in UNCTAD decision making.[4]

Until the Third Ministerial Meeting of the Group of 77 (26 January–7 February 1976) in Manila, Philippines, the sole basis for membership was regional. To become a member of the G77 a state first had to be admitted to one of the three regional groups — Africa, Asia and Latin America. Any country admitted to one of the three regional groups automatically becomes a full member of the G77.[5] The issue of non-regional membership arose with the applications of Malta and Romania, both of whom applied for G77 membership

Table 5.1   *The members of the Group of 77 categorised according to membership in the regional groups, 1988*

Africa (52)	Asia (43)	Latin America (33)
Algeria	Afghanistan	Antigua and Barbuda
Angola	Bahrain	Argentina
Benin	Bangladesh	Bahamas
Botswana	Bhutan	Barbados
Burkina Faso	Brunei	Belize
Burundi	Burma	Bolivia
Cape Verde	Cambodia	Brazil
Central African Republic	Cyprus	Chile
Chad	Democratic People's	Colombia
Comoros	Republic of Korea	Costa Rica
Congo	Democratic Yemen	Cuba
Djibouti	Fiji	Dominica
Egypt	India	Dominican Republic
Equatorial Guinea	Indonesia	Ecuador
Ethiopia	Iran, Islamic Republic	El Salvador
Gabon	Iraq	Grenada
Gambia	Lao People's Democratic	Guatemala
Ghana	Republic	Guyana
Guinea	Lebanon	Haiti
Guinea-Bissau	Malaysia	Honduras
Ivory Coast	Maldives	Jamaica
Kenya	Malta	Mexico
Lesotho	Nepal	Nicaragua
Liberia	Oman	Panama
Libyan Arab Jamahiriya	Pakistan	Paraguay
Madagascar	PLO	Peru
Malawi	Papua New Guinea	St Kitts and Nevis
Mali	Philippines	St Lucia
Mauritania	Qatar	St Vincent and the Grenadines
Mauritius	Republic of Korea	Surinam
Morocco	Samoa	Trinidad and Tobago
Mozambique	Saudi Arabia	Uruguay
Namibia	Singapore	Venezuela
Niger	Solomon Islands	Romania
Nigeria	Sri Lanka	
Rwanda	Syrian Arab Republic	

Sao Tomé and Príncipe	Thailand
Senegal	Tonga
Seychelles	United Arab Emirates
Sierra Leone	Vanuatu
Somalia	Vietnam
Sudan	Yemen
Swaziland	Yugoslavia
Togo	
Tunisia	
Uganda	
United Republic of	
Cameroon	
United Republic of	
Tanzania	
Zaire	
Zambia	
Zimbabwe	

without first having been accepted into one of the three regional groups.[6] A non-regional member is entitled to participate in all meetings of the G77 and may be invited to participate in the work of a regional group on an informal basis. Proposals from non-regional members have to be channelled through one of the regional groups.[7] Non-regional members are admitted on the proviso that they 'participate in the work and positions of the Group of 77 in all forums and not only on specific topics and aspects of international relations.'[8]

Membership of a regional group does not in itself guarantee active participation. Cuba was admitted to the G77 at the Second Ministerial Meeting of the Group of 77 (28 October–7 November 1971) held in Lima, Peru but was not invited to attend certain meetings of the Latin American Group in Geneva until summer 1973.[9] Cuba was never banned from attending formal meetings of the group but was never invited to informal ones. Since these informal meetings constituted the bulk of the Latin American Group's activity Cuban participation was kept minimal.[10]

It is the level of representation in Geneva rather than total group membership which is of greater importance when discussing the organisational structure of the G77 in UNCTAD. The economic disparities in the G77 are reflected in the relative sophistication of the various foreign ministries, economic departments and the general bureaucratisation of governmental machinery. This economic heterogeneity of the G77 results in a constantly changing organisational scope. In other words, although all states are theoretically involved in all major decisions, the day-to-day machinery is effectively entrusted to those states with representation in Geneva.

Divergencies in economic and technical resources are noticeable in three different ways with respect to the representation of individual states to UNCTAD.

The first concerns the establishment of permanent missions in Geneva. For foreign exchange and other reasons developing countries cannot usually afford to have many foreign missions. Geneva is a major centre of international organisational activity; thus a mission situated there minimises cost and maximises access to a variety of international institutions. Despite both the importance attached to UNCTAD by the developing countries and despite Geneva's position as a nexus of international organisational activity there is a serious under-representation of the G77 in Geneva.[11] Table 5.2 presents data on G77 representation in Geneva for two years, (1978 and 1980) at the height of the NIEO debate. In March 1978 only 56 per cent of the G77 had missions in Geneva and in March 1980 this had risen slightly to 59 per cent. The largest regional group, Africa, also contains a greater proportion of poorer states and, consequently, has less representation in Geneva than the other two regional groups. This lack of representation affects the politics of the African Group. First, the members always have to renegotiate their group position before any major meeting. Secondly, there is an element of disorganisation because in order to canvass as many opinions as possible the Chairman of the African Group has to circulate current issues to resident missions in other European capitals.

Table 5.2 *Diplomatic missions in Geneva, by region March 1978 and March 1980**

Region	1978			1980		
	Total group membership	Number of missions	Percentage of total	Total group membership	Number of missions	Percentage of total
Africa	(48)	17	35.4	(48)	18	37.5
Asia	(40)	27	67.5	(41)	30	73.2
Latin America†	(28)	21	75	(30)	22	73.3
G77	(116)	65	56	(119)	70	58.8

*Included are those missions in Geneva or its immediate vicinity.
†Including Romania.

Members of the G77 not represented in Geneva are consulted before any major UNCTAD meeting, such as the Trade and Development Board or one of the main committees. A meeting to reassess the common agreed position of the G77 is usually held a day or two before the relevant UNCTAD meeting between the resident G77 members and the newly arrived participants. Despite the absence of on-the-spot representation, members of the G77 are nevertheless always provided with an opportunity to register their views before a major meeting. Furthermore, states without a permanent mission in Geneva sometimes designate another state from its regional group to act on its behalf within the regional group and the G77 as a whole. Failing these provisions the regional group occasionally designates on an *ad hoc* basis a spokesperson for a non-represented state.

Secondly, the size and strength of the missions vary enormously from the large and highly efficient missions such as Argentina, Brazil and India to the poorly staffed ones like Nicaragua which once operated for some time in the 1970s with only one professional diplomat. The larger, better staffed missions are more able to cope with the huge volume of complex information that needs to be processed and can more effectively represent their interests in the G77. For example in 1979, the staff at G77 missions in Geneva had to cover 2,083 official meetings in UNCTAD, numerous meetings of other international organisations and countless regional group and plenary G77 meetings. The documentation is also overwhelming, for example from January to November 1979, apart from summary records, UNCTAD produced approximately 14,000 pages of documents.[12]

Thirdly, the relationship between the permanent missions and their national capitals is not a uniform one. The larger countries with sophisticated foreign services and good channels of communication usually maintain close contact between the home capital and the mission. In this relationship the ambassador is very dependent on orders from the centre. On a declining scale of bureaucratic control are those countries which attempt to maintain some control over the ambassador's freedom of action but lack the necessary communications system to do so as effectively as the former group. In this situation, a general directive is usually given to the mission providing it with a certain orientation. The ambassador then has a certain degree of freedom in the interpretation and execution of state policy. Finally, some ambassadors have a completely free hand; state policy being effectively decided by the mission in Geneva. All states — from those with a high degree of centralisation to those with a high latitude of discretion for the Geneva mission — frequently strengthen their diplomatic team by sending experts from the home state to take part in important negotiating conferences.

Organisational infrastructure of the Group of 77

The organisational infrastructure of the G77 shows an increasing degree of institutionalisation over time. The First Ministerial Meeting in Algiers in 1967 began a process which has served to maintain the existence of the group.[13] The key organisational elements are the regional groups, the Preparatory Committee, the Senior Officials Meeting and the Ministerial Meeting. These developments are indicative of increases in both the scope and level of the G77 as an organisation. UNCTAD is both a continuing machinery and a periodic conference, and developments in the G77's organisational infrastructure have been shaped by the UNCTAD context. First, we will discuss the organisational aspects of the G77 pertaining to the continuing machinery and then we will examine infrastructural development in relation to UNCTAD conferences.

The basic organisational unit of the G77 is the regional group which represents the most fundamental decision-making centre in the group. All organisational features are based on the three regional groups. And the final G77 position on any issue is first discussed in the regional groups and only when the regional groups have arrived at separate decisions on the specific items are they discussed at the level of the G77 as a whole. In Geneva the three regional groups meet frequently to discuss common issues and to reach a group position to be presented to the G77 as a whole. Of the three regional groups, the Latin American Group is the most structured, meeting informally once a week and formally at least once every two months to elect a new chairman. The African Group meets at least once a month to elect a new chairman but the Asian Group does not have a timetable for regular meeting. The deliberations of the regional groups provides the agenda for the meetings in plenary of the G77 before meetings of the TDB and the main UNCTAD committees.

Apart from the regional groups the G77 in Geneva consists of an interlocking web of working groups and sub-committees of a transient nature. These sub-groups are created to consider a specific proposal or series of proposals currently being debated in UNCTAD or of interest generally to the G77. When UNCTAD's deliberations on the specific item are completed the working group is then disbanded. It is in these sub-groups, normally composed of equal representatives from each regional group, that most intra-G77 bargaining takes place. To maintain the balance of equality between the three regional groups, the offices of chairman, vice-chairman and rapporteur of any G77 working group or sub-committee are always distributed so that each regional group holds one of them.

The organisational proliferation is not restricted to these formal working groups. Numerous contact groups of an informal nature exist for the conduct of serious negotiations between G77 members. These informal contact groups are formed by members of the G77 on specific issues in which they have an interest. Membership of these contact groups is determined by the interested states themselves and includes states which are members of the formal working groups and states outside the formal structure. The creation of specifically G77 contact groups arises from the UNCTAD political process where informal and formal contact groups consisting of members of the G77, Group B and Group D are a general feature of the negotiating process.

For both intra-group relations and negotiations with other groups there was a necessity to provide for the coordination of member state policies. Initially the Group of 31 member developing countries of the TDB began coordinating G77 policy in UNCTAD. This led to a jurisdictional dispute between the Geneva and New York delegates over the leadership of the G77. Prior to UNCTAD II in 1968 meetings of the TDB were split between Geneva and New York and because the G77 had first appeared in New York representatives to the UN argued that they should take precedence over delegates to UNCTAD. This dispute was settled at the Algiers Ministerial Meeting when it was decided that the Group of 31 should be the official coordinating body for G77 activities.[14]

This was an important decision for the future growth of the G77. In ruling in favour of the more technical Geneva location it provided a less political atmosphere in which the G77 was to develop. At the height of the NIEO negotiations when a more political impetus was needed there was a concerted attempt to transfer leadership back to New York. With the expansion of the TDB in 1972 the Group of 31 ceased to exist and the coordination function passed to the Chairman of the G77 and the Chairmen of the regional groups. G77 meetings are convened by the Chairman of the G77 either at the request of one of the regional groups or when the negotiation of a specific issue in UNCTAD has reached a stage where it is deemed necessary to have a G77 meeting.

The coordination of G77 negotiating positions for UNCTAD conferences has led to the creation of new organisational forms. The Preparatory Committee, Senior Officials Meeting and the Ministerial Meeting provide further avenues for joint policy making. During the third session of the TDB (25 January–17 February 1966) the Group of 31 decided that the G77 should be convened at ministerial level prior to UNCTAD II. Pursuant to this decision the Group of 31 decided in September 1966 to create a coordinating committee to carry out 'effective preparation' for the ministerial meeeting.[15] This Coordinating Committee was the forerunner of the Preparatory Committee. Following the success of the Algiers Coordinating Committee, the Group of 31 decided that in preparing for UNCTAD III a Preparatory Committee should be established on the basis of equitable geographical representation of the three regional groups (ten countries from each region), but that its deliberations be kept open to all members of the G77.[16] A Preparatory Committee has been convened prior to all subsequent UNCTAD conferences. The Preparatory Committee meets in Geneva and its sessions last on average for eight months. Its main task is the production of the documentation required for the ministerial meeting and a draft agenda. The work of the Preparatory Committee is carried out by a number of working groups and sub-committees. The expansion of these groups and their specific areas of concern reflect the major issues dominant in UNCTAD and scheduled to be discused at the forthcoming Conference.[17] The work of the Preparatory Committee proceeds in three stages. In the first stage organisational details are discussed, namely the organisation of the Preparatory Committee, the creation of sub-committes, etc. At this stage the chairmen of the existing working groups and senior UNCTAD secretariat officials brief the Preparatory Committee on the major policy issues for the forthcoming Conference. In the second stage, the Preparatory Committee begins the formulation of the G77's position on Conference agenda items. The third stage is concerned with the drafting of position papers and recommendations for the ministerial meeting.[18]

The Senior Officials Meetings is the next stage in the process of formulating a common G77 position.[19] This has developed from a meeting concerned almost exclusively with procedural and organisational matters at Lima in 1971[20] to one in which detailed substantive work was undertaken at Arusha in 1979.(21)The turning point in this process came with the Senior Officials Meeting in Manila in 1976 when consideration was given to the substantive items on the provisional agenda of UNCTAD IV.[22]

The highest policy-making organ of the G77 is the Ministerial Meeting held before the four-yearly UNCTAD Conferences to coordinate the position of the G77. The supreme authority of the Ministerial Meeting was decided by the Algiers Conference.[23] The Ministerial Meeting as the supreme organ of the G77 sets the policy guidelines until the next meeting at ministerial level. The outcome of the Ministerial Meeting is two-fold. First, a declaration which provides an overview of the global economy, reaffirms the solidarity of the G77 and demands certain changes in the international economy. Secondly, a programme of action which sets out in an itemised fashion the various areas in which 'technical' change should be forthcoming.[24] The G77's platform for UNCTAD VII was an exceedingly brief document which perhaps revealed an acceptance of the limited usefulness of these texts in stimulating a positive response from the industrialised world. The Ministerial Meeting usually has before it a synoptic table comparing the texts of the three regional groups, the report of the Preparatory Committee and the report of the Senior Officials Meeting.[25] Discussions are held in plenary and in a series of working groups established to prepare the declaration and the programme of action. The organisational infrastructure of the Ministerial Meeting has changed over time. First, with the increased participation of the Senior Officials Meeting in substantive areas since Lima in 1971, the work carried out by the Drafting Committee and the four main committees of the whole has decreased. Secondly, the composition of the bureau has been enlarged to include the regional coordinators and the Chairman of the Senior Officials Meeting. These developments in the organisation of the Ministerial Meeting are a result of the increased institutionalisation of the G77 and the mode of decision making. The existence of the group is no longer in doubt and with working methods clearly established ministers feel able to delegate the preparations of a common group position to politically junior officials. Moreover, it is unlikely that a severe crisis would arise and should it do so the consensus method of decision making effectively protects national autonomy. High-level officials (ministers) are necessary for the final agreement but negotiations can be entrusted to their subordinates.[26]

The previous sections in this chapter have charted the increasing growth and expansion of the G77 as an international organisation. It has been argued that the proliferation of sub-groups, the creation of new institutional mechanisms and the increase in areas of joint decision making strengthens the coalition. The development of stable and persistent patterns of behaviour create expectations concerning future behaviour and outcomes. This analysis suggests that the institutionalisation of group procedure enhances cohesion and lessens fractionalisation. The creation of new institutional patterns, however, only reveals part of the picture. Apart from documenting the positive developments, it is also necessary to examine those areas in which there was a failure to increase the scope and level of the coalition. In exploring the dynamics of the G77 we also need to examine the limits to institutional cooperation. This is most clearly revealed in an examination of the attempts to increase coordination between the different regional centres of the G77. The most radical proposal in this context is that which envisages the creation of a G77 secretariat. We will therefore discuss the debate on the creation of a secretariat in the context of the wider debate on strenghtening the organisational infrastructure of the G77.

The relationship between the Group of 77 in UNCTAD and the Group of 77 in other geographical centres

The organisation of the developing countries into the G77 for the purpose of coordinating policy positions in international organisations has not been confined solely to UNCTAD. International policy is discussed in a number of global fora and the interest of the developing countries in all areas of international economic relations has led to the mushrooming of the G77 in other international organisations. This process has been aided by the relationship of UNCTAD itself to other international organisations, most notably the United Nations. The close constitutional relationship between UNCTAD and the General Assembly of the United Nations and the importance of the General Assembly in initiating global strategies of economic development led to the creation of the first centre of the G77 away from Geneva, in New York.

The G77 is now a multi-centric organisation with further branches in Rome (Food and Agriculture Organisation), Vienna (United Nations Industrial Development Organisation and the International Atomic Energy Agency), Washington (the IMF and the World Bank), Paris (UNESCO) and Nairobi (United Nations Environment Programme). The developing countries meet as the G77 in all the specialised agencies and during various global conferences, for example the Law of the Sea negotiations. Even when the Group is not recognised by the organisation concerned for instance in GATT, the developing countries still act in concert. The organisation and structure of the G77 varies in the different regional centres and at *ad hoc* global negotiations. This study is not concerned with the operation of the G77 in other fora.[27] But the problem of coordination between the different centres of the G77 is of interest in so far as it affects the functioning of the G77 in UNCTAD. We will therefore investigate the key organisational issues pertaining to the coordination of the different centres of the G77.

The different Groups of 77 are not subsidiaries of one central organisation but rather autonomous bodies with certain minimal features in common. These include a similarity in membership, the use of the group system and the ministerial meeting as the highest policy-making organ. This autonomous development is reflected in the relations between these different centres of G77 activity. Despite the interrelationship between the activities of the various organisations within which the G77 acts no formal methods of coordination have been created. The few attempts at coordination that have been attempted have proved to be singularly ineffective in developing any flows of communication. Many delegates in Geneva are aware of the absence of effective coordination but no consensus exists on the problems caused by this, or on the necessary measures to improve consultation between the different centres of the G77. The need for liaison between the different centres of the G77 arises from the similarity of the issues considered and the institutional links between the various parts of the UN system. The failure of the G77 to develop effective coordination procedures reflects the coordination problems experienced in the UN system.[28]

Some delegates regard the lack of coordination as serious, and would like to see some institutional development to remedy what they consider to be an impediment to the effective working of the G77. Two main arguments are made by the proponents of the creation of liaison group or some form of liaison mechanism. The first concerns the need for consistency in national policy. Some delegates claim that the individual delegations in one city are often unaware of the position taken by their counterparts in another city on the same issue. This schizophrenia in national policy can arise when missions in different cities attach different priorities to the same issue.[29] Secondly, it is argued that coordination would increase the consistency of the G77's policy. Given that questions of interest to UNCTAD are discussed in other international fora, coordination would improve the ability of the G77 to mount a sustained campaign to reform the international economic order. At the moment no means exist for discovering what is happening in other international organisations.[30] Some delegates are content with the existing situation which in their estimation does not hinder the working of the G77. They argue that the creation of a liaison group is unneccessary and would be needless bureaucratisation. Proponents of this view deny that there has been any evident contradiction in G77 policy. Furthermore, they argue that it would be illogical to ask the representatives of a government in one international organisation to confer with representatives of that government in another international organisation when the representatives get the same set of instructions from the national capital. This view does not accept that a state may follow inconsistent policies in two different organisations. This argument, however, in assuming a single model of governmental behaviour is seriously flawed. It is true that some governments will have resolved differences between different segments of the bureaucracy and will maintain a consistent policy but this will not be the case for all governments. Moreover, many ambassadors have a great deal of leverage and are not dependent on their national capitals for precise instructions.

Four related explanations can be given to account for the failure of any effective network of consultation to develop between the different geographical locations of the G77.[31] First, the petty jealousies and rivalries between diplomats in the major cities unwilling to forgo any of their prestige has inhibited any moves toward closer coordination. Secondly, most of the G77 ambassadors in Geneva feel that UNCTAD is the centre of the G77's activities and they are unwilling to allow outside interference in their activities. It is also argued that the G77 first emerged in UNCTAD and it is felt that if any precedents are made then they shoud be made in Geneva. Thirdly, rivalries between the missions in New York and Geneva inhibit efforts at increased coordination. Delegates to the General

Assembly apparently feel that the political importance of the General Asembly gives them precedence over delegates in Geneva. Finally, the UNCTAD secretariat has been lukewarm to the idea of greater G77 coordination because it fears that some of its influence might be eroded.

Proposals to strengthen the organisational infrastructure of the G77 through the creation of a secretariat have to date met with failure. The debate on the creation of a secretariat can be traced to Second Ministerial Meeting of the G77 in Lima in 1971.[32] We do not need to rehearse the history of attempts to strengthen the negotiating capacity of the G77 through the creation of a secretariat. The conclusion of a Working Group set up to study the issue by the Third Ministerial Meeting sets out clearly the impasse reached in the G77 on this issue.[33] The Working Group concluded that a fully independent secretariat 'would not fit well with the G77.'

The Group is an informal and flexible association of developing countries and the secretariat set up to serve it should also be informal and flexible. There is also political opposition by some members of the Group to the establishment of such a secretariat.[34]

Those countries in favour of the creation of a secretariat argue that one is necessary in order to enhance the expertise of developing country delegations in negotiations with the developed countries.[35] The poor economic knowledge and tactical skill of many developing country negotiators is openly acknowledged. Only a handful of developing countries, for example Argentina, Brazil, India and Mexico, possess the administrative and professional expertise to service their delegations to a sufficiently high level on all major policy questions. In negotiations with the developed countries the developing countries are seriously disadvantaged. For not only do the developed countries have substantial national resource pools of expertise, they are also able to draw on their collective expertise in the OECD for Group B and Comecon for Group D. A secondary consideration related to an increase in bargaining power is the increased scope for coordination betweeen the G77 in Geneva and the different regional centres that such a secretariat would provide.

Those countries which oppose the creation of a secretariat do so for a variety of reasons. Some are hesitant about the extent of any proposed operational functions. These states are worried not only about the nature of its initial role but also about its future development. Other countries are apprehensive concerning the financial implications; namely, the source of financing and the extent of country contributions. Other states express concern over the exercise of influence within the secretariat. Satisfactory answers to the following questions would have to be obtained before they committed themselves to supporting the creation of a secretariat. What would be its administrative structure? Would it reflect the present equal balancing of the three regional groups? What scope would a Secretary-General have for independent initiative? Some states express doubts concerning the ability of a G77 secretariat to service meetings in the different regional centres of the G77. Allied to this is the tricky problem of agreeing a suitable headquarters for the location of the secretariat.[36] Finally, although never explicitly stated, some of the more developed countries are against the creation of a secretariat because they do not need its research resources but more importantly perceive that their influence in the G77 and in their region would be lessened.[37]

The failure to create a G77 secretariat is the direct result of the conflicting political interests and perceptions outlined above. Another obstacle to this type of organisational reform is presented by the UNCTAD secretariat. The existence of the UNCTAD secretariat and its performance of a variety of functions for the G77 masks to some extent the need for an independent secretariat. Moreover, the UNCTAD secretariat has opposed the creation of a G77 secretariat fearing a loss of its own political influence in the light of such a development. The UNCTAD secretariat has thus used its considerable political influence in the G77 to support those states sceptical about the benefits to be gained by the creation of a G77 secretariat. Thus, although the UNCTAD secretariat is not part of the organisational infrastructure of the G77 an examination of the relationship between the G77 and the UNCTAD secretariat is vital for understanding the operation of the G77 in Geneva.[38] Such an examination also provides a link to the political processes of the G77 which will be examined in the second part of this chapter.

The UNCTAD secretariat and the organisational infrastructure of the Group of 77

The relationship between the G77 and the UNCTAD secretariat is conditioned by the absence of an independent secretariat of the G77[39] and the political commitment of the UNCTAD secretariat to the developing countries.[40] A formal link between the G77 and the UNCTAD secretariat was instituted in 1971 with the creation of a Liaison Office in the Office of the Secretary-General.[41] This office was specifically created to provide a channel of communication and to facilitate liaison between the G77 and the secretariat. Communication between the G77 and the secretariat occurs through a variety of channels but the Liaison Office is the nodal point of the system.

The UNCTAD secretariat provides three different types of services for the G77.[42] First, it fulfils a logistic role for meetings of the regional groups and also of the G77 as a whole. These services include note-taking, the provision of interpreters, the collection, duplication and dissemination of documents and the provision of records of these meetings for the participants. Secondly, the secretariat fulfils a research function for the G77; conducting research and preparing reports requested by individual members of the G77, by one of the regional groups or by the G77 as a whole or by initiating such studies itself. The secretariat also gives economic briefing sessions to members of the G77. Thirdly, the secretariat provides an input into the strategic-political operations of the G77. It helps the G77 to draft its resolutions and it often mediates in intra-G77 disputes. The logistic provisions are not only confined to the activities of the G77 in Geneva. The secretariat also provides conference facilities for the ministerial meetings of the G77. These services include the preparation of a synoptic table of the Preparatory Texts of the three regional groups. The costs of the services provided to the ministerial meetings are borne by the host state. Apart from this open provision of services, the secretariat also provides discreet informal advice to the regional groups and to the G77 as a whole.

The relationship between the G77 and the UNCTAD secretariat is subject to differing assessments by members of the G77.[43] The UNCTAD secretariat despite its close working relationship with the G77 does not enjoy the full support of all members of the Group. Three contrasting perspectives are discernible — (i) satisfied; (ii) dissatisfied; and (iii) critical. These views are summarised below:

(i) The UNCTAD secretariat performs a valuable and important role for the G77. Its positive commitment to the developing countries ensures that it produces relevant and helpful research. It is a unit which is useful in getting the developing countries to articulate their interests. Its research facilities are adequate for the needs of the G77.

(ii) Although the UNCTAD secretariat performs some important functions for the G77, these services do not go far enough. The UNCTAD secretariat as part of the United Nations secretariat has inherent limitations which restricts it from developing into an adequate secretariat of the G77. Officials of the secretariat are international civil servants and are bound by UN rules. The organisation itself has to serve the interests of all its members. As a global body it cannot be a lasting organisation of LDC interests. Furthermore, the UNCTAD work programme is a political compromise resulting from the interplay of the G77, Group B and Group D. And UNCTAD's economic ideology still operates within the confines of the liberal economic paradigm. UNCTAD cannot, for example, research the best methods available for the creation of primary producer cartels, nor can it recommend policies of national self-reliance.

(iii) The secretariat oversteps its constitutional provisions; initiating policy when it should be responsive to the needs and wishes of its members. Secondly, its staff is of low calibre and its economic judgements are questionable. Moreover, it produces far too many reports. It is impossible for even the best staffed mission to adequately process and digest the large number of documents circulated.

The political process

Political dynamics of the regional groups

The previous section on organisational structure demonstrated that the regional group is the basic organisational unit of the G77. All proposals discussed by the G77 originate within the regional groups and there is a high level of group discipline. Moreover, the three geographical groups have precise identities of their own and often within the various UNCTAD bodies designated spokesmen present the regional view as distinct from the G77's view. Salient factors relating to conflict and consensus in UNCTAD relate to (a) the experience of cooperative ventures in the region; (b) the influence of extra-regional powers on regional politics; (c) the homogeneity of the region; (d) the level of institutionalisation in the region. In this section we assess the relevance of these factors on political dynamics and identify influential regional actors and their sources of influence. It should be noted that it is not an easy task to assess the influence exercised by any state in a regional group, or the G77 as a whole partly because the larger states afraid of appearing too dominant occasionally get a smaller member of their region to represent their views. Thus, for example at UNCTAD V, although Costa Rica was the main proponent of the view that petroleum should be included on the agenda, many delegates have privately expressed the view that it was Brazil which was behind the move.[44]

The Latin American Group is the most structured with a long history of Pan-American diplomatic cooperation. The creation of ECLA provided a focus for the underdeveloped countries in the region to develop a separate identity. ECLA philosophy emphasised small market size and the lack of economies of scale as being prime hindrances to Latin American industrialisation. The favoured solution to these problems was the creation of regional markets to supersede national markets. Following this doctrine the Latin American states initiated a series of cooperative projects in the 1950s and 1960s — the Latin American Free Trade Area (LAFTA), the Central American Common Market (CACM), the Andean Common Market (ACM) and the Cuenca del Plata River Basin Project.[45] Apart from these integrative schemes the Latin American countries created frameworks for trade policy coordination. The Special Latin American Coordinating Committee (CECLA) created in February 1964 was the first such attempt. The initial purpose of CECLA was to plan for UNCTAD meetings, but by 1968 it had become a permanent arrangement with a mandate to negotiate with the United States and the EEC and to coordinate bloc action in multilateral organisations, such as the IMF and World Bank. CECLA existed until December 1975 when it was replaced by the Latin American Economic System (SELA).

The policy coordinating and regional integrative frameworks exist in the context of Latin American dependence on the United States.[46] Traditionally Latin America depended on the United States as its largest single export market and the source of its largest single flows of private capital. In their relationships with the developed world the Latin American countries have a predisposition to respond to US initiatives and during the 1960s the Alliance for Progress provided a rudimentary framework within which to conduct developmental efforts. The supervisory role of the United States meant that until 1971 Cuba was excluded from participation in the activities of the Latin American group.

Conflicts of an economic nature in the group mainly arise from the disparate size and levels of development in the region and the consequent unequal distribution of gains and losses. The LAFTA experience showed that Argentina, Brazil and Mexico generally benefited disproportionately from trade but were unwilling to grant concessions to the less advanced countries. Conflicts of an ideological and political nature centre around specific inter-state disputes, like the 1970 'Football War' between El Salvador and Honduras; the struggle for regional power between the more economically prosperous states, that is Argentina, Brazil and Mexico; and regional conflict, for example Central America.

The relative cultural homogeneity of the Latin American Group was disrupted by the admission to the group of the English-speaking Caribbean states with their traditional links to Europe. For example, the Caribbean states are linked to the EEC through the Lomé Convention. These countries are also outside the Latin American integrative system. They have their own regional economic arrangements — the Caribbean Community and Common Market (CARICOM) and the Caribbean Development Bank. The political processes in the Latin American Group are therefore influenced by relations with different metropolitan powers; two separate common historical experiences; local conflict and rivalry and different levels of development.

Leadership in the group is related to these extraneous factors and to the calibre of national representatives in Geneva. The main actors in the group have been the largest, most developed states — Argentina, Brazil, Mexico and Venezuela. But other states have held leadership positions for more limited periods, for example Colombia and Jamaica. Colombia's prominence in the Latin American Group and the G77 between 1976 and 1980 was due in large measure to the personal qualities of Ambassador Jaramillo. His influence stemmed from his expert chairmanship of the G77's Coordinating Committee on the Multilateral Trade Negotiations (MTN). Under the (1972–80) government of Michael Manley, Jamaica played a leading role in the G77 and the NAM. Jamaica's role arose from its prominent position in the Commonwealth Caribbean, Manley's interest in Third World issues and the calibre of its diplomatic staff in Geneva and New York.

The Latin American Group can be differentiated from the other two groups by its collective view on preferences, LDCs, commodity problems and the institutionalisation of the G77. Specific conflicts exist in the group, for example between Bolivia and Chile over the right of land-locked countries to have a guaranteed access to the sea.[47] On the other hand, there are certain specific alliances, such as the coffee producers of Brazil, Colombia and Central America, which tend to present a common front against the African coffee producers. The Latin American Group is the most homogenous of the three regional groups and was the first to develop regular institutional processes in the G77.

Two issues dominate policy making in the African Group. First, the existence of a rift between the French-speaking countries and the English-speaking ones. The first Lomé Convention in 1975 removed the rift beteen Anglophones and Francophones over the issue of trade preferences but fundamental differences in outlook still create divisions. This is especially noticeable in relation to post-colonial economic arrangements. For example, whereas the ex-British colonies have largely freed themselves from direct control over their economies the Francophone countries are still largely dependent on the French Treasury and the French Central Bank to handle their affairs. Secondly, the under-representation of African states in Geneva seriously affects decision making. Problems arise because before decisions can be taken it is frequently necessary to consult missions in other European capitals thus prolonging the time the process takes. Furthermore, even when consensus has been reached, there is the necessity of reopening the issue when non-resident delegates arrive for an important meeting.

Like the Latin American Group the African Group has an institutional focus separate from UNCTAD. This is provided by the OAU which through its Liaison Office in Geneva services the meetings of the group and prepares position papers to be discussed at higher levels. The OAU Liaison Office is not a coordinating body but it functions as an embryonic secretariat to the group, for example arranging meetings, note-taking and providing limited research facilities. A further institutional feature of the African Group is that issues discussed in UNCTAD can be transmitted to African Ministerial Meetings and OAU Heads of States meetings in order to provide a sharper political thrust to the group's work. The political framework is supplemented by the OAU's Economic Committee and the Economic Comission for Africa.

There is no stable pattern of leadership in the African Group. The major causal factors accounting for change are the personal qualities of diplomats and the importance attached to UNCTAD deliberations by governments. For example, Algeria's leadership role between 1964–70 and 1974–80 reflected the priority attached to UNCTAD and Third World issues by the Algerian government. A combination of good diplomatic staff and relative economic prosperity accounts for Nigeria's high profile in the group since 1966. Some states are influential on specific issues, such as Ethiopia on LDDCs and Ghana on commodity negotiations. The African Group is fairly homogenous in terms of levels of development and also contains the majority of countries belonging to the special interest groups of the LDDCs and land-locked countries.

The Asian Group is the least homogenous of the three regional groups. It has no history of pre-UNCTAD regional cooperation similar to that of Africa or Latin America. Its membership is extremely diverse ranging from oil-rich states such as Saudi Arabia, Bahrain, Iran, Iraq, Kuwait, Qatar and the United Arab Emirates to the small islands lacking in resources such as Fiji, Samoa and the Maldives to the large populous states such as India, Pakistan and Bangladesh. The Asian Group also has three European members. With this wide-ranging and diverse membership regional integration schemes where they exist provide low-level, institutional patterns.

Overall leadership of the Asian Group has remained relatively constant. India, Pakistan and Yugoslavia and after 1973 Saudi Arabia have been at the forefront of group politics. For the smaller states influence is heavily dependent on the personal attributes of their delegates, for example. Indonesian influence between 1977-1978 was largely due to Ambassador Alatas and his work on the Common Fund negotiations and the Philippines enjoyed a long period of influence due to Ambassador Brilliantes' uninterrupted tenure as chairman of the Asian Group. On specific issues certain states are recognised as being influential. In this category would come Afghanistan on the problem of land-locked states and Malta on the problems of developing island economies. Conflict between member states, such as India and Pakistan, Iran and Iraq and the civil war in Afghanistan, spill over into group politics. This is compounded by the influence of competing external powers on the region.

Decision making

This section describes the process through which decisions are reached and assesses the main influences on decision making and the importance of the mode of decision making for the maintenance of G77 unity. The process of arriving at collective decisions among a group of sovereign states is never an easy one. States are generally unwilling easily to forgo their right to a unit veto and although in many formal bodies the principle of majoritarianism has triumphed, in informal arrangements unanimity still prevails as the basic method of arriving at decisions. The decision-making structure of the G77 reflects this reluctance to submit to majority decisions. It is not surprising that this is so, given the diversity of interests among the members and the over-protective attitude most new states have towards their newly gained sovereignty. Moreover, it must be remembered that the G77 is not a policy-making body, although in practice this often happens, it is principally a forum for the harmonisation and coordination of individual viewpoints. To change from a unanimous to a majority rule procedure would to a large extent sanction a policy-making role.

The method by which actors seek to reconcile conflicting objectives or to reach agreement on common positions without the resort to force is negotiation. That is to say, in negotiations the parties aim at reaching a collective agreement through the discussion of proposals on certain issues identified as salient for the negotiating process.[48] The G77 strives to reach agreement on a set of issues where it is felt that agreement is better than no agreement at all. In doing so they use techniques of mixed bargaining. Mixed bargaining encompasses features of distributive bargaining (bargaining over the way something should be divided with emphasis on one's own share) and integrative bargaining (trying to increase the joint gain without worrying about distribution).[49]

In the G77 both within and between regional groups the emphasis in bargaining has been on a mixed strategy. States are concerned to preserve their interests and reluctant to forgo any present benefit without some equivalent advantage. This can be illustrated by the refusal of the Francophone African countries to surrender their preferential access to the EEC without adequate compensation.[50] But on the question of international financial transfers the G77 has followed an integrative approach, trying to increase the total quantity of aid and to improve the terms of this transfer. This integrative approach was seriously tested over the issue of debt relief because when the G77 first presented proposals for Generalised Debt Relief the developed countries' response was one which forced the developing countries into a distributive framework. The resulting clash in the G77 at the Ninth Special Session of the Trade and Development Board[51] arose as a result of a dispute between those states which were most likely to benefit from any scheme to reschedule debt and those states which would only benefit from a scheme of comprehensive Generalised Debt Relief.[52] The mode of intra-G77 bargaining therefore is as much a reflection of the issues under discussion as of the political attributes of the states themselves. Negotiations between the G77 and Groups B and D, whilst of a mixed nature, correspond more closely to distributive rather than integrative bargaining.

Decision making in the G77 is based on consensus and this applies to all aspects of the organisational infrastructure. In Geneva, the first stage of decision making is the regional group, and after consensus has been reached at the regional level attempts are made to form a common group position. Often within specific UNCTAD bodies it is the regional groups which present a common position rather than the G77 at the beginning of the negotiations. Indeed, the necessity of getting regional group consensus is such an important part of the decision making process that plenary and other meetings are often postponed because one or more regional group has not arrived at a consensus. This necessity for regional consensus and the compromises that are necessary to achieve it makes it difficult to reach a common G77 position since the regional compromises have to be safeguarded.[53] In this context issues are viewed not in terms of individual country interests but in terms of regional group interest. Decision making in the working groups and sub-committees created to cover specific negotiations is also by consensus and when agreement has been reached it is forwarded to the regional group for approval.

The origination of a common G77 position is both a simple and a tortuous process. Within the framework of UNCTAD the demands of the G77 on any issue is first the result of pressures by one state or a group of states. A country with an interest in a particular issue will first present a draft resolution to a meeting of its regional group. Normally, before a resolution is formally presented informal consultations are held with several members of the group to see what the likely reaction to the proposal will be. The draft resolution is then debated in the regional group. If the resolution fails to gain consensus in the regional group it generally dies at that stage, but it is possible for states to resurrect their proposal at a meeting of the G77 as a whole, especially if members of other regional groups are likely to give support to the proposal.[54] If the resolution is successful it is then adopted as an official position of the regional group for presentation to the G77 as a whole.

Objections to any proposal are generally based on two divergent types of reasoning. On the one hand, states will invoke considerations of their national interests and, on the other, they will invoke the likely reactions of Groups B and D to the proposal; either as a call for moderation or to argue in favour of more far-reaching demands. Because decisions are by consensus every state has a theoretical veto. The possession of this automatic veto would severely restrict the activities of the G77 if the custom had not been adopted of states entering reservations on any resolution with which they fundamentally disagreed. Persuasion is the normal method of arriving at collective decisions in a context of minimal sanctions. This is done through appeals to higher shared values or longer-run self-interest considerations and through the use of economic argument to show that the proposed policy really would benefit the state in question. There is very little conscious trade-off between different proposals. Any trade-offs take place within the parameters of a specific issue. There is an in-built hostility to the use of a conscious trade-off strategy. Negotiations among the G77 are conducted in a hard-headed bargaining atmosphere and within these negotiations two different approaches may be emphasised. I have termed these approaches 'maximalist' and 'minimalist'. Maximalists argue that G77 positions should contain far-reaching demands. Proponents of this approach argue that this would force Group B to upgrade its offers. Maximalists criticise the present G77 approach which is based on obtaining group cohesion. They argue that it provides Group B with the opportunity of making offers below the G77 position which will be acceptable to some countries. This argument appears misguided since given the internal G77 negotiating process it is difficult to envisage circumstances in which the resulting negotiating position cannot be undercut to the satisfaction of some members. Minimalists argue that G77 positions should provide a meaningful basis for negotiations with Group B and therefore should not contain excessive demands. This strategy is based on two questionable assumptions. It assumes that Group B is interested in meaningful negotiations on a wide range of issues and that the G77 can be maintained as a viable coalition if it consistently refuses support to positions held to be important by large sections of the membership.

Although various writers have categorised G77 decision making as conforming to the mode identified here as maximalist,[55] it is not really possible to identify which method pertains most widely over the range of G77 decision making. Decision making in regional groups is a closed process and one cannot arrive at firm conclusions regarding the type of outcome reached. The accommodation of regional positions into that of the group as a whole is a more open process and some more definite conclusions can be drawn. Although decision making here seems a compromise between the maximalists and the minimalists because it tends towards portmanteau resolutions covering all points of view, it approximates more readily to the maximalist strategy. Once compromise has been reached at the regional level it usually proves difficult to renegotiate positions in the G77 as a whole. This inflexibility arising from the need to balance the intricacies of the internal agreement gives G77 'final' positions a forceful and uncompromising air.

Although it is often claimed that the NAM plays an important role in G77 decision making,[56] in Geneva the NAM is not constituted as a formal group and does not have an input into G77 deliberations. We do not observe the patterns of influence in the NAM being replicated in the G77 in Geneva. But it should be noted that both Algeria and Cuba used the chairmanship of the NAM to exercise an effective degree of persuasion in the G77. It is at the global level that the NAM links into the negotiating process. Together with the G77 the NAM forms a

Third World coalition campaigning for regime change. Since the NAM took a decisive interest in international economic issues following its third Heads of State conference at Lusaka in September 1970 it has provided an input into the policy formulation of the G77. The continued support for the objectives of the G77 given by successive NAM conferences represents some input into G77 decision making at the global level. The NAM raised the political profile of regime change and became the originator of ideas. It was certainly useful in setting the agenda for the NIEO but the deliberations of the G77 in UNCTAD have not been affected by specific NAM inputs. To claim that the NAM is important in the G77's decision making we need to go beyond enumerating a coincidence of objectives and similarity of topics discussed by the G77 and the NAM and to show the specific influence of the NAM in G77 decision making. The process of influence is diffuse and difficult to isolate. In so far as the NAM took a leading role in agenda setting during the NIEO discussions then it was an influential actor in the G77's decisional process but we also need to recognise that most NIEO proposals were long-established G77 demands.

The structure of influence

The concepts of power and influence, central as they are to political science, have as yet not been reduced to definitions widely acceptable to political theorists.[57] In what follows influence will be defined as the ability to affect the distribution of goods and services and the formulation of value consensus in the negotiating process. We can identify two types of influence — negative influence and positive influence. Negative influence is exercised when an actor plays a blocking role preventing some proposal from being accepted and positive influence is exercised when an actor initiates a successful proposal. This analysis is primarily concerned with the exercise of influence over time and not specific, discrete acts. The following analysis is largely based on interview material.

Given the decision-making structure of the group the exercise of influence is first noticeable in the regional context. Here we can identify three factors which account for influence. First, there is a correlation between the main actors in UNCTAD regional groups and in the regional sub-systems at the global level. Thus in the Latin American Group, Argentina, Brazil, Mexico and Venezuela were consistently regarded as the most influential states. Similarly in the African Group, Algeria, Egypt, Ghana, and Nigeria,and in the Asian Group, India and Pakistan were acknowledged as being influential. The relatively high status of these states in the political and economic institutions of their region and their wide-ranging interests and political activity contributes to their prestige and effectiveness in UNCTAD. Indeed, it is precisely those attributes which determine their regional preponderance that enhances their roles within UNCTAD. Secondly, the ability to maintain a diplomatic mission in Geneva with a large and competent professional staff with good communication links with the national capital is an invaluable asset for any member of the G77. This is important because despite the outpourings of rhetoric UNCTAD is essentially an organisation concerned with technical issues the understanding of which is important if any meaningful negotiations are to take place. Moreover, the expanded agenda, proliferation of issues, reports and meetings place a severe strain on resources. In these circumstances, those G77 members with the administrative capacity equipped to cope with these demands enjoy a tremendous advantage over those states unable to prepare an adequate response. As J. M. Thomas and W. G. Bennis argue 'power will accrue to those organisations and positions within organisations which can develop access to and control of the knowledge and information needed for complex problem-solving.'[58] Only a handful of countries enjoy this administrative advantage, namely Brazil, India and Yugoslavia and to a lesser extent Argentina, Nigeria and Pakistan. Harassed missions with one or two professional staff members cannot cope with the wide range of issues with any degree of competence and so they specialise in a few areas and rely on a general approach in others.[59] The third factor is the influence of delegates. Influence exerted by a delegate may be due to diplomatic skill and wide range of experience enhancing negotiating ability in the context of consensus politics. The ability to be a moderator, to facilitate agreement between opposing sides and to construct compromises contributes to the esteem in which a particular representative is held. The possession of expert knowledge in a certain area and general economic expertise also contribute to a representative's high standing within the G77. The two categories are not mutually exclusive and long tenure, importance of the problem to the diplomat's government and personal interest are common features. Finally, some diplomats are able to exercise influence because they are not constrained by orders from their national capitals. Because of this they are relatively free to initiate proposals and are not subject to the confusion that can stymie national policy due to jurisdictional conflicts between different ministries.

The influence of individual states in the decisional process of the G77 therefore varies over time. For the larger states it has been relatively constant but for the smaller states it is very much a function of issue and the personal qualities of the diplomatic staff. Although the regional group is the basis of wider influence in the G77 it does not follow that leading regional actors exert a wider leadership role. For example, between 1976 and 1979 Egypt, the Ivory Coast, Morocco and Tunisia (African Group), Indonesia, Sri Lanka and Malaysia (Asian Group), and Peru and Trinidad and Tobago (Latin American Group), although major regional actors, were not in the forefront of the group as a whole.

The UNCTAD secretariat as a *de facto* secretariat of the G77 exercises two particular functions which contributes to its influence in the G77's political process. The first is what I term an informational role. Beginning with Prebisch's 'Towards A New Trade Policy for Development', the UNCTAD secretariat has consistently provided the developing countries with an economic rationale for their political objectives. It is the secretariat which conducts the research on which the common G77 positions are so often dependent. Although some countries have become less dependent on secretariat research, for example Brazil and

India, and some G77 members do criticise the work of the secretariat, most countries are dependent on the secretariat for almost all of their economic arguments. Thus G77 policies are largely formulated on the basis of the UNCTAD secretariat's statistical information and economic interpretation. Furthermore, members of the secretariat are often able to get delegates to sponsor resolutions largely drawn up by the secretariat. The second function can be termed a brokerage role. The secretariat plays an important role as a mediator in the decision-making process of the G77. For example, as the two case studies demonstrate Prebisch played a significant role in the attainment of compromise on the GSP at UNCTAD II and Corea was instrumental in securing consensus on the Common Fund resolution at UNCTAD IV. Furthermore, the Special Unit for Liaison in the Office of the UNCTAD Secretary-General plays a day-to-day brokerage role and is important in reconciling the diverse interests of the group members at the various levels of meetings.

Conflict and conflict resolution

Three types of cleavages — ascriptive (different levels of development, and the differing structures of economies); attitudinal (ideology and preferences); and behavioural (activities within UNCTAD and membership in other organisations and groupings) — determine the conflictual process within the G77.

Ascriptive cleavages determine the heteogeneity or homogeneity of a group. The G77 is a very heterogeneous group because of the huge economic and political differences among the members.[60] Economic differences can be measured in terms of GNP or other economic indicators or they can be plotted in terms of specific issues. But while ascriptive cleavages signify the existence of difference it is the intensity of the cleavage which is important. In other words it is the political importance attached to the ascriptive cleavage which determines the degree of unity or disunity attained by the G77. Examples of ascriptive cleavages to which political importance has been attached in the G77 are special categories of economic or geographical disadvantage. The G77 has been reluctant to accept the subdivision of the developing country category.[61] As a pressure group which accepts its necessary heterogeneity but subordinates this to the pursuit of common interests, the identification of sub-categorisations within the group based on a separate developmental axis poses fundamental problems for group unity. But three groups have been successful in getting recognition of their special status. The identification of and support for the category of least developed countries (LDDC) constituted a serious problem for the G77. It caused a cleavage along regional group lines since most of the designated countries belonged to the African Group.[62] And it also led to intra-group conflict, for example between Bangladesh and India. The cohesion of the LDDCs and the support of major Western donors for this grouping has ensured both its continued importance in the G77 and the provision of special measures by the international community.[63] The identification of a land-locked country (LLC) is largely unproblematical.[64] The conflicts concerning LLCs centre around their relations with their transit neighbours and the drafting of rules to safeguard the right of access to the sea for the LLCs. The importance of security concerns in this context brings an added political intensity to the debate. The category of developing island countries (DIC) is one that by its very nature creates a high degree of political opposition. Many states, particularly those in the the LDDC category resent the creation of another special-interest group in the G77 which diverts resources away from their interests. The category of DIC is so wide as to be intellectually meaningless. In creating such a category in the first place the island countries were ascribing a political commitment to their geographical status[65] and it is difficult to envisage them agreeing to a more restricted definition which makes some economic sense.

The existence of cleavages poses problems for G77 unity but the proliferation of interest groups in the coalition need not create disunity. Interest groups are contained in the G77 and become enmeshed in its political process. The ability of states to pursue specific interests in an organisational forum to some extent enhances the degree of unity achieved by the G77. Furthermore, the mode of decision making protects national autonomy and the proliferation of interest groups increases the scope of the G77 as an international organisation. It also provides a stable pattern of expectations concerning the behaviour of disaffected group members.

There are two types of attitudinal cleavages in the G77. Those of a political nature relating to the relations between member countries and developed countries and the bearing this has on the collective efforts of the developing countries. And those resulting from particular ideological and political conflicts between developing countries. There is a wide range of opinion in the G77 concerning relations with the developed world. The developed countries attempt to exploit these attitudinal differences in order to undermine the unity of the G77. Attempts to increase these divergent tendencies are made through designing bilateral and multilateral arrangements, with specific developing countries, on issues which directly affect G77 demands.[66] Strenuous attempts are made to limit the impact of the second type of attitudinal cleavage on G77 unity. Whilst at the regional and global levels there are many political disputes between G77 members these are very rarely allowed to intrude into the group's deliberations in UNCTAD. There is an unwritten agreement that UNCTAD is a technical body and that extra-political considerations should not interrupt its work programme. Nevertheless, there are ocassionally disputes of a political nature which surface and lead to a degree of antagonism between states.[67]

Behavioural cleavages are of two types. Those relating to behaviour in UNCTAD are covered extensively in this study and need not detain us here. The second type of behavioural cleavage relates to the conflicting membership some states have outside the UNCTAD framework. For example, preferential arrangements with the EEC have caused a great deal of divisiveness in the G77.

We have already outlined the main features of conflict resolution in the group in the section on decision making. The avoidance and diminution of conflict is a continuous process within the G77 and of utmost importance for its continued unity. Given the level of common interests, variations are bound to arise on matters of detail. The consensus mode of decision making and the nature of conflicting objectives have resulted in the absence of dispute settlement procedures within the group. Whenever there is a major dispute a working group is created to try to formulate a compromise solution. This is a tortuous and slow process and seriously affects the G77's effectiveness as a negotiating instrument. The necessity of arriving at a compromise on all issues and the refusal of parties to negotiate on other issues until the outstanding issue is resolved affects the progress of conference deliberations and imparts an air of crisis to G77 decision making. The conscious use of a trade-off policy would alleviate some of these problems of conflict resolution.

The level of conflict and dissensus in the group has not to date produced any defections from the coalition. This is not because there have not been severe strains on G77 unity but because the benefits to date outweigh the costs. The economic costs of membership are minimal. There are no real direct participation costs, since the cost of a mission in Geneva is not an essential prerequisite of membership. Moreover, a mission in Geneva is a multi-purpose one since it provides representation to a cluster of international organisations. The economic cost of sending missions to ministerial meetings and UNCTAD conferences are not unduly high and states can reduce their level of participation without absenting themselves from the organisation. Of greater importance are those benefits which would be forgone if membership of the G77 prevented a state from joining a bilateral or multilateral agreement. But to date membership of the G77 has not acted as a restraint on the pursuit of other economic goals.[68] It is possible that a political cost can exist if a country feels that a G77 resolution or common position is unwise and likely to lead to a worsening of relations with the developed countries. But in that case a government can ignore those positions in which it has no interest and those which it finds embarrassing.

Conclusions

We began this chapter by considering the importance of changes in scope and level for organisational performance. Having considered the evidence it is now possible to assess the relevance of our amended concepts for an understanding of the nature and stability of the G77. The scope of the organisation has incresased considerably. Beginning with the first Ministerial Meeting in Algiers in 1967 a permanent structure has gradually developed. Secondly, the number of groups involved in policy making increased with the proliferation of the G77 in various international fora. Moreover this proliferation can be taken to signal the importance of the G77 as a coordinating body for national governments. Thirdly, within the UNCTAD context two different sets of groups developed i.e.

organisational bodies e.g. working groups and interest groups like LDDCs. These developments have contributed to the continuity of joint decision making thus increasing the level of organisational activity. The creation of the Preparatory Committee and the changes in the Ministerial Meeting reveal not only increased institutionalisation but also the creation of a stable pattern of expectations. We have argued that the consensus method of decision making, because it protects national autonomy, contributes to the stability of the G77. This argument is the reverse of the findings of organisational theory but far from being perverse merely recognises the special characteristics of the G77. From the viewpoint of organisational development, that is increasing the autonomy of the G77, this stress on national sovereignty had an inhibiting effect on the creation of a secretariat or the implementation of coordination between the various regional centres. In the absence of a G77 secretariat the UNCTAD secretariat through its command of material and ideological resources exercises a significant degree of influence over the group.[69]

Developments in organisational structure and the mode of decision making provide effective checks on the tendency towards disunity. This analysis shows that the importance of cleavages for the G77's stability cannot be inferred from rational actor assumptions. The enmeshment of state actors in a complex organisational web and the methods of conflict resolution significantly condition group outcomes. The two case studies which follow in Chapters 6 and 7 will examine the importance of organisational context on the outcomes of negotiations.

Notes

1. P. C. Schmitter, 'Three Neo-Functional Hypotheses About International Integration', *International Organization* (Winter 1969), pp.161–6.
2. Ibid., p.163.
3. Ansari, *UNCTAD: Ojectives and Performance,* p.183.
4. China with sufficient resources and influence potential is able to eschew membership of the G77.
5. The principle of regional group autonomy on questions of membership was maintained when the PLO, a non-state actor was admitted to the Asian Group. See *Jakarta Declaration 1976* 77/MM(III)/6. Annex I. Resolution on the PLO.
6. Malta had applied for and been refused membership of the Asian Group. See *Jakarta Declaration,* ibid. But during the course of the Manila Conference Malta was admitted to the Asian Group.
7. See 'Working Group on Membership: Report on Procedures for the Admission of New Members to the Group of 77 and on Membership of the Group' (Geneva, 28 April 1976) in K.P. Sauvant (ed.), *The Collected Documents of the Group of 77,* vol.III (hereinafter referred to as *Collected Documents*).
8. *Manila Declaration and Programme of Action. TD/195* and 77/MM(III)/49. Annex I. p.9. These stipulations were made because Romania's application had been greeted unfavourably by some countries who were annoyed that at a UNIDO meeting immediately preceeding Manila it had supported the Group D position.

9. Cuban membership was sponsored by the African and Asian Groups. The Latin American Group agreed largely as a result of the pressure brought by the Allende regime in Chile, the hosts for UNCTAD III in 1972.

10. Cuba's integration into fully active membership came at the insistence of Mexico, Jamaica and Chile and coincided with a less hostile attitude towards Cuba in Latin America and the Caribbean.

11. This is compounded by lack of professional staff and a rapid turnover of important officials.

12. K. P. Sauvant, *The Group of 77* (New York: Oceana, 1981), p.52.

13. Prior to the Algiers meeting the G77 was riven by disunity particularly over the GSP and LDDC issues. See Dick Wilson, 'Unity of the South', *Far Eastern Economic Review* (20 October 1966), p. 130; Edith Rebecca Lenart, 'The Algiers Charter', *Far Eastern Economic Review* (9 November 1967), p.266.

14. See *The Charter of Algiers* TD/38. Add.1 p.28.

15. TD/B/Misc.60/Rev.2 (23 September 1966).

16. TAD/31(X)/Misc.6/Rev.3 (10 March 1971).

17. See the reports of the Preparatory Comittees for the second, third and fourth ministerial meetings in *Collected Documents*, vol.I, pp.476–96; vol.II, pp.337–78; vol.III, pp.151–241.

18. Sauvant, *op.cit.*, p.32.

19. The Group of 31 in its preparations for the Second Ministerial Meeting requested a preparatory meeting of 'high officials'. See TAD/31(X)/Misc.6/Rev.3.

20. See MM/77/II/4(27 Oct.1971), Report on the Meeting of Senior Government Officials (*Collected Documents*, vol.II).

21. See 77/MM(IV)18 (4 February 1979). Senior Officials Meeting (*Collected Documents*, vol.III).

22. See 77/MM(III)/2 (27 January 1976). Senior Officials Meeting *Collected Documents* vol.II).

23. TD/38. Add.1. p.28.

24. See The Charter of Algiers (1967), The Declaration and Principles of the Action Programme of Lima (1971), the Manila Declaration and Programme of Action (1976), the Arusha Programme for Collective Self-Reliance and Framework for Negotiations (1979), the Buenos Aires Platform (1983), the Havana Assessment, and Proposals by the Group of 77 relating to UNCTAD VII (1987).

25. See for example 77/MM(IV)/5 – 77/MM/(IV)/15 for the Arusha Ministerial Meeting.

26. See Sauvant, op.cit., pp.38–43, for more details on the institutionalisation of the ministerial meeting.

27. See Sauvant, op.cit., pp.54–86.

28. On coordination problems in the UN system see M. Hill, *The United Nations System* (Cambridge: Cambridge University Press 1978); Joint Inspection Unit, *Some Reflections on Reform of the United Nations*, prepared by Maurice Bertrand, JIU/REP/ 85/9, Geneva 1985 (the Bertrand Report).

29. A Yugoslavian diplomat reported that the Yugoslavian missions to New York and Geneva held differing views pertaining to the agenda of UNCTAD V.

30. A Jamaican diplomat reported in 1978 that in eighteen months in Geneva he had never seen nor heard anything of the G77 in Rome or Vienna.

31. Two key attempts at developing coordination were made between 1975 and 1980. The first concerned coordination between the Group of 19 developing countries

attending the Conference on International Economic Cooperation (CIEC) in Paris and the Geneva and New York based groups of the G77. The second, concerning an initiative in the Committee of the Whole in the UN, did lead to a limited amount of coordination.

32. *The Declaration and Principles of the Action Programme of Lima*, Part Four (IV).

33. See 'Working Group of the Group of 77 — Manila Decision No.2: Report on the Proposed Establishment of the Group of 77', Geneva, 27 April 1976. UNCTAD/CA/843 (28 April 1976).

34. Ibid., para, 30.

35. See Kenneth O. Hall, 'Technical Assistance and Organizational Support for Developing Countries on International Economic Negotiations: A Report', in *The Group of 77: Strengthening Its Negotiating Capacity* (Nyon: Third World Forum, 1979), p.18.

36. States are afraid that if the headquarters are situated in a developing country then that country might be able to exert unwanted influence on the secretariat. On the other hand, although Geneva is the obvious site, many countries would like the headquarters to be in the Third World.

37. I was told by a Brazilian diplomat that the creation of a G77 secretariat would be 'unneccesary bureaucratisation'. He added somewhat revealingly that a secretariat would be 'unhelpful or too efficient'.

38. For a discussion of the effect of the G77 on the UNCTAD secretariat see Weiss, *op.cit.*, pp.89–101.

39. There are, however, a range of economic and political Third World organisations which provide support services for developing countries, for example regional organisations and producer alliances. The creation of the 28-member South Commission in July 1987 does not really fill the institutional void. The Commission's objective is to 'find out how the South can work together and bring about a much more fruitful dialogue with the North'.

40. See R. N. Gardner, 'The United Nations Conference on Trade and Development', *International Organization* (Winter 1968), pp.99–130; A. K. Bhattacharya, 'The influence of the international secretariat: UNCTAD and generalized preferences', *International Organization* (Winter 1976), pp.75–90; J. S. Nye, 'UNCTAD: Poor Nations Pressure Group' in R. W. Cox & H. K. Jacobson (eds), *The Anatomy of Influence* (New Haven, Conn.: Yale University Press, 1973), pp.334–70.

41. Regularised contact between the secretariat and the G77 had been taking place before this process was given an institutional focus.

42. The G77 in other international organisations only receive administrative services.

43. These assessments are based on interviews.

44. Marc A. Williams, 'The Group of 77, UNCTAD V and the North/South Dialogue', *IDS Bulletin* (January 1980), p.7.

45. See for example E. S. Milenky, *The Politics of Regional Organization in Latin America* (New York: Praeger 1973); W. R. Cline & E. Delgado (eds), *Economic Integration in Central America* (Washington, DC: Brookings Institution, 1978); A. Gauhar (ed.), *Regional Integration: The Latin American Experience* (London: Third World Foundation, 1985).

46. See W. A. Agor, 'Latin American Inter-State Politics: Patterns of Cooperation and Conflict', *Inter-American Economic Affairs* (August 1972), p.19.

47. Bolivia lost its coastline in the 1879 War of the Pacific with Chile and refuses to recognise the permanency of Chile's acquisition.

48. See K. Midgaard, 'Cooperative Negotiations and Bargaining: Some Notes on Power and Powerlessness' in B. Barry (ed.), *Power and Political Theory* (London: John Wiley, 1976), p.117.

49. See P. Warr, Psychology and Collective Bargaining (London: Hutchinson, 1973), pp. pp.17–20.

50. This was usually phrased as follows, 'The new system of general preferences should ensure at least equivalent advantages to developing countries enjoying preferences in certain developed countries'. See the *Charter of Algiers*.

51. 5–10 September 1977; 23–7 January 1978 and 6–11 March 1978.

52. See TD/B/SR.478-494.

53. A similar process occurs in Group B where the EEC common position has to be safeguarded.

54. This occurs when interest group membership cross-cuts the regional groups.

55. See, for example, Gosovic, 'UNCTAD: North–South Encounter', op.cit, p.30; I. M. D. Little, *Economic Development* (New York: Basic Books, 1982), p.382.

56. See O. Jankowitsch K. P. Sauvant, 'The Initiating Role of the Non-Aligned Countries' in K. P. Sauvant (ed.), *Changing Priorities on the International Agenda* (Oxford: Pergamon, 1981), pp.41–77; R. A. Mortimer, *The Third World Coalition in International Politics* (Boulder: Westview, 1984), pp.74–94.

57. See Cox Jacobson, op.cit., pp.20–1 for an attempt to operationalise the concepts of influence and power in international organisations.

58. J. M. Thomas & W. G. Bennis (eds.), *Management of Change and Conflict* (Harmondsworth: Penguin, 1972), pp.9–10.

59. For example during the 1979 Code of Conduct on the Transfer of Technology negotiations some African delegations had no negotiating expertise. They presented a position which stated, 'we support the position on a legally binding code in principle' but were unable to discuss details. Brazil and India who both opposed a legally binding code were able to argue their case persuasively.

60. See also Jean-Phillipe Colson, 'Le Groupe des 77 et le problême d'unité Des pays du tiers monde', *Revue Tiers Monde* (October–December 1972), pp.813–30; B. Gosovic, *UNCTAD*, op.cit, pp.297–86; B.Gosovic, 'UNCTAD: North–South Encounter', op.cit., pp.1–80.

61. For example, in the wake of the oil and debt crises World Bank reports divide the developing countries into a number of distinct analytical categories.

62. None of the countries included in the least developed category (Bolivia, Ecuador and Paraguay) as defined in Latin American integration schemes were included in the UNCTAD secretariat's list, thus provoking the opposition of the Latin American Group to special measures for the LDDCs.

63. The UNGA adopted the Substantial Programme of Action for the 1980s for the Least Developed Countries (SNPA) in 1981. Forty countries are now classified as least developed. UNCTAD was entrusted with the focal role of monitoring the implementation of SNPA at the global level. See also T. G. Weiss & A. Jennings, *More for the Least? Prospects for Poorest Countries in the Eighties* (Lexington, Mass.: Heath, 1983).

64. Although Zaïre with only a small outlet to the sea would like to be included in this category.

65. I have been informed privately, however, that this category was created by the Latin American countries in an attempt to proliferate special categories. The rationale behind this is to limit any special benefits gained from special status.

66. For example, CIEC.
67. See, for example, the dispute over the representation of Kampuchea at UNCTAD V. *Proceedings (1976)*, vol.1, Report and Annexes, Part 2, paras 1–229.
68. A Pakistani diplomat did however inform me that Pakistan had refrained from making some bilateral deals because of its G77 commitments. He admitted nevertheless that Pakistan gained from pressure the G77 exerts in fields outside UNCTAD's immediate range because bilateral deals reflect the multilateral agreements of organisations such as UNCTAD.
69. Nye, *op.cit.*, pp.334–370.

Part III
Conflict and conflict management

6 The negotiations for a Generalised System of Preferences, 1964–70

Negotiations on the GSP dominated UNCTAD politics in the first five years of the organisation's existence. The unity of the G77 was put to a severe test during these negotiations and therefore an examination of this process will illuminate group cohesion and fractionalisation. This chapter attempts to provide answers to two central questions: how, given the initial differences, did the G77 construct a common negotiating position? And what effect did the existence of various cleavages have on the shape of the final agreement? This chapter, therefore, analyses both the development of a joint negotiating strategy by the G77 and the UNCTAD decision to implement a GSP.

Economic analysis and the debate on preferences

Before discussing the bargaining which took place over the issue of preferences it is important that some attention is given to the economic considerations underlying the GSP. It is not the aim of this section to assess the benefits which have flowed from the operation of the scheme[1] or to debate the limitations of the scheme that was agreed.[2] Rather it is to examine the underlying economic arguments for and against the granting of wide-ranging preferential access for the manufactured and semi-manufactured exports of the developing countries to the markets of the developed countries. We will be examining divergent opinion on two sets of arguments. First, those relating to any form of preferential access for LDC manfactured exports (to developed country markets) and, secondly, those relating more specifically to the concept of the GSP.

It is essential to open up the bargaining space to this kind of consideration because of the role played by ideas and ideology in the determination of outcomes.[3] Economic analysis and the struggle between competing theories is a crucial aspect of negotiations. In other words, economic analysis is not an unproblematical element in international economic negotiations. Negotiating positions are based to a large extent on economic analysis, and economic theories and ideas serve to shape choice and to define the arena of the possible.

Preferential schemes seek to expand the exports and export earnings of developing countries. This objective is accomplished through static price advantages which make developing country goods more competitive *vis-à-vis* domestic producers and third country non-preferred exporters. They also seek to create dynamic incentives for investment in export capacity. We can distinguish three aspects of the economic argument in favour of preferences. The first highlights the necessity to grant favourable entry conditions to developed country markets for infant industries in the Third World. In the context of economic development the infant industry argument rests on three considerations[4]: the importance of increasing returns to scale, i.e. as output grows costs diminish until the point is reached when the industry becomes competitive; the role of externalities, i.e. an industry tends to produce secondary industries, services and infrastructure investment; and the importance of the learning effect in the development of technical, organisational and managerial skills. It is argued that producers of manufactured goods in developing countries are unable to compete with developed country producers because of the existence of certain conditions germane to underdevelopment.[5] For example, high import costs for capital equipment, the low productivity of domestic labour and the absence of internal economies of scale. The second aspect of the argument stresses the way in which the tariff structures of the developed countries act as a disincentive to developing country exporters. One of the basic features of tariff regimes in the developed countries is the escalation of rates from the lower to the higher stages of processing. Duties on imported raw materials tend to be low or even nil, but increasingly duties are levied on products manufactured from the same raw materials. The effective degree of protection given to domestic producers is hence far in excess of the nominal rate of protection.[6] This kind of tariff structure discourages the processing of raw materials in the exporting country and encourages the export of raw materials instead. Taking the steeply escalated tariff structures of developed countries in conjunction with the high dependence on imported materials and components characteristic of developing countries, tariffs do then provide a sizeable barrier to LDC export of manufactured and semi-manufactured products. Preferential tariff reductions would give developing country exporters advantages in two categories. It would reduce the degree of protection given to domestic producers and give the LDC exporters a competitive edge over competing exports from non-preferred third countries. The third aspect of the argument stresses welfare considerations. As Murray states the 'redistribution of world income in favour of developing countries might increase the welfare value of a constant (or even declining) level of world income.'[7] This argument is based on analysis of the trade diversion and trade creation effects of preferential systems. But the welfare gains may be greater than this analysis with its assumption that factors of production have alternative employment opportunities envisages. In the case of developing countries the new exports may use previously unemployed or under-employed factors thus increasing welfare, that is welfare equals producer surplus plus the entire factor wage bill. It is also possible that factors displaced in preference-giving and preference-receiving countries are likely to be re-employed.[8]

Before turning to the case against preferences it is worth noting some additional arguments tangential to and supplementary to the three major ones outlined above. Increased productivity in developing countries would lead to increased income which in turns leads to increased market size, investment etc. Improved access to world markets leads to improved opportunities for large-scale production and enlarged domestic markets. Furthermore, there might be a new export flow of new products which were previously uncompetitive in the preference-giving country and of products previously only exported to other developing countries. Indirect dynamic gains would include incentives for investment by local firms and transnational corporations, the establishment of new market linkages in developed countries, and the diversification of supply source by the developed country importers to include LDCs. Finally, given the wide-ranging import substitution policies in developing contries any scheme to encourage export promotion is desirable.[9]

The case against preferences rests on a denial of the benefits claimed by the proponents of the scheme and an argument that the objectives could be attained through more cost-effective means. The objection to the GSP rested on three main arguments. The first stresed the inappropriatenes of the proposed measures. Tariff preferences were held to be inappropriate for a variety of reasons. First, it is argued that the case that is presented is too general. The infant industry argument cannot be generalised to cover the wide range of industries and countries proposed.[10] Secondly, as Hindley observed, LDCs' failure to be competitive arises from their lack of complementary factors, capital, technical know-how, managerial and marketing skills which in turn are magnified by overvalued exchange rates and other policy measures.[11] If infant industries cannot compete this is primarily due to internal problems in developing countries which will not be solved by changes in the commercial policies of the developed countries. Thirdly, opponents of the GSP rejected the claim that developed country tariff regimes were prohibitive to LDC exporters. Fourthly, they asserted that the creation of preferences could be double-edged and backfire in that they could give producers in the developed countries a better opportunity to press for legislation implementing restrictive safeguards than would be possible under a non-discriminatory regime.[12]

The second objection was based on the claim that better alternatives existed to achieve the same objectives. First, in so far as preferences attempt to stimulate exports then devaluation is a better alternative. Devaluation as an export stimulating measure only fails when trading partners take retaliatory measures and since LDCs are relatively insignificant in world trade the industrialised states are unlikely to risk upsetting the structure of exchange rates to retaliate against an individual developing country.[13] Secondly, the LDCs could subsidise their industrial exports. Thirdly, from the perspective of global redistribution preferences are an inferior form of aid giving, and result in aid costs being distributed unequally.[14] If the goal is to increase revenue accruing to LDCs then this could best be satisfied by an increase in aid.

The third was a specific objection to the concept of a GSP. It was argued that such a system would be difficult to negotiate and administer and therefore was a costly and time-consuming exercise best abandoned given the previous economic arguments against preferential systems. For example, Johnson identified seven main problem areas in the negotiation and administration of a GSP ranging from equity (for both receivers and givers) to the likely duration of the preferential scheme and the necessity to provide compensation for countries currently enjoying preferences.[15]

Cleavages

In this section the specific cleavages which existed in the G77 over preferences will be examined. The nature and salience of particular cleavages were of crucial importance in the bargaining process. The significant ascriptive traits are those relating to the ability of a country to benefit from the operation of a GSP. This is dependent on the level of development achieved and the ability to export manufactured and semi-manufactured products. It is also dependent upon whether a GSP might interfere with existing patterns of trade in a detrimental manner. The significant attitudinal traits relate to the perception of whether a general system or a more selective arrangement might enhance a country's access to markets. The significant behavioural traits relate to the use made of organisational membership outside the UNCTAD framework and to actions within UNCTAD. Although inevitably there is an element of overlap involved the analytical separation of the three categories rests on distinctions between material conditions (ascriptive), perceptions (attitudinal) and actions (behavioural).

An examination of the immediate or short-term potential of the developing countries to benefit from the introduction of a preferential scheme shows that only a handful of them were sufficiently competitive to be able to take advantage of the improved access to developed country markets. The ability to benefit from the GSP was also dependent on the extent of product coverage. And here on the wider question of principle there was an argument for extending the system to cover processed and semi-processed agricultural products. The expansion of manufactured and semi-manufactured exports from developing countries to the developed countries between 1961 and 1965 was confined to a small number of countries. The biggest growth in exports was achieved by Hong Kong, Taiwan, Israel, South Korea, Brazil, Mexico and Chile. The principal manufactured exports consisted of a limited range of products, mainly textiles and other light manufactures. In 1961 five developing countries supplied 51.8 per cent of all developing countries' manufactured exports. In 1965 these same five (Hong Kong, India, Yugoslavia, Mexico and Algeria) supplied 50 per cent. With the addition of Taiwan and Brazil these seven countries accounted for 56.7 per cent and 57.7 per cent of developing countries exports of manufactures and semi-manufactures in 1961 and 1965 respectively. As Table 6.1 shows twenty-five developing countries account for 85.9 per cent of total exports of manufactures and semi-manufactures from this group in 1965. Moreover, in 1965 the export of processed agricultural products accounted for the total manufactured and semi-manufactured exports of Somalia, El Salvador, Togo and Yemen; and for more than 50 per cent for Cuba, Algeria, Paraguay, Senegal, Iraq, Morocco, Nicaragua, Ethiopia, Argentina, Uruguay and the Dominican Republic.[16]

Table 6.1 *Imports of manufactures and semi-manufactures into developed market economy countries from developing countries, by main countries of origin, 1965*

Developing countries which are major suppliers	Exports in value ($US million)	Per cent distribution
Developing countries total	3,585.3	100.0
Hong Kong	723.6	20.3
India	472.2	13.2
Yugoslavia	255.7	7.1
Mexico	178.2	5.0
Algeria	161.8	4.5
Taiwan	146.0	4.1
Brazil	130.5	3.6
Argentina	101.4	2.8
Iran	101.0	2.8
Israel	95.5	2.7
Malaysia/Singapore	87.4	2.4
Philippines	87.4	2.4
Morocco	72.7	2.0
Pakistan	71.2	2.0
Republic of Korea	61.2	1.7
Chile	61.0	1.7
Jamaica	50.6	1.4
Thailand	41.2	1.1
Panama	37.8	1.1
United Arab Republic	34.0	0.9
Peru	25.6	0.7
Guinea	25.1	0.7
Paraguay	21.3	0.6
Cameroon	21.0	0.6
Trinidad and Tobago	16.4	0.5
Sub-Total	3,080.1	85.9
Others	505.2	14.1

Source: UNCTAD Review of Trade in Manufactures and Semi-Manufactures (TD/10/ Supp.1).

At the outset of the negotiations two main preferential systems were in operation — the Yaoundé Convention linking the EEC with the Association of African and Malagsy States (AASM) and the Commonwealth preference system.[17] Evaluation of the importance of these selective preferences for the beneficiaries at the outset of the negotiations is difficult given the limited evidence available. The following discussion is based on an analysis attempted by the UNCTAD secretariat.[18]

Preferential imports from the AASM amounted to some $580m. or about half the total EEC imports from this source in 1965. But manufactures (SITC 5–8) constituted a very small part of the total exports of the AASM. Although virtually all their exports to the EEC were covered by preferences, manufactures accounted for only $10m, i.e. 2 per cent of total preferential flows. About 60 per cent of the preferential imports into the EEC came from three of the eighteen associates. The Ivory Coast, Cameroon and Senegal had preferential exports of more than $100m. each. At the other end of the scale, six countries, Burundi, Chad, Mali, Mauretania, Rwanda and Upper Volta, had preferential exports of less than $1m. There was also a wide variation in market concentration from country to country. The Associated States as a group shipped on average nearly 60 per cent of their total exports to the EEC but whereas Dahomey, Senegal and Togo had an 80 per cent concentration in the EEC market, export concentration for Mali and Upper Volta was 17 per cent and 6 per cent respectively.

The pattern of preferences and the preference margin enjoyed by individual Commonwealth developing countries was determined by the composition of their exports to Commonwealth developed countries. In the United Kingdom most manufactured products entered duty-free. In Canada, Australia and New Zealand, although preferences fell short of duty free entry, there was still a considerable margin of preference over third countries. But it was the United Kingdom which was the most important market since in 1965 this market accounted for 79 per cent of all exports of Commonwealth developing countries to the more developed members of the Commonwealth. In the United Kingdom preferential system manufactured products (including foodstuffs) accounted for about half the preferential trade. Preferential trade in manufactures was spread over a wide area. The bulk of the trade, i.e. $360m.(63 per cent) consisted of manufactures of SITC classes 5–8; food industry products contributed $200m. (35 per cent) and processed raw materials accounted for $14m.(2 per cent). The main preferred suppliers were India and Hong Kong, followed by Nigeria, and about one-third of the countries had preferential exports of about $10m. or less. Some countries, such as Hong Kong, Malta and Gibralta, enjoyed preferences for a relatively high share of their manufactured exports. Trade dependence was less than that of the EEC's African Associates. The developing Commonwealth countries only relied on the UK market for one-fifth of their exports. Concentration of exports also varied widely from country to country. Only a few countries shipped more than half their exports to the United Kingdom, namely Sierra Leone, Mauritius, Barbados and the Gambia, whereas for Malaysia and Singapore the proportion was less than 10 per cent each.

In terms of the relationship between preferential trade and world exports the EEC Associates exhibited a higher level of dependence. For about a third of them, notably Senegal, Cameroon and Dahomey, preferential trade amounted to between one-half to two-thirds of their world exports; for another third this proportion ranged between 10 per cent and 40 per cent. For the remaining six countries, Burundi, Chad, Mali, Mauretania, Rwanda and Upper Volta, the proportions were between 1 per cent and 10 per cent. Only for three Commonwealth countries, Mauritius, the Gambia and Barbados, did preferential trade exceed half of their world exports; for most countries the proportion ranged between 1 per cent and 10 per cent. And for countries such as Ghana, Malaysia, Singapore, South Yemen and Zambia, preferential exports to the United Kingdom were insignificant. This evidence shows that the heterogeneity of the G77 varied not only across the two trait cleavages, that is the ability to export manufactures and semi-manufactures and membership of an existing selective preference scheme, but also within these two identifiable groups.

In the absence of any concrete evidence to support or refute the proposition that selective preferences seriously damaged the export prospects of third countries, the G77 was divided between those countries which felt that the existing system of selective preferences was detrimental to their own development efforts and the preference holders who refused to countenance giving up their 'advantages' without some form of compensation. However, not all countries currently enjoying vertical preferences took the attitude that these should be preserved. In the Commonwealth the Asian members were willing to forgo this special treatment in return for a satisfactory GSP. The AASM countries on the other hand, although having no significant preferential exports into the EEC, insisted on the granting of equivalent advantages before they would consider abandoning selective preferences. The Latin American countries, particularly Brazil, Argentina and Chile, called for the immediate abolition of existing preferential schemes upon the introduction of the new scheme.[19] Some Latin American states frustrated at the continuation of vertical preferences proposed as a counter the creation of a preferential system linking the United States and Latin America. It is difficult to assess whether this was viewed as an alternative to the GSP or if it was being used to put pressure on those countries in receipt of special preferences to abandon their systems. In this context, given that most LDC preference receivers did not stand to gain much from the GSP it seems more a serious proposal than a bargaining ploy. This counterbalancing policy was especially favoured by Colombia and it was a Colombian national, who as chairman of the Inter-American Committee of the Alliance for Progress(CIAP) proposed such a scheme in a letter of 10 August 1965 to the presidents of the American republics.[20] The view was also taken that existing preferential arrangements were exploitative since they perpetuated colonial structures of production and export. Apart from different perceptions concerning existing preferential arrangements, conflicting viewpoints existed on a number of other issues. These included the purpose and the likely duration of the scheme, country coverage and the treatment to be accorded to the LDDCs. These conflicts of interest will be discussed in greater detail later. The behavioural cleavages form the substance of the remainder of the chapter and arise from the trait and attitudinal cleavages discussed above. The bargaining process in UNCTAD was affected by membership of other organisations and the attempt of G77 protagonists to mobilise support within these organisations for positions taken in the negotiations. In this respect the African Associates of the EEC were able to use both their diplomatic missions in Brussels and also the institutionalised structure of the association to put pressure on the EEC to safeguard their special interests. The relevant joint institutions were the Association Council, the Association Committee and the consultative Parliamentary Conference.[21] Latin American states used their membership of the GATT and two regional organs, the CIAP and the Inter-American Special Committee for Consultations and Negotiations (CECON) to exert pressure on the United States.[22] Similarly, the developing Commonwealth countries could exert pressure on the United Kingdom and other developed Commonwealth countries.

The regional group structure of the G77 tended to produce conflict in the GSP negotiations along regional lines. The degree of fractionalisation was greatest between the African and Latin American groups but within each group a diversity of interest and attitude also existed. For example, not all Latin American countries supported the demand for a vertical preference system with the United States,[23] and Bolivia and Ecuador stressed the necessity to build safeguards for LDDCs within any agreed GSP. In the African Group both Ghana and Guinea argued against the continuation of vertical preferences.

The bargaining process

Agreement among the developing countries could not in itself bring into being a generalised system of preferences. The developed countries had to be convinced of the economic sense and practicality of the idea. The G77 thus had to secure internal agreement through the reconciliation of different regional group positions and the accommodation of individual state interest and secondly, persuade the major developed countries of the political necessity of the GSP. The examination of the bargaining process therefore traces developments in both areas.

UNCTAD I

When the Geneva Conference convened the subject of preferential treatment for the manufactures and semi-manufactures exports of developing countries had been on the international agenda for about a year. The GATT Ministerial Meeting of May 1963[24] had considered two proposals concerning special tariff treatment for LDCs and had accepted the principle of non-reciprocal tariff concessions to the developing countries. Of most interest for subsequent developments was the proposal by Mr Maurice Brasseur, the Belgian Minister of Foreign Trade and Technical Assistance.[25] Subsequently developed and expanded, the Brasseur Plan was submitted as part of a French memorandum to UNCTAD I.[26] Brasseur envisaged the creation of temporary, selective and degressive preferences. A series of bilateral negotiations would be held between individual preference givers and preference receivers. On a case by case basis they would reach agreement on the preferential margins, duration of the preferences and the size of tariff quotas. Each preference-giver, although ostensibly engaged in solely bilateral talks with interested developing countries, would nevertheless be making its decisions in the light of what other developed countries were doing. In this sense an element of multilateral negotiations would be imposed on the bilateral system. Preferences would be selective in respect of country and product and a declining level of preferences would be given for industries in developing countries that were not yet competitive. In the early discussions this plan was the main alternative to a GSP.

Both developing and developed countries came to UNCTAD I with prepared views on preferences. The common group positions of the three developing regions are contained in the Niamey Resolution (African Group), the Tehran Resolution (Asian Group) and the Charter of Alta Gracia (Latin American Group). All three groups welcomed the creation of a global system of preferences but the Charter of Alta Gracia called specifically for the abolition of vertical preferences.[27] Among the major developed countries both Italy[28] and the United States[29] rejected the concept of a preferential system for LDC manufactured exports. The other industrialised countries gave varying degrees of welcome to the idea. Both France and Belgium favoured the introduction of selective preferences. The United Kingdom signalled a willingness to extend preferences currently granted to Commonwealth countries to all developing countries provided that the other major industrialised countries also instituted a scheme thereby ensuring benefits in these markets for the Commonwealth developing countries. West Germany, which had not really gained from EEC preferences with the AASM, supported the British approach and Kurt Schmucker, the Federal Minister of the Economy, also stressed the need to decrease preferences 'beyond the general reduction of tariffs which we expect from the Kennedy Round of negotiations.'[30] Japan adopted an equivocal position, pointing out that a GSP would only prove effective when all the developed countries agreed to it and stressing the need to ensure equality of treatment among the LDCs.

In the ensuing negotiations two major lines of conflict in the G77 had to be resolved in order to present a united front to the developed countries. First, between countries in receipt of vertical preferences and those outside such schemes and, secondly, between the LDDCs and the more advanced developing countries. The search for unity was affected by the mood of the conference and the embryonic stage of the coalition. The confrontational atmosphere of the conference tended to exacerbate differences between the developed and developing countries. The developing countries had come to Geneva with a new found solidarity but one which had not as yet been tested on any substantive issue. The conflict over preferences was thus very important for the unity and future effectiveness of the group. On one hand, the very diversity of the group created disagreements and, on the other, there was an intense belief that it was only through solidarity that they could hope to extract any concesions from the indus-trialised countries. The problem was therefore posed in terms of improving their effectiveness in the inter-group discussions and adjusting their conflicting interests so that the distribution of any gains would be shared equitably.

The majority of countries enjoying special preferential access to major Western markets refused to accept the potential loss of their privileged treatment. The EEC African Associates were the most militant members of this group. This is not too difficult to understand when one considers the close relationship between France and many of its ex-colonies and the fact that these countries had only recently negotiated as independent states their first aid and trade agreement with the EEC — the Yaoundé Convention — which only entered into force whilst the conference was under way. The EEC Associates argued that they could not be sure that new preferences in developed country markets would compensate for the loss of existing preferences; that their existing industries would have to undergo a long and costly adjustment process if they lost their special access and that they had experienced difficulty in expanding tropical exports to the EEC despite preferential treatment and therefore did not think that a new general system for the export of manufactured goods would be of much use to them. They gave their support to the Brasseur Plan. The EEC Associates received strong support from some Commonwealth countries, in particular, the Commonwealth Caribbean. The Jamaican Minister of Trade and Industry declared that 'In all frankness we cannot identify ourselves with the proposal to dismantle all the existing preferences for the developing countries . . . we would strenously resist any effort to bring about the removal of the preferences we now enjoy so long as Britain is prepared to continue their application.'[31] The Com-monwealth countries had to be slightly more cautious in their opposition since whilst unity prevailed between France and the AASM on selective preferences the United Kingdom was quite willing to dilute Commonwealth preferences into a wider system. Moreover, India with one of the more developed industrial bases among developing countries announced that it was willing to forgo Common-wealth preferences for access to a wider generalised system. The developing countries were unable to agree on a common position when discussions on the preference issue began in the Second Committee. Four draft resolutions were submitted[32] and an intense effort was made to find a compromise formula. Disag-reement was settled by an appeal to unity and the promise of compensation for the loss of existing preferences.[33]

It was quite obvious that preferences would benefit the more advanced among the developing countries. The economically weaker countries (and once again this included the AASM) pressed for some recognition of their special problem. The more advanced developing countries, fearing that the preference-givers might discriminate against them and their products, argued in favour of a non-discriminatory scheme among all preferred suppliers and for the category of preferred supplier to be self-selecting. The poorer countries were worried that they would be unable to compete with the more advanced ones and that even if they became competitive in a few years, under a general scheme with a fixed duration, they would find it difficult to break into developed country markets. They therefore argued in favour of some system which would reserve some of the market for themselves by means of a system of quotas, higher preferential margins or selective preferences. India, Pakistan and the more developed Latin American countries objected to the proposal that preferences should be granted on a sliding scale with the higher margins being given to the least developed by arguing that the sliding tariff scales in existence in developed countries would render the preferential concessions meaningless. The conflict over special measures for the LDDCs was settled by an agreement that special measures (to be established at a later date) would be granted to the LDDCs. On the duration of preferences it was agreed that preferential treatment began from the date when a particular industry in a developing country began to benefit from the full application of the preferential tariff. Since the more advanced countries needed the support of the LDDCs they were prepared to accept this compromise formula. But at base the draft resolution was deeply contradictory.[34] It called both for a non-discriminatory application of a preferential system *and* for discrimination in favour of the LDDCs.

The outcome on both conflictual issues was the result of the deep divisions in the group and the consensual nature of group decision making. This method of reconciling group diversity was to become a favoured way in the future. For the moment all parties could go away satisfied. There was a commitment to abolish vertical preferences which pleased those countries currently not receiving any favoured treatment and a commitment to provide compensation for the loss of preferences which pleased the current preference receivers. On the other hand, this formula was an empty agreement which allowed each group to continue supporting its pre-agreement position. Agreement in principle to protect LDDC interests was not wholly satisfactory to them since in the absence of concrete proposals there was no guarantee that they would benefit, but it was better than no agreement at all. The developing countries thus maintained solidarity by aggregating all their interests.

The pressure applied to developed countries was unable to change the positions as they existed at the beginning of the conference. The participants failed to reach agreement in principle on a general system of preferences. General Principle 8 which embodied this idea found the developed countries either abstaining[35] or voting against.[36] Indeed despite the compromise reached in the G77 five countries — Brazil, Republic of Vietnam, Rwanda, Uganda and Venezuela — abstained. Further, Special Principle 3 on preferences was shelved. Recommendation A.III.5 marked the highest degree of unanimity possible on the preference issue at Geneva. Adopted without dissent it called on the UN Secretary-General to set up a committee of government representatives to look at preferences and to work out the best method of implementing non-reciprocal preferences. Agreement had thus been reached only on the necessity of investigating the issue further. The developing countries had reconciled their differences but only at the highest level of principle. No serious consideration had been given to the precise nature of equivalent advantages or to the special measures to be initiated for the LDDCs. A start had been made but a GSP still had to be negotiated. The fragile solidarity of the G77 still had to be cemented and the developed countries still had to be convinced of the merits of the scheme. Events between the first and second UNCTAD conferences created the circumstances so that when UNCTAD II convened in New Delhi the prospects for agreement on the GSP were propitious.

Between UNCTAD I and UNCTAD II

A solution had to be found to two conflicting objectives before a GSP could be agreed. Any system needed to find adequate safeguards to protect the developed countries against market disruption and also to offer increased market access to the developing countries. The search for agreement was pursued within three interactive frameworks — intra-developed country consultations, developed–developing country consultations and intra-developing country consultations. We will now examine each of these frameworks in the 1964–8 period. Events here show the increasing institutionalisation of the G77 and its influence on the group's bargaining strategy and tactics; the limited discipline imposed by group membership, so that outside UNCTAD G77 members are free to pursue policies which conflict with their stated aims in the organisation; and the limitations of G77 pressure politics in changing developed countries' positions.

Discussion among the major industrialised countries on the subject of preferences took place within the framework of the OECD, the *de facto* secretariat of Group B. The key negotiations were held by a group known as the 'Four Wise Men' consisting of senior trade officials of the United States, United Kingdom, France and West Germany. The early meetings of the group failed to shift positions beyond the stalemate of the Geneva Conference. It was not until President Johnson's announcement on 14 April 1967 that the United States was willing to 'explore the possibility of temporary preferential tariff advantages for all developing countries in the markets of all the industrialised countries'[37] that the way was opened for serious discussion. In the wake of this announcement France dropped its insistence on selective preferences. The resulting OECD consensus was presented in the report of the 'Four Wise Men'.[38] This report set the OECD position which was maintained throughout the subsequent negotiations. Agreement was reached on the following main features of a non-reciprocal scheme of preferences: (a) product coverage — this would conform with chapters 25–99 of the Brussels Tariff Nomenclature (BTN), but other products could be negotiated on a case-by-case basis; (b) beneficiary countries — by the method of self-election, that is any country claiming developing country status; (c) duration — an initial period of ten years, preferences should be temporary and degressive; (d) donor countries — all major developed countries. Agreement was not possible, however, on safeguards and exceptions, tariff arrangements then in force and the depth of tariff cuts.

Members of the G77, notwithstanding the compromises reached at UNCTAD I continued to pursue individualistic policies in respect of the preferences issue. Some African countries entered into negotiations with the EEC to create special preferences for themselves. Nigeria concluded a separate agreement,[39] the East African Community embarked on the talks that would lead to the Arusha Agreement[40] and the Maghreb countries began discussions with the EEC in 1968. In response to the possible extension of the existing EEC preferential arrangements the majority of Latin American countries pressed the US government to establish a selective preference system for the region.[41] Prebisch, concerned both for the task expansion of UNCTAD and the solidarity of the developing countries, waged a vigorous campaign against this sectarianism. His interventions were made both inside the UNCTAD framework, where he used his reports to the TDB to argue against special preferences, and to put his weight firmly behind the GSP,[42] and in Latin America where he waged an intensive lobbying campaign.[43] He also created an informal group of Latin American diplomats to convince the United States that general preferences were needed to supplement the results of the Kennedy Round.

The US decision to opt for the GSP was taken for political reasons. The Johnson administration was faced with the prospect of deteriorating relations with Latin America unless it agreed to some preferential scheme. The global responsibilities of the United States ruled out instituting a vertical preference scheme for Latin America since this would create difficulties with developing countries in other regions. The GSP also had the advantage of seeming to provide a means to control the spread of the EEC selective preferential schemes by incorporating them under the GSP. Moreover, a general scheme made political sense if the impact on domestic industry could be minimised through safeguards and exceptions. The United States could then minimise its political losses and use the GSP as a bargaining counter in its push for a free trade system.[44]

As UNCTAD II approached, the omens for the creation of a GSP were good. The industrialised countries had signalled their willingness to implement a general scheme and the United States had clearly rebutted the proposal for the creation of a US–Latin America preference scheme. In this context the developing countries could respond collectively or on an individual basis. The conflicts among developing countries which surfaced at UNCTAD I continued to prevent a common negotiating position.[45] But the debate on preferences was taking place in the context of the G77's overall strategy. This strategy was based on the assumption that concessions could only be wrested from the rich countries through collective action by the developing countries. Solidarity and unity were essential for this strategy to work and initially it was thought that the mere application of collective pressure would be sufficient to get significant concessions. And yet the period since UNCTAD I had been one of almost unmitigated disappointment. The recommendations of 1964 still remained to be implemented. In the commodities field, universally agreed as the most important for development purposes, only a few agreements had been concluded and not all of these could be attributed to UNCTAD.[46] The confrontational attitude in UNCTAD was not conducive to the resolution of differences between the G77 and Group B. And in the G77 the various conflicts ensured that the unity displayed was more apparent than real. It was with this background that the First Ministerial Meeting of the G77 was held, 10–25 October 1967, in Algiers. Algiers was important then in re-establishing G77 unity[47] and helping to improve the chances of the forthcoming UNCTAD Conference having a successful outcome.

Although convened in a spirit of compromise the Algiers Conference was wracked by dissension and disagreement. The issue of preferences provided one of the most important areas of contention. This was basically a rehearsal of the splits outlined earlier. The conference opened with the regional groups reaffirming positions taken in 1964.[48] The compromise achieved at UNCTAD I was seemingly forgotten and the sectarianism of the previous three years given prominence. In the search for compromise the agreement that decisions should be by consensus, following the practice of G77 meetings in Geneva and New York, proved an important procedural rule.[49] Without the recourse to majority-vote, decisions could only be taken on the basis of approval by the entire membership of the G77. This meant that decisions would reflect the lowest common denominator; be the result of a splitting of the difference; or an aggregation of conflicting demands. After exhaustive discussions a compromise on vertical preferences was reached which involved splitting the difference. The Latin American states gave up their demand for the immediate abolition of special preferences and the African Associates accepted that they would relinquish their special preferences because the new scheme would ensure them at least equivalent advantages. This compromise was hardly an advance on the stage reached in 1964.[50] But it was an advance in the sense that in papering over the cracks and restoring the level of unity to 1964 it marked the end of the 'free-for-all' period which had been in existence from the close of the Geneva Conference.

The LDDCs continued to insist that any GSP should secure advantages for them as a distinct sub-group in the G77. At this stage an official list of LDDCs had not been compiled[51] and the issue of differentiation within the G77 was an intensely political one. Tensions in the G77 were heightened because differentiation also ran along regional lines with most states claiming LDDC status originating in Africa. In the Latin American Group Bolivia, Ecuador and the Central American countries (none eventually classed as LDDCs) vigorously supported and defended the claims of the LDDCs.[52] Before Algiers the LDDC delegates to the TDB had used every available occasion to demand special treatment in any GSP.[53] At Algiers the LDDCs formed a distinct sub-group which pressed not only for recognition within the G77 but also for a series of wide-ranging measures tailored to suit their needs.[54] The cross-regional alliance between African, Asian and Latin American LDDCs was a novel feature of G77 politics and helped them to achieve their goals. The LDDCs stressed the need for continued G77 unity but argued that this could not be maintained if they were unable to benefit from any measures negotiated in UNCTAD.[55] The intransigence of the LDDCs succeeded in persuading the more advanced countries that some safeguards must be written into the GSP which would protect the poorest countries. Hence the inclusion in the Algiers Charter of special measures for the LDDCs on preferences and a widening of product coverage to include processed and semi-processed products.

In the context of the Algiers Conference an agreement on preferences was vital for the continued unity of the G77.[56] Preferences for manufactured goods had become the most important issue in North–South economic relations. This was a result both of the abject failures experienced in commodity negotiations and the seemingly imminent agreement on a GSP. In the light of the well-publicised divisions within the Southern coalition it had become the acid test of unity. There were certain salient factors which made the compromise in the G77 a likely result. The more advanced developing countries wanted a GSP and had prior to Algiers identified it as a possible area for progress at New Delhi. But in the search for agreement with Group B they needed the support of the remainder of the G77. They were thus predisposed to accept some of the demands of the poorer members of the G77. It was also clear by now that the various extensions of the EEC's preferential schemes meant that any general scheme would have to co-exist with these vertical preferences. The African Associates who stood to make no immediate gains from a GSP could therefore pursue a damage limitation strategy in the context of an agreement on a general scheme because they knew that their special preferences would be safeguarded.

Developments in the three interactive frameworks had thus produced by the time UNCTAD II convened on 1 February 1968 the firm expectation that a GSP would be concluded in New Delhi. At the very least the main outline of such a scheme would be agreed. UNCTAD II, it was felt, would mark the culmination of one stage in the bargaining process. As we have seen, these conclusions did not mean however that differences had ceased to exist either between the G77 and Group B or within the G77. A wide gap still separated the G77 position and that of the OECD countries and the agreement reached at Algiers did not constitute a negotiating document. The Algiers agreement on preferences was a broad set of principles which would need considerable tightening up before it could serve as a joint negotiating platform for the G77.

UNCTAD II

When UNCTAD II convened on 1 February 1969 many observers had high expectations that one outcome of the conference would be an agreement on the GSP. In the event although Conference resolution 21(II) recognised 'unanimous agreement in favour of the early establishment of a mutually acceptable system of generalized non-reciprocal and non-discriminatory preferences' and created a Special Committee on Preferences to finalise the arrangements for such a scheme, most observers were disappointed. This resolution clearly revealed the failure to make any substantive progress on preferences at the conference. This failure can be attributed to the interplay of a number of factors. As I have already pointed out, the conflicting perspectives held on UNCTAD's role by the G77 and Group B restricts the functioning of the organisation. Group B refuse to accept UNCTAD as a proper negotiating forum and approached the New Delhi conference with the intention of restricting its scope to the discussion of trade policy issues and the formulation of principles. The G77 and the UNCTAD secretariat were both looking for substantive progress and anger at Group B's limited approach pushed the G77 into a more confrontational posture. In addition the common positions of both groups had been arrived at after hard internal bargaining and group members were reluctant to unravel the compromises. Thus two opposed positions were presented face-to-face with little prospect of agreement. The resultant discussions were acrimonious in the committees and in the contact groups established at the end of every committee's deliberations to try to work towards consensus. It was in such an atmosphere that agreement was sought on preferences.[57]

As we have noted the Charter of Algiers did not provide an adequate negotiating platform for the G77. However, continued division in the group over vertical preferences and the LDDCs hindered the adoption of a common negotiating strategy. It was not until 11 March at the twenty-sixth (out of thirty-two) meeting of the second committee that a G77 draft resolution (58) was presented.[58] It took over five weeks for this stage to be reached. Indeed it was not until the contact group had been established to consider in greater detail the main elements of a scheme of preferences and to discuss a possible timetable for implementation that the G77 draft resolution was produced.

The outcome of intra-G77 negotiations revealed a move away from splitting the difference as a mode of conflict resolution to an aggregation of conflicting demands. In deciding to upgrade the common interest the conditions relating to special preferences were more extensively spelt out than they had ever been and constitute a definite advance on the Charter of Algiers in two respects. First, it accepted that a transitory period of at least five years would be necessary before special preferences were abolished and, secondly, the safeguards for those states enjoying special preferences were to be adjudicated by an impartial international body.[59] A similar aggregation approach was taken to the demands of the least developed countries. Following on from their limited success in Algiers they were determined not to retreat and made support for the G77's position conditional on the granting of certain concessions. The LDDCs insisted that the G77 should demand wider product coverage. The OECD report had suggested that preferences only be granted to products in BTN 25–99. The LDDCs argued in the intra-G77 negotiations for the inclusion of products in BTN 1–24 and succeded in having this demand accepted by the other members of the coalition although the more advanced countries, such as India, were prepared to accept the limited product coverage offer made by the OECD countries. The draft resolution went a very long way towards attempting to meet the needs of the LDDCs and articles 5, 8, 12 and 13 all sought either to exempt the LDDCs from the general exceptions clauses or to provide specific commitments which would enable them to benefit from the scheme. The G77 had survived its internal dissension and had managed to preserve its unity.

It proved impossible at UNCTAD II to reach agreement beyond the need to set up a system and to create appropriate machinery to enable countries to continue consultations regarding the scheme. The developed market-economy countries refused to go beyond the position worked out in the OECD. The minimal OECD compromise was an inadequate bargaining position since it failed to cover important elements of any future preference scheme, namely safeguards, exceptions, the depth of tariff cuts and reverse preferences. The G77 had spent most of the conference unable to agree on a negotiating position and the final compromise which aggregated a set of conflicting demands pushed the G77 position even further away from Group B. Major differences between Group B and the G77 existed on all significant elements of a preference scheme — product coverage, exceptions, safeguards, duration and existing preferences. New Delhi thus marked the beginning of another stage in the process of negotiating a GSP. From a maverick concept it had become the centrepiece of international economic diplomacy. After UNCTAD II this was particularly so since it was one of the few positive achievements of a disappointing conference. The next phase marked a move away from discussion on lofty questions of principle. In the negotiation of a concrete agreement intra-G77 conflict would prove largely irrelevant. In this new phase the developed countries presented their preference schemes to the scrutiny of the developing countries. This was a process of negotiation and consultation fundamentally different from what had taken place before.[60]

Towards implementation, 1968–70

At the second part of its fourth session (21 September–12 October 1970) the Special Committee on Preferences adopted 'Agreed Conclusions' in respect of a GSP.[61] The culmination of the post New Delhi process was greeted as an important event. Manuel Perez-Guerrero, the UNCTAD Secretary-General, acclaimed 'a far reaching and unprecedented undertaking. Never before to the best of my knowledge, has there been such a concentration of concerted efforts in favour of developing countries in the field of trade.'[62] The timetable envisaged by Resolution 21(II) had been exceeded but that was not altogether surprising given the complexity of the process involved.

The period between 1968 and 1970 was characterised by activity on two different levels. On the first the developed country preference-givers — Austria, Belgium, Canada, Denmark, Finland, Ireland, Italy, Japan, Luxembourg, Netherlands, New Zealand, Norway, Switzerland, Sweden, United Kingdom, United States and West Germany — negotiated within the OECD framework to harmonise the various 'national' offers.[63] It was soon obvious that the GSP would never be general in the sense of all the developed countries having identical schemes. The specific circumstances of the individual countries made harmonisation rather than uniformity a more realistic choice, although until May 1970 the US administration insisted upon uniformity. US opposition to reverse preferences and special preferences also slowed down the decision-making process. But once broadly comparable schemes were agreed the next stage of the process could be entered into. This was in the UNCTAD Special Committee on Preferences (SCP), where the developing countries responded to the offers made by the donor countries. The first part of the fourth session of the SCP (March–April 1970) was spent in examining these initial preference offers.[64] Incremental changes were suggested by the spokesmen of the developing countries who adopted a pragmatic approach. Realising that they were not in a position where confrontational tactics would work, they sought to make realistic suggestions in order to improve the benefits they would gain from the proposed schemes.[65] After detailed discussions the donor countries reconsidered their proposals and made revised offers in September.[66]

Various factors accounted for the new mood of realism and pragmatism in the G77's approach. The different nature of the bargaining process, the move away from questions of principle to practical issues of commercial policy and the shift of the discussion from intangibles to tangibles helped to transform the manner in which conflicting interests in the G77 were expressed and its effect upon the strategies pursued by individual group members. Those countries with most to gain from the new scheme felt that something was better than nothing. They believed that it was better to accept a flawed scheme which would be implemented quickly rather than to continue arguing for an ideal scheme which might never be attainable. Those states which had been keen to preserve the benefits they gained from existing preferential systems realised that the GSP as envisaged would not hurt their market access. The EEC Associates so worried previously about losing their privileged access to the Community market were assured that the Community's scheme did not seriously threaten their interests. The rearguard action that they had mounted had been successful in preserving their interests. Partly as a result of their pressure on the EEC its GSP offer excluded those processed agricultural goods of major interest to the Yaoundé associates.[67] And the qualified schemes which the other OECD countries were implementing gave only limited benefits to the more advanced LDCs. For their part the LDDCs realised that the GSP, as it stood, although not helping their export earnings, was the best that could be achieved. It was also clear that they would not be able to mount a successful campaign to improve the schemes in their favour. This was partly due to the loss of influence of the LDDC sub-group in the G77 decisional process. Official identification of LDDCs had weakened the cross-regional alliance when only Haiti (a marginal member) from the Latin American Group had been granted LDDC status. Moreover, in this period the LDDCs shifted their pressure from concentration on preferences, which held only marginal gains at best and these were all in the future, to issues such as aid — in which gains were both immediate and substantial. The LDDCs perceived that unity of the G77 was crucial if the developing countries as a whole were to wrest further concessions from the industrialised states. Any attempt by the LDDCs to delay an conclusion of a GSP would therefore be self-defeating.

Conclusions

Negotiations on the GSP presented the first concentrated challenge to the maintenance of effective G77 unity. From the outset attitudinal, ascriptive and behavioural cleavages threatened to undermine the coalition. The salience of the GSP negotiations for intra-G77 relations arose from the centrality of these negotiations in the development dialogue between 1964 and 1970. The fact that the GSP was a collective good neccessitated joint action on the part of the G77. Nevertheless, the members of the group were forced into a distributive bargaining mode because of the unequal distribution of gains. On the other hand, because an overall increase in trade liberalisation would benefit all members the coalition also engaged in integrative bargaining. Hence a mixed bargaining strategy prevailed in which group members oscillated between stressing the distributive and integrative aspects. A purely distributive strategy would have resulted in even greater strains on group unity but the possibility of joint gain and the necessity to press Group B members to agree as wide-ranging a scheme as possible provided a degree of solidarity and a cause around which the G77 could coalesce.

Two further factors tended to unite rather than increase the divergent strains in the group. The first stems from the nature of the coalition. The solidarity achieved by the G77 is primarily a diplomatic solidarity which exists for the purpose of multilateral commercial diplomacy. Group members agree on common positions for the purposes of multilateral negotiations but possess the freedom to pursue on a bilateral basis policies which may conflict with agreed joint ventures. Members of the coalition were prepared to accept this dualism in national policy during the period of the GSP negotiations. This was justified partly on the grounds of safeguarding vital national interests and partly because the coalition was able to function despite these deviations from the common position. Secondly, the G77's organisational structure developed considerably over this period in response to these fissiparous tendencies. The development of structures and decision-making procedures widened and deepened the levels of interest aggregation and interest articulation. The political process of the group ensured that members could effectively represent their interests. The development of common institutions and the institutionalisation of procedures created a framework in which a stable pattern of expectations could develop. Thus the G77 became not just a constant factor in national policy making but also the relevant body for the discussion of the GSP and other issues. But the level of coordination achieved, that is diplomatic solidarity, in so far as it did not jeopardise vital interests, made it easier for governments to compromise. The G77 could reconcile divergent viewpoints because effective decision-making lay elsewhere and because growth in organisational competence enmeshed members without threatening national autonomy.

Disintegrative tendencies, however, continued to have an effect on the bargaining process. Coalition members were hesitant to sacrifice real or perceived benefits without engaging in strenuous defence of their national interests. Hence the LDDCs and the preference receiving countries insisted on special treatment. Recognition of these claims by Group B undermined the position of those members of the G77 opposed to differential treatment of GSP beneficiaries. Furthermore, the commitment to special measures for disadvantaged countries, although discussed mainly as a matter of principle, was in the final analysis a practical question. Preference-givers were free to design schemes which contained exceptions from the standard principles. The hard-fought battle by the preference-receivers and the LDDCs resulted in some minor concessions but the final agreements reached owed less to G77 interests and pressures than the autonomous actions of the industrialised countries.

Negotiations on the GSP showed the limited role of UNCTAD as a negotiating forum. The demand for a GSP originated with the G77 and the UNCTAD secretariat but the implementation of any agreed scheme depended on the industrialised states. Third World pressure politics had succeeded in procuring a new device for the management of international trade but the design, implementation and execution of the GSP was largely the result of negotiations among the industrialised states. The UNCTAD forum therefore although important as a centre for discussion was largely irrelevant as a decision-making body. UNCTAD's main role lay in providing a forum through which pressure could be exerted and as a legitimising instrument through which any agreement needed to be ratified.[68] These constraints arising from the global distribution of power and the organisational context were important conditioning factors on the behaviour of the G77.

The G77 had campaigned for a reform which would only benefit a few of its members and had managed to maintain a degree of unity despite widely conflicting interests. This pragmatic unity recognised the demands of special-interest groups in the coalition. Common G77 positions of necessity had to accommodate diverse interests. The success of the group in maintaining a united bargaining front in the context of the UNCTAD negotiations was a result of an organisational process biased in favour of group bargaining. In addition the UNCTAD group system tended to push the developing countries together. The powerlessness of the G77 to effect meaningful regime change underlines the weakness of individual members of the coalition. Joint action may be a second-best solution but it does offer the possibility of limited gain. The GSP negotiations demonstrate both the necessity for collective action and the limits to cooperation.

Notes

1. For analysis of the operation of the GSP see Tracy Murray, *Trade Preferences for Developing Countries* (London: Macmillan, 1977); R. E. Baldwin & T. Murray, 'MFN Tariff Reductions and Developing Country Trade Benefits Under the GSP', *Economic Journal* (March 1977), pp.30–46; and various UNCTAD studies, for example, TD/232 — 'Review and evaluation of the generalized system of preferences'; TD/B/C.5/15 and TD/B/C.5/42 — 'Operation and effects of the generalized system of preferences'; TD/B/C.5/111 and Add.1 — 'Eleventh general report on the implementation of the generalized system of preferences'.

2. See, for example, B. Hindley, 'The UNCTAD Agreement on Preferences', *Journal of World Trade Law* (November–December 1971), pp.694–702; P. Tulloch, *The Politics of Preferences* (London: Croom Helm & ODI, 1975), pp.88–100; Z. Iqbal, 'The GSP Examined', *Finance and Development* (September 1975), pp.34–9.

3. See S. Lukes, *Power: A Radical View* (London: Macmillan, 1974); J. C. Isaac, *Power and Marxist Theory* (Ithaca, NY: Cornell university Press, 1987).

4. Tulloch, op.cit., p.16.

5. K. S. Sundar Rajan, 'Tariff Preferences and Developing Countries', *Proceedings of the American Society of International Law* (1966), pp.87–8.

6. ET = 100 (NT/VA) where ET is effective tariff; NT is nominal VA tariff and VA value added.

7. Murray, op.cit., p.20.

8. It was precisely the fear that this would occur which led some domestic producers in the industrialised countries to oppose the GSP. For an account of the activities of such pressure groups in respect of the EEC, see Tulloch, op.cit., chap. 7.

9. J. Pincus, *Trade, Aid and Development* (New York: McGraw-Hill, 1967), p.198.

10. See Tulloch, op.cit., for the extension of this argument. He asserts that 'Discriminatory preferential access terms may not have much meaning for some products and some import markets' p.15.

11. Hindley, op.cit., p.698.

12. Pincus, op.cit., p.199.

13. Murray argues that it would be much easier for the developing countries to negotiate joint currency devaluations than to negotiate tariff preferences. Murray, op.cit., p.18.

14. Pincus, op.cit., p.199.

15. H. G. Johnson, *Economic Policies Toward Less Developed Countries* (London: George Allen & Unwin, 1967), pp.196–7.

16. TD/12/Supp.1 — 'A System of Preferences for Exports of Manufactures and Semi-Manufactures From Developing to Developed Countries, (31 October 1967).

17. Special (vertical) preferences also existed between the United States and the Phillipines; during the period under study the EEC concluded agreements with Nigeria and the East African Community.

18. TD/16/Supp.1 — 'The Problem of Special Preferences — some illustrations of special preferential arrangements' (11 January 1968).

19. See also A. K. Bhattacharya, 'The influence of the international secretariat: UNCTAD and generalized tariff preferences', *International Organization* (Winter 1976), p.78.

20. The letter is reprinted in TD/16 — 'The Problem of Special Preferences — Trade Policy Aspects' (12 Jan 1968).

21. See Tulloch, op.cit., pp.65–72, for an analysis of AASM pressure on the EEC.

22. Bhattacharya, op.cit., p.85.

23. The Argentine delegate to the first session of the TDB stated that Argentina refused to join any system of vertical preferences. See TD/B/SR.12 (14 April 1965).

24. The previous year Mr Edward Heath the President of the Board of Trade had announced the United Kingdom's willingness to extend Commonwealth preferences to all developing countries providing other industrialised countries implemented similar preferential schemes. See Tulloch, op.cit., p.37.

25. Press release, GATT/750 (17 May 1963).

26. Reprinted in *Proceedings 1964*, vol. VI, pp. 23–25.

27. OAS Inter-American Economic and Social Council, Special Committee on Latin American Co-ordination: the Charter of Alta Gracia. Reprinted in *Proceedings 1964*, vol.VI, pp.57–66.
28. Bernardo Mattarella, the Italian Minister for Foreign Trade rejected the concept as being misplaced. See *Proceedings 1964*, vol.II, p.240.
29. For a discussion of US policy on preferences see S. Weintraub, *Trade Preferences for Less Developed Countries* (New York: Praeger, 1967); G. Patterson, *Discrimination in International Trade: The Policy Issues 1945–1965* (Princeton, NS: Princeton University Press, 1966), pp.353–6.
30. *Proceedings 1964*, vol.II, p.192.
31. Ibid., p.264.
32. E/CONF.46/C.2/L.5 submitted by Niger; E/CONF.46/C.2/L.22 submitted by India, Indonesia, Lebanon, Nepal and Saudi Arabia; E/CONF.46/C.2/L.23 submitted by Argentina, Brazil, Bolivia, Chile, Colombia, Costa Rica, Dominican Republic, Ecuador, El Salvador, Guatemala, Haiti, Honduras, Mexico, Nicaragua, Panama, Paraguay, Peru, Uruguay and Venezuela; E/CONF.46/C.2/L.27 submitted by Ghana, Kenya, Liberia, Nigeria, Tanganyika and Zanzibar, Sierra Leone, Sudan and Trinidad and Tobago.
33. E/CONF.46/C.2/L.40 and Add.1-5.
34. Ibid. 35. Belgium, Denmark, Federal Republic of Germany, Finland, France, Greece, Ireland, Italy, Japan, Luxembourg, Netherlands, New Zealand, Portugal, Spain, Turkey plus Holy See, Monaco and San Marino.
36. Australia, Austria, Canada, Iceland, Norway, South Africa, Sweden, Switzerland, United Kingdom, United States plus Lichtenstein. 37. See Department of State Bulletin, vol.LVI No.1454 (8 May 1967) p.709.
37. See *Department of State Bulletin*, vol.LVI No.1454 (8 May 1967), p.709.
38. TD/56 — 'Report by the Special Group on Trade with Developing Countries of the OECD'.
39. The Lagos Convention signed in 1966 never came into force because of the Nigerian Civil War.
40. The Arusha Convention was signed in 1968 and revised in 1969.
41. This demand met with a receptive response among some influential Americans, for example George Ball, Walt Rostow, David Rockefeller and Thomas Mann, former Under Secretary of state for Economic Affairs. See Weintraub, op.cit., p.156, and Bhattacharya, op.cit., pp.84–5.
42. See, for example, TD/B/SR.25.
43. See Weintraub, op.cit., p.150; and Bhattacharya, op.cit., pp.82–3.
44. See R. I. Meltzer, 'The politics of policy reversal: the US response to granting trade preferences to developing countries and linkages between international organisations and national policy making', *International Organization* (Autumn 1976), pp.663–8 where he argues that the change in the American stance was the result of bureaucratic politics.
45. In UNCTAD debates the absence of a coherent G77 position was readily apparent. See, for example, the two meetings of the Group on Preferences (26 July–5 August 1966 and 4–18 July 1967) established as a subsidiary body of the Committee on Manufactures. See TD/12 (1 November 1967) and TD/B/C.2/AC.1/7.
46. Successful agreements were the International Tin Agreement negotiated in 1965, the United Nations Conference on Olive Oil, March 1967, which adopted a protocol for the extension of, 1963 Olive Oil Agreement, and the International Grains Agreement, August 1967.

47. See Dick Wilson, 'Strategy for the South', *Far Eastern Economic Review*, 20 October 1966, p.130.

48. The *Bangkok Declaration* of the Asian Group did not even mention this issue! See the *African Declaration of Algiers* and the *Charter of Tequenedama* for the respective positions of the African and Latin American countries.

49. See MM.77/I/7.

50. TD/38 — *Charter of Algiers* p.9.

51. See UNCTAD, Research Memoranda No.6/1 — Preliminary Identification of the Least Developed Among Developing Countries [Typology Study] (10 January 1967) and No.6/1 Rev.1 — The Least Developed among Developing Countries in the Context of UNCTAD Policies and Measures. Part 1: The Problem of Identifying the Least Developed among the Developing Countries (5 July 1967), for early efforts in this direction.

52. The least developed countries in the Latin American region had failed at the CECLA meeting in Bogota to get regional support for special measures. See Gosovic, 'UNCTAD: North–South Encounter', *International Conciliation* May 1968 p.19.

53. See the summary records of the TDB first to fifth sessions. TD/B/SR.1–157.

54. See First Ministerial Meeting of the Group of 77, Algiers October 1969 in Sauvant (ed.) *Collected Documents*, vol.I pp.174–325.

55. See Provisional Summary Records of the Plenary Session, (MM.77/I/SR.1–14) in *Collected Documents*, vol.I, pp.215–314.

56. See two articles by Edith Rebecca Lenart in the *Far Eastern Economic Review*, 2 and 9 November 1967 and Y. Yelutin, 'Rehearsal before the Delhi Conference', *International Affairs [Moscow]* (January 1968), pp.38–42, for contrasting perspectives on the Algiers Conference.

57. On general features of the conference see D. Howell, 'Failure at UNCTAD II: Divided Rich and Embitterd Poor', *Round Table* (July 1968), pp.249–53; C. Miles, 'Trade and Aid: the Second UNCTAD', *World Today* (July 1967), pp.297–302.

58. TD/II/C.2/L.5 — 'Basic principles and procedures covering an agreement on the general system of preferences'.

59. TD/II/C.2/L.5, Article 14.

60. Whether the discussions in the Special Committee on Preferences constituted negotiations or not is a moot point. See Tulloch, op.cit., who argues, p.34, that they were not but on p.63 writes 'there were still many detailed areas . . . which would be settled through negotiation in the UNCTAD Special Committee'.

61. See TD/B/329 (12 Oct 1970).

62. Cited in R. Krishnamurti, 'The Agreement on Preferences. A Generalized System in Favour of Developing Countries', *Journal of World Trade Law* (January–February 1971), pp.45–6.

63. The EEC countries submitted a joint proposal. On the continuing conflict in Group B see V. Walker-Leigh, 'The GSP: Background to the Recent UNCTAD Agreement', *World Today* (January 1971); Gosovic, UNCTAD, op.cit, pp.183–7; and various UNCTAD documents — TD/B/243 (19 May 1969); TD/B/256 (3 July 1969); TD/B/262 (14 July 1969); TD/B/AC.5/24 (14 November 1969) and TD/B/309/Add.1 (16 July 1970). The final Group B offer is contained in TD/B/AC.5/34 and Add.1–3 (21 September 1970).

64. See TD/B/300 and Add.1–2 (27 April 1970).

65. On the move from 'confrontation to strategy' see D. Cordovez, '*UNCTAD and Development Diplomacy*' (*Journal of World Trade Law*, 1971), pp.144–65.

66. See TD/B/329; and TD/B/AC.5/L.13.
67. See Tulloch, op.cit., p.59 and pp.65–71.
68. Even this was a limited role since, before the scheme could be implemented, it was necessary to obtain a waiver in GATT.

7 The negotiations for an Integrated Programme for Commodities, 1974–80

The negotiations for the Integrated Programme for Commodities (IPC) are comparable to the GSP negotiations with respect to its centrality in the North–South dialogue and the salience of the issue for intra-G77 relations. A major difference between the two sets of negotiations resides in the wider environmental setting and this is one of the key variables in explaining the higher degree of politicisation in the later bargaining process. The aim of this chapter is to examine the internal divisions within the G77 in relation to the IPC and the attempts to maintain unity in the face of these differences. Two central questions are posed for the analysis: how, given the existence of various cleavages, did the group manage to maintain unity and what was the exact nature of this unity? And what effect did the existence of these divisions have upon the G77's negotiating position and how did they affect the 'final agreements' covering the Common Fund (CF) and the individual commodity agreements?

Economic analysis and the commodity debate

As we pointed out in the previous chapter the attitudes of countries and the positions they adopt to the reform of the international political economy are based to a significant extent on economic analysis of the relevant subject matter. Economics, many claims to the contrary notwithstanding, is not and cannot be a value-free science. The conclusions reached as a result of economic reasoning are based on a number of stated and unstated assumptions. In the field of international political economy no topic is more subject to controversy, conflicting research findings, inadequate methodologies and a general paucity of research as commodity policy. Hence, when the Integrated Programme was launched by the UNCTAD secretariat a fierce polemic arose between supporters and defenders of the scheme based in large measure on ignorance and prejudice. The existence of these conflicting views and the tentative state of much of the existing knowledge was used by many governments (mainly Group B) as a stalling device in the negotiations. The aim of this section is not to reproduce the argument between defenders and opponents of the IPC but rather to examine the competing theories, methodologies and research findings in order to establish the intellectual uncertainty which constituted an important environmental variable circumscribing the negotiating process. Competing analyses of international commodity policy and specifically the IPC affected the negotiations throughout their history and at different levels.

A cursory glance at the starting points for an economic analysis of international commodity policy reveals the analytical and empirical difficulties found in a multi-commodity and multi-country world. At the most basic level no generally agreed definition of what constitutes a primary commodity exists. But all definitions, whether statistical (for example, SITC classification) or not, stress that they are natural products produced by agriculture or extracted by mining and including some element of processing. Secondly, the classification of commodities does not conform to any accepted usage.[1] This analytical complexity is reinforced by empirical reality, where contrary to popular opinion the developing countries are not the main exporters of primary commodities. The developing countries, share of primary commodity exports is only some 40 per cent in total and under 30 per cent if fuels are excluded. Further, the export concentration on primary commodities varies widely among developing countries. Thus, generalisations concerning the experience of developing countries as primary commodity exporters and the effects of this dependence on domestic economic activity is unlikely to meet with general agreement and it follows that international policy prescriptions will also be the subject of disagreement.

The IPC proposals embodied seven specific objectives: (a) reduction of excessive fluctuations in commodity prices and supplies; (b) establishment and maintenance of prices remunerative to producers and equitable to consumers; (c) improvements of access to supply for importing countries; (d) improved market access; (e) improved competitiveness of natural products *vis-à-vis* synthetics; (f) expansion of processing of commodities in developing countries; (g) improved food aid provisions.[2] The two key objectives can be seen as price stabilisation to diminish fluctuations and price increases above the long-term trend to improve real income. The UNCTAD scheme aimed at price stabilisation rather than revenue stabilisation and this immediately raised doubts concerning its efficacy because price stabilisation and revenue stabilisation are not commensurate and can in fact be opposed objectives. Price stabilisation may destabilise revenue or may lead to revenue stabilisation at the cost of a reduction in revenue. This is not a question that can be settled in theoretical terms: it is essentially an empirical issue depending on the slope of the demand and supply curves, risk aversion, elasticities and the causes and nature of the shifts, i.e. multiplicative or additive.[3] Price stabilisation would not lead to revenue stabilisation if competition increased or higher prices led to substitution. Moreover, the welfare effects of price stabilisation measures on producers and consumers are shrouded in uncertainty and dependent on the technical assumptions made.[4] The second key objective was also ill considered. In this jungle of assumptions, methodologies, computer simulations and research findings, the futility of attempting to increase prices above the long-term trend, is the one issue on which a degree of consensus exists. Such attempts are bound to fail because consumers will turn to substitutes. It might be possible to have short-run success in commodities that are demand inelastic but even here the welfare and equity implications argue against adopting such a strategy. As the OPEC example so clearly demonstrates some Third World importers will suffer economic losses.

The twin goals of price stabilisation and price augmentation are based on an analysis of LDC trade problems that identifies declining terms of trade and instability of export earnings as the major defects which need to be remedied. The meaning, nature and economic implications for development of these two concepts became the subject of heated debates. Stated simply, the 'terms of trade' refer to the exchange of commodities or the 'price' in physical terms of one good for another. But there are three conceptions of the terms of trade and seven different measurement indices. Results tend to vary depending upon which measurement is used and, in so far as one index might show deterioration in terms of trade and another an improvement over the same time period, there is widespread disagreement amongst economists concerning the usefulness of any data collected. The factual evidence is also open to dispute and at best can be called inconclusive. Rangarajan concluded that the facts do indicate a downward trend in the terms of trade of developing countries,[5] and Behrman found that for the UNCTAD core commodities and others of interest to developing countries there was a negative secular trend in prices between 1950 and 1975.[6] Paul Bairoch, on the other hand, in an analysis of the period 1948–70 found that a marked fall in the terms of trade was a phenomenon limited mainly to the period 1952–62 and concluded that the evidence did not support the thesis of a long-run deterioration in LDC terms of trade.[7] A Group of Experts convened by the UNCTAD Secretary-General came to a similar conclusion.[8] The healthy scepticism felt by most economists on this issue is clearly expressed by John Spraos who concluded a survey article with the opinion that 'while the deteriorating tendency cannot be decisively refuted, it is open to doubt when the record up to the 1970s is taken into account.'[9]

Traditionally it was thought that primary commodities were significantly more unstable than manufactures and that for countries heavily dependent on primary commodities for their export earnings, such instability hindered long-range planning of investment both in the public and private sectors. By the time the IPC was formulated this pessimism had been challenged by a number of studies and there were, broadly speaking, two schools of thought on the problem of export instability. Three key questions can be identified: does instability exist 'that is, do developing countries experience larger fluctuations in their export earnings than developed countries)? What are the causes of instability? And does instability matter (i.e. is it detrimental to economic growth)? Coppock[10] and MacBean[11] argued that developing countries did not experience greater instability than developed countries. Their conclusions were challenged by a number of later studies which, using a variety of indices, different time periods and assessing a wide range of effects (export prices, quantities and proceeds), found the export instability of developing countries to be more than twice as high as that of developed countries.[12] Most economists would now agree with Thoburn's statement that 'There is little doubt that primary commodity markets exhibit greater instability than those of manufactures.'[13] Even greater confusion

surrounds the causal explanation of instability. No single factor has been found
with sufficient power to explain the phenomenon and to some extent this reflects
the lack of definitional clarity with regard to the concept, that is instability of
income or export proceeds? Numerous variables have been investigated[14] and the
ones currently thought to be of most relevance are the size of domestic markets,
the openness of the economy and the relationship between aggregate export
earnings and earnings derived from particular commodities subject to high levels
of instability. Empirical research on the effects of export instability has also
produced inconclusive findings. The relationship between export instabilty and
overall economic activity and/or an important domestic variable is unclear from
the available evidence.[15] It should also be noted that countries can suffer adverse
effects even if domestic variables are left untouched, for example, the competive-
ness of their exports could suffer in relation to substitutes with more stable prices.

The inconclusiveness and contradictory nature of these findings is due to poor
theoretical formulation and inadequate methodologies. Wilson, in his survey of
export instability theory, argues that the failure to specify the transmission
mechanism envisaged and to link this with testable structural and behavioural
hypotheses sufficiently grounded in economic theory, especially the theory of
choice under uncertainty, results in serious shortcomings.[16] In his survey of the
empirical work he notes the problems of comparison inherent in using highly
aggregative cross-section methodology and suggests greater disaggregation. The
casual adoption of instability indices, failure to link the empirical work strongly
enough with economic theory and crude quantitative methods contribute to the
ambiguity surounding the concept.[17] These criticisms, I would contend, have a
wider relevance to the entire commodity debate and are not specific to analyses
of instability.

Support or opposition to the IPC was based in large part on analysis of the
terms of trade and export instability but it was also based on an examination of the
detailed proposals. The IPC contained four main elements — the integrated
approach, the Common Fund, buffer stocking and 'Second Window' measures.
I will now discuss the main points of contention with respect to these issues in
order to highlight the importance of different perspectives in the bargaining
process.

The integrated approach was based on an analysis which stressed the failure
of commodity by commodity negotiations, the financial gains that would accrue
from a common source of funds and increased market management. Many critics
doubted whether the causes of the failures both to conclude and maintain international commodity agreements arose from the lack of an integrated approach
and doubted the wisdom of market intervention on this scale. Technical considerations of the costs and benefits of an integrated approach focused on attempts
to calculate financial gains for both producers and consumers. Once again
different studies came to different conclusions. Paul MacAvoy and John Cuddy
both assessed the expected annual net benefits accruing to producers and
consumers as a result of the stabilisation of the ten core commodities. MacAvoy
estimated producer gain at $250m., consumer gain at $75m. but a net global loss

of $590m. because of storage and interest costs of $915m. Cuddy on the other hand, estimated that producers would gain $1,022m.,consumers would gain $1,097 m., and that the net global benefit would be $1,204m.[18] Behrman calculated that the consuming countries would make substantial gains because of the reduction of inflationary pressures.[19] Thus according to the estimates of Cuddy and Behrman the major beneficiaries from the IPC would be consumers in developed countries!

Supporters of the Common Fund argued that it was necessary in order to generate financial savings given the negotiation of a series of ICAs. This would be accomplished through offset savings if the stockable commodities moved in variance. Behrman's computation of the correlation coefficients of the ten core commodities supported the the idea of a Common Fund since he found that less than a third were significantly positively correlated over the period 1954–72.[20] Supporters also hoped that the CF would attract investors, command better borrowing terms and play a catalytic role in the conclusion of commodity agreements. Helen O'Neill argued that 'the greatest constraint on the operation of buffer stock schemes has been the cost to the producing countries of financing the stock funds.'[21] Opponents of the scheme criticised both the financial and operational aspects. The UNCTAD secretariat's estimate of $6bn. capital funding was universally dismissed as being inadequate.[22] Furthermore, critics argued that the offset savings would be dependent on the number and type of commodities stocked and that the provision of a CF would generate unnecessary buffer stocks.[23]

In the IPC proposals buffer stocking was frequently mentioned as the most appropriate instrument for market control in that it was more flexible, intervened less with the market, was more easily negotiable and was capable of covering a wider range of commodities than either of the other two types of commodity agreements, that is multilateral contracts and export restriction agreements. Critics doubted whether the historical evidence supported the contention that buffer stock operations had been successful in the past. Doubts were also expressed concerning the number of commodities for which stocking arrangements could be made. The World Bank and the OECD estimated that only five commodities (coffee, cocoa, copper, tin and rubber) were good candidates with sugar, tea, cotton and tin as possible candidates.[24]

A wide variety of 'other measures' which subsequently became 'integrated' under the Second Window were envisaged in the proposals. These included diversification, increasing productivity, supply management, promotional measures, transport and marketing improvements and compensatory finance. These activities were distinguished by a low rate of return and long-term lending requirements. In the light of this it was not these measures *per se* which were criticised but the source and size of the financial requirements and the allocation of priorities among them.[25]

This discussion of economic analysis and the commodity debate has been concerned with outlining the various controversies and differing interpretations of LDC trade problems and international arrangements for commodity trade. No attempt has been made to assess the merits of the various arguments partly because this is widely available in the literature and partly because considerations of space do not permit the detailed technical discussion which would be necessary. But such discussion has been excluded mainly because the aim of this section was to establish the existence of competing perspectives, the inconclusiveness of economic research and the wide range and complexity of the issues involved. I am arguing that economic analysis did not present a pre-existent set of answers to which policy makers could turn but was itself an integral part of the attempt to create an IPC. The manner in which governments and bureaucrats supported their case, the use they made of evidence and the skill they demonstrated in refuting economic arguments was an important feature of the negotiating positions taken by the participants in the negotiations. Neither am I claiming that particular theories influenced particular phases of the negotiations. My contention is that the economic debate was part of the discursive process whereby interests in the bargaining process were constructed. In this context the 'battle' between competing theories and rival explanations form one dimension of power in the bargaining process. We have shown that it was unlikely that any particular proposal would attain widespread support given the state of economic knowledge. This tended to heighten the conflict between supporters of the IPC and its critics. The intellectual support for most of the G77's demands came from the UNCTAD secretariat and although the secretariat recognised the political role played by economic theory its tendency to reduce economic objections to political ones meant that it failed to respond creatively to academic critics of its proposals.[26] This in turn devalued the research undertaken by the secretariat, eroded its credibility and ultimately limited the value of its assistance to the G77.

Cleavages

This section will examine the specific cleavages which existed in the G77 in relation to the IPC. The cohesion of the group was dependent on its ability to suppress the effects of these cleavages. The significant ascriptive traits are derived from the role of a country as a producer or consumer of the commodities included in the integrated programme and any benefits they might gain from Second Window activities. Positions within specific commodity markets, share of world production and efficiency (and cost) of production are key variables. The net costs and benefits of the IPC to a particular developing country and levels of development are important considerations. The salient attitudinal traits relate to (a) the perception of whether the IPC as a whole is beneficial to a country, and if not, the extent to which political gains outweigh economic losses; (b) the perception of the working of specific commodity markets of particular interest to the country concerned and views concerning future market arrangements. The most important behavioural traits are related to the use made of organisational membership outside the UNCTAD framework, such as producer associations and ICAs, and to behaviour in UNCTAD. The large number of countries, multiplicity of commodities and wide range of market conditions (mainly free, protected or distorted, closed, partly open and partly closed and oligopolistic buyers)[27] do not determine the degree of fractionalisation or cohesion of the G77 but condition the outcome of intra-group bargaining.

The potential benefit of the integrated programme to a developing country can be assessed by examining the country's overall balance of trade in the commodities covered by the scheme. The total effect of the IPC was not the only important consideration to governments, however, since as producers of particular commodities they had specific interests which would dictate attitudes to the scheme whatever the overall calculation suggested. It was apparent at the outset that the IPC could not provide positive gains for all developing countries. A significant ascriptive trait therefore related to the expected gains or losses from the operation of the scheme and the size of the gain or loss. The impact of the IPC was dependent on the commodity coverage,[28] techniques of regulation, other measures and financing. An early UNCTAD analysis covering a hundred developing countries for the 1970–2 period showed that twenty of these countries were net importers, that is potential losers.[29] Of these countries, thirteen had high incomes or enjoyed fast growth in their export earnings; the remaining seven were small food deficit countries. Of the countries that stood to gain sixty had a higher than 3:1 ratio of exports to imports in the relevant commodities. The category of net importer was not a static one since the calculations are based on moving averages. Despite the difficulties surrounding such an exercise, that is the tentative nature of the statistical data and the lack of comprehensive treatment, we will examine the differential impact of the integrated programme on the G77 by looking at some calculations made by the UNCTAD secretariat in 1976.[30] This analysis reveals that only twenty-four out of the 113 G77 members for which data was available would suffer a negative impact. But these statistics also clearly show the inadequacy of relying solely on trait cleavage (heterogeneity) to predict the behaviour of the G77. Brazil and India were among the main beneficiaries, indeed Brazil stood to gain the most, and yet both countries adopted conservative and lukewarm attitudes to the IPC. Although this is to some extent explained by the fact that the UNCTAD analysis is very crude and unsophisticated[31] and does not for instance include the effect on economies of a rise in food prices (a likely consequence of the IPC), an event of great importance to a food-importing country like India, it does provide preliminary evidence on which positions could be formulated. Secondly, it is interesting that Malta and Romania, both net importers, joined the G77 after the beginning of the IPC dialogue. Thirdly, the division along regional lines expressed particularly in bargaining over the CF cannot be predicted from these figures. Given the importance of regional groups in the structure and functioning of the G77 the regional group with the largest number of 'losers' would be expected to be the least receptive to the proposals. Of the twenty-four disadvantaged states eighteen were in the Asian Group, four in the African Group and two in the Latin American Group. Conversely four out of the ten top beneficiaries were Latin American countries. And yet the Latin American Group was not very supportive of the scheme.[32] This perverse result shows the limitation of relying solely on aggregative data and the necessity to take perceptions, existing patterns of organisational behaviour and links with extra-UNCTAD groups and organisations into account. The Latin American Group adopted a more reserved position to the IPC negotiations than the Asian Group, an outcome based on the strong reservations held by some leading members of the group, such as Brazil and Colombia, to many features of the proposal, rather than the influence of the most disadvantaged members of the group, the Bahamas and Romania, in group decision-making. On the other hand, some leading members of the Asian Group, for example Yugoslavia, Iran, Singapore and Saudi Arabia, were potential losers. Algeria and Libya, potential losers from the African Group and influential members of the group were unable to affect group policy significantly because they represented such a small constituency. The weak conclusions derived from this preliminary analysis suggests that other trait cleavages were important in determining support for the IPC. We therefore examine briefly ascriptive cleavages in respect of export concentration, level of development and individual commodity markets:

The contribution of the ten core commodities to total export earnings provided another basis on which support for the integrated programme could be built. Behrman calculated that for eight countries the ten core comodities accounted for more than two-thirds of their export earnings and for a further twenty-two countries, more than one-third of their export earnings.[33] Almost half of these countries with a high export concentration in the ten core commodities are African and this was another factor behind the African Group's support for the IPC. In contrast some heavily populated non-OPEC members of the coalition had an export concentration in these ten core commodities below one-third.[34]

The impact of the integrated programme on countries at different levels of development was another pertinent trait cleavage. In the bargaining process this was most readily observable in terms of the special interests of the LDDCs. One study showed a substantial interest by the twenty-nine LDDCs in the eighteen Nairobi commodities since they accounted for 56 per cent of their total exports (44 per cent for the ten core commodities) and 8 per cent (6 per cent for the core commodities) of total imports (1970–75).[35] Nine countries were overall net importers of the 18 commodities. Five countries had substantial trade surpluses in the eighteen commodities and also a high dependence on two or three commodities for the bulk of their export earnings. The authors concluded that

Given the trade position of the least developed countries in the Integrated Programme for Commodities . . . it would appear that these countries are likely to gain relatively more from the operation of the Integrated Programme than any other group of developing countries in that many of them rely heavily for their export earnings on the commodities currently envisaged for the Programme, while the significance of their imports of these commodities is very minor in aggregate.[36]

Market position provided another relevant ascriptive cleavage. In commodity negotiations it is possible to identify two types of conflicts, one between producers and consumers and the second between producers. Developing countries as producers and consumers of various commodities were therefore influenced by their market interests. The integrated programme was launched in the wake of the successful OPEC price hike and although this had been given rhetorical support by the developing countries the deleterious effects of the quadrupling of oil prices on the economies of the oil importing developing countries was a factor which could not be ignored. Although most developing countries were not significant importers of the eighteen commodities and therefore lacked bargaining strength they were nevertheless likely to be hurt by higher import prices. For example, countries like Singapore, South Korea and Yugoslavia with their growing manufacturing sector needed access to cheap raw materials. Similarly, Pakistan was a substantial importer of jute and tea. The conflict between producers has a theoretical and historical dimension. In other words, previous international commodity arrangements had witnessed conflicts of interest between developing country producers; and the different cost structures, market shares, bargaining strengths and product quality made conflict likely. Of course, elements of cooperation are not wholly absent, since no producer alliance or commodity agreement could ever be negotiated unless the competing interests are reconciled.

Attitudinal cleavages were based on perceptions of overall benefit from the operation of the scheme, satisfaction with existing market arrangements in commodities of particular interest and importance attached to the unity of the G77. The inconclusive nature of the economic evidence and the wide diversity of interest meant that there would be no simple consensus formation. The negotiating process divided as it was between the CF and the individual commodity negotiations gave rise to constantly shifting perceptions and changing attitudes. That is to say there was an element of feedback between the two sets of negotiations and governments could maintain some degree of consistency in policy or choose not to do so depending on the state of the negotiations. For example, a country could be very self-interested within an individual commodity negotiation and yet play a 'positive' role in the CF negotiations. This is not just hypocrisy or the failure of communications but arises from the attempt to reconcile two competing objectives. In this instance economic self-interest in the commodity negotiations and diplomatic solidarity with the G77 in the CF negotiations. I will argue below that the high degree of politicisation of the CF talks was not only an outgrowth of the G77 decision-making structure but necessary to maintain the coalition. Without the solidarist element provided by the CF the G77 would have ceased to be a coalition since the diverse interests took precedence in the commodity negotiations. This is not to deny the existence of conflicting perspectives on the CF but to argue that removing the CF from its central position, or insisting that it should be negotiated after the conclusion of the commodity negotiations, would have meant removing the collective good or its most potent symbol.

The attitudes of G77 members were shaped not only by the specific organisational context but also by wider environmental considerations. Brazil and India, two of the most disaffected G77 members on the IPC issue, remained in the coalition because the unity of the G77 was politically important in the North–South dialogue.[37] The IPC negotiations and intra-G77 politics cannot be understood unless this important factor is not forgotten. The IPC was the centrepiece of the attempts to establish a NIEO but its failure did not entail the failure of attempts to get incremental/radical change in other areas. The debate begun in UNCTAD in 1964 was finally almost front-page news and extended into other international organisations. Defection from the G77, especially when interests in commodities of special concern could be safeguarded, just did not make political sense. Most G77 governments took a pragmatic attitude to the IPC. Strategies varied from damage limitation, in the case of those governments which felt their interests threatened, to goal maximisation, in the case of those which saw the potential for real benefits.

The attempt to create an IPC met with difficulty because many producers were already members of inter-governmental organisations which they felt satisfactorily protected their interests and they did not want these organisations to be brought under UNCTAD's umbrella. Moreover, the existence of various consultative groups and cartels revealed conflicting producer aims and values. In other words, governments exhibited a variety of modes of behaviour in the international political economy and an integrated programme was in direct conflict with various vested interests. Existing arrangements and membership provided a complex picture of attempts to regulate commodity trade. Before the Nairobi resolution ICAs existed for tin, coffee and cocoa. A variety of regional associations exist; for example among coffee producers; the Organisation of Coffee Producers of Africa and Malagasy (OAMCAF), a Francophone grouping; the Inter-African Coffee Organisation(ICAO), covering all African producers; the Central American, Mexican and Caribbean Coffee Federation (FEDECAME), which includes all Latin American producers except Brazil and Colombia; and the Pan-American Coffee Bureau. Cartels of interest included the Intergovernmental Council of Copper Exporting Countries (CIPEC), the Union of Banana Exporting Countries (UPEB) and the International Bauxite Association (IBA), but in each case leading exporters were non-members. Examples of consultative fora are those engaged in by the tea-producing countries on a regional basis in Asia (India, Indonesia and Sri Lanka) and in Africa (Kenya, Uganda and Tanzania). The existence of these organisations had two consequences for G77 unity and the IPC negotiations. First, producer governments had a history of dialogue and various working arrangements. In so far as they felt in control of their market share under existing arrangements then the UNCTAD scheme was an irrelevance. They therefore used their membership of these organisations to preserve autonomy and to resist encroachment by UNCTAD. Secondly, both regional organisations and cartels reflected existing disputes and the IPC did not provide suitable mechanisms to solve them. For example, the Latin American and African coffee producers had fundamentally opposed interests. ICAs already in existence reflected different bargaining strengths under prevailing rules, which indicated that some countries were satisfied with the rules and the outcomes. Participating in the IPC would jeopardise their interests, for example the Latin American coffee producers. Similarly countries outside a cartel arrangement or ICA had taken that decision on perceived self-interest. Why join the integrated programme which might mean a loss of market share? This was a consideration behind Brazil's self-exclusion from the IBA. On the other hand, countries seeking the conclusion of commodity agreements were those which felt that they might gain from new market share quotas, such as East African tea producers. In so far as existing organisational arrangements were in accord with the interests of some producers the IPC represented a challenge to their control.

Alignments with developed countries, particularly close economic cooperation and market arrangements, produced another cleavage in the group. The Lomé Convention between the EEC and the African, Caribbean and Pacific states (ACP) is the most significant agreement in this context. Lomé provides preferential access to the EEC market for the ACP and also in the innovative Stabex provision compensatory financing for shortfalls in earnings from selected commodities. Non-members, particularly the Latin American countries, complained about this discrimination. Unlike the GSP, association with the EEC was not a crucial issue and the increase in the number of beneficiaries ensured greater support for discrimination. A key development was the geographical extension of association to the Pacific and most importantly the Caribbean. The existence of ACP members within the Latin American Group was important in reducing that group's hostility to the EEC's association system. The Commonwealth Caribbean countries vigorously defending the Lomé Agreement in the Latin American Group were effective in moderating that group's hostility.

The bargaining process

From the origins of the concept to Nairobi, 1974–76

The UNCTAD secretariat's proposal for the creation of an Integrated Programme for Commodities in August 1974(38) was a response to a request of the UNGA.[39] It is not clear why the UNCTAD secretariat responded in this particular manner but a number of factors can be suggested. Gamani Corea assumed office as the new Secretary-General of the organisation in April 1974, the same month as the Sixth Special Session and the launching of the NIEO. An approach with a high political profile would establish him firmly in his new post. UNCTAD, labouring under the sobriquet Under No Circumstances Take Any Decisions, was sorely in need of new dynamism. By 1974 after a decade in existence UNCTAD had few concrete achievements to show. A new programme which would see it once again as the centre of UN development activities and contribute to its struggle to be accepted as a legitimate negotiating body was therefore attractive to secretariat officials. Moreover, GATT had finally thrown off its post-Kennedy Round lethargy and launched the Multilateral Trade Negotiations (MTN) in September 1973. The influence of personalities and other idiosyncratic variables cannot be weighted precisely but a combination of the ambitions and career aspirations of secretariat officials combined with the necessity for task expansion and increased legitimisation all combined to provide both the initial impetus behind the proposal of an integrated programme and subsequent support and development of the concept.

Efforts to reform the international economic order were undertaken in a number of fora, but UNCTAD became the central organ of the UN system spearheading the thrust and within UNCTAD the IPC became the focus of attention. This is attributable to the political commitment of the UNCTAD secretariat, the importance of commodities in the economies of the developing countries, trends in the world economy and the slow pace of reform on other issues. The UNCTAD secretariat functioned as a *quasi de facto* secretariat of the G77 and its continued influence depended on its ability to design programmes favoured by the majority of the G77. It was the G77, with its numerical majority, which was capable of generating new programmes within the United Nations and in deciding which agency would be charged with the research and implementation. The UNCTAD secretariat was therefore ready and willing to tailor its programme to suit its constituency. But the secretariat was also imbued with its own organisational ideology which favoured these goals and therefore the intellectual justification for the IPC did not require a departure from its normal mode of operation. The rebuttal of the secretariat's economic analysis by Western academics was not a new phenomenon and, perhaps because the secretariat had from its inception been subject to hostile criticism of its economic competence and the soundness of its ideas, it self-protectively retreated into a cocoon and refused to recognise pertinent criticisms of its approach.[40]

The original note by the UNCTAD Secretary-General on the integrated programme was expanded at the request of the TDB[41] into a series of studies published in December 1974.[42] These documents formed the basis on which discussion within the G77 and between the G77 and Groups B and D took place in the TDB and the Committee on Commodities. Attempts to coordinate the G77's position for these meetings were made in the regional groups in Geneva but from the outset it was recognised that group support would be at the broad level of principle and that in working out the detailed nature of the programme the interests of individual states would have to be protected. This was a realistic assessment based not only on the nature of the IPC but also reflecting a sober reappraisal of the centrifugal tendencies within the group exacerbated by fundamental changes in the global economy.

The effects of higher oil prices were evident in the worsening balance of payments position of the non-oil-rich developing countries. As the economic disparities within the Third World widened, so a plethora of categories reflecting a political attitude to the increasing diversity sprang up. To the existing categories of LDDCs, LLCs and DICs were added the most seriously affected countries (MSA) and the newly industrialising countries (NICs). Analysts also began dividing the Third World into fourth and fifth worlds. The existence of new groups claiming special status added to the strains within the group. This was further exacerbated when it was asserted that the newly prosperous group members, OPEC members that is, should contribute to the development of the poorer countries. OPEC members resisted the claim that higher oil prices had contributed to the plight of developing countries and pointed to the level of their economic aid commitments which in terms of GNP were higher than those of the OECD countries. Group B attempted to exploit these differences by adopting a strategy which stressed the diverse nature of the Third World coalition. Apart from attacking OPEC as the cause of global inflation, Group B spokesmen attempted to initiate studies concentrating on the problems of the LDDCs and MSAs and altered their aid programmes so that a clear distinction was made between the poorest countries and other developing countries.[43]

Countering these centrifugal tendencies were two centripetal tendencies which helped to maintain the coalition. Increased turbulence in the global economy ushered in the concept of Economic Cooperation Among Developing Countries (ECDC). The developed countries reacted to the collapse of the Bretton Woods regime, higher oil prices and global inflation by turning inwards and increasing protectionism. ECDC was conceived as an alternative to reliance on developed countries' markets and financial institutions. At the same time the more developed members of the G77 looked to the MTN talks to provide them with real benefits but felt that without the support of the developing countries as a whole their interests would be marginalised in the GATT.

The original proposal stressed five kinds of international action required under an integrated programme: (a) the creation of a series of international stocks; (b) the establishment of a common fund to finance the stocks; (c) the negotiation of multilateral trade commitments; (d) the creation of a compensatory financing facility; (e) the expansion of processing in developing countries. The three radical elements of the programme, that is the comprehensive coverage of problem commodities, the common fund and the multi-dimensional approach, were retained throughout the discussions. By the time the integrated programme reached Nairobi two elements had come to dominate the discussions — international stocks and the common fund. The IPC, following previous commodity discussions in UNCTAD, soon became a dispute about principles. Before the negotiations on individual commodity agreements could begin it was first necessary to reach agreement on the nature and shape of the programme. Buffer stocks and the common fund were more amenable to general discussions on principle than the other three measures. The UNCTAD secretariat argued that the common fund (CF) would play a catalytic role and therefore it was imperative to negotiate the CF before the individual commodity agreements. It was argued that failure to create a CF would result in fewer ICAs being successfully negotiated. The secretariat ensured that buffer stocking became an important question of principle by, first, making a distinction between core and other commodities and, second, insisting that the core commodities would be subject to buffer stocking. Compensatory financing was not a contentious issue since both the IMF and the EEC operated such schemes. The expansion of processing in developing countries was more a medium-term than a short-term goal. Multilateral contracts suffered in comparison to buffer stocks as an approach to market management because they were more complicated to negotiate and politically inappropriate since they were not applicable to the core commodities.

The G77 endorsed the integrated programme with varying degrees of enthusiasm from the outset. In response to the UNCTAD Secretary-General's note in August 1974 some developing countries made radical speeches supporting producer associations, indexation and the arrival of a new phase in North–South negotiations.[44] But some leading members of the G77 gave very lukewarm support to the proposal.[45] The discussions in the Committee on Commodities and the TDB reveal the absence of unity in the G77. The expected differential impact of the proposed scheme led to five areas of disagreement. First, countries that felt that the costs would outweigh the benefits argued for special consideration of their needs. Instead of jettisoning the entire programme those countries that stood to gain had little to lose by agreeing to the inclusion of special measures for the developing importing countries. In a similar vein the special needs of the LDDCs and MSAs were taken into consideration. Secondly, it was obvious that indexation would only benefit certain exporters, that is exporters of metals and minerals, and although at this stage indexation was included in the package it did not have a great deal of support. Thirdly, the benefits to be gained depended on commodity coverage and the programme was increased from the original ten commodities (coffee, cocoa, cotton, tea, copper, tin, jute, sisal, sugar and rubber), in response to sectional interests, to seventeen with the addition of wheat, rice, bananas, meat, wool, iron ore and bauxite. Fourthly, some producers (particularly Brazil and Colombia in respect of coffee) had serious reservations concerning the inclusion of their commodities in the IPC since they were satisfied with existing arrangements. At this stage they were willing for the sake of solidarity to allow its inclusion, since they knew that in any detailed negotiations they could protect their interests. Finally, the emphasis given to buffer stocking in the secretariat's proposal did not meet with the approval of all countries, particularly those like India, which did not expect to benefit from the operation of stocks.[46] These countries therefore insisted that the other measures in the programme should be given the same weight as the buffer stock proposal. At this stage no concerted attempt was made to devise a common G77 negotiating position. The task of so doing fell to the Third Ministerial Meeting of the G77 (26 January–6 February 1976) which met in Manila, Philippines, to prepare a joint G77 position for UNCTAD IV.

The Manila conference came at a critical time in the history of the G77. Two important developments since the Second Ministerial Meeting in 1971 posed problems for the organisational coherence of the group. First, the G77 had mushroomed in other organisational contexts and the importance of the General Assembly in initiating the NIEO had given an impetus to the G77 in New York with a resultant challenge to the dominance of the Geneva-based G77 on economic issues.[47] The G77 was therefore subject to problems of coordination between the different centres of the G77 and the campaign for an independent secretariat by some members increased divisions. Secondly, the G77's competence as the Third World's main organ in the attempt to harmonise and formulate policy on international economic relations was increasingly being challenged by the NAM. The increased activism of the NAM in seeking regime change was resented by some G77 members (non-members of the NAM), especially diplomats in Geneva who felt that extraneous political considerations were being introduced into development diplomacy.[48]

The regional group meetings prior to Manila revealed the existence of potential lines of conflict in the G77. Although all three groups posited support for the aims and objectives of the IPC and called for the creation of new institutional structures in UNCTAD to negotiate the CF and to oversee the individual commodity negotiations, the emphasis of their deliberations was on the necessity to negotiate a set of measures which best protected their sectional interests. The African Group changed the commodity coverage of the integrated programme. Rice, wheat and wool products of limited or part interest to African countries were excluded and vegetable oils, timber and phosphates added; and sisal was extended to cover all hard fibres. The African Group also called for special account to be taken of the needs of the least developed.[49] The Asian Group also changed the commodity coverage of the integrated programme, extending cotton to cotton yarn, jute to cover jute goods and sisal to cover all hard fibres. Special emphasis was placed on the needs of net importers and at India's insistence the Jakarta Declaration stressed the necessity to award equal status to all the proposed measures in the IPC.[50] The rather lukewarm support given to the programme by leading members of the Latin American Group was expressed in the defence made of existing institutions. The Declaration and Action Guidelines adopted by SELA's Latin American Council argued that the IPC 'should be conceived as a complementary global action and not as a substitute for other trade and financial measures and machinery'.[5]

The reaffirmation of unity and solidarity at Manila was more than rhetorical since the coalition was in danger of being thrown into crisis in the event of failure to agree a common position for the forthcoming UNCTAD conference. The salience of the IPC in the NIEO discussions and on UNCTAD IV's agenda helped to bring a spirit of compromise to the deliberations. Two different methods of conflict resolution were used, upgrading the common interest and splitting the difference. In respect of commodity coverage the Manila Declaration expressed the wishes of the African and Asian producers and also included manganese as a suitable commodity. Indian diplomacy was successful in obtaining commitment to the importance of measures other than buffer stocking since these had not been included in the Report of the Preparatory Committee.[52] Those countries wishing to limit the role played by the IPC in respect of commodites of interest to them also secured agreement that preserved the autonomy of state action.[53] In these instances agreement had been reached by upgrading the common interest, that is including the demands of the dissatisfied states in the final compromise. This did not resolve the conflcit but it contained the potential divisiveness. This form of dispute settlement did not however prevail over the issue of special measures for the LDDCs. Many Latin American states, angered by the conclusion of the Lomé Convention the previous year, refused to agree special measures for the African states since they argued that special treatment was provided under Lomé. The Latin Americans refused to accept the LDDCs as a special category and placed them with the developing importing countries. The UNCTAD secretariat had suggested that a range of special measures might be instituted for the LDDCs including 'exemption from the obligation to share the financial costs and risks of stocks, and specially favourable treatment in the allocation of export quotas.'[54] Latin American objections meant that the Manila Declaration could only promise 'appropriate differential and remedial measures within the programme'. The G77 thus arrived at Nairobi with a unity which masked important disagreements. Nevertheless, in the context of the NIEO discussions it was of crucial importance that they had agreed a common position. Unity ensured the continuation of North–South confrontation and collective G77 support for the creation of an institutional structure in UNCTAD to negotiate a CF, set in motion negotiations on individual commodities, and investigate measures other than buffer stocking.

Nairobi (1976)

The three most important topics at Nairobi were commodities, aid and debt rescheduling and the transfer of technology. High oil prices, the collapse of the commodity boom, Western worries about investment in commodities, concern about the relationship between commodity price instability and domestic inflation, the still present threat of producer associations and the Third World's insistence on structural transformation of the world economy resulted in commodities becoming the most important topic at the conference.

Group B had prior to the conference attempted to adopt a common position. But the divisions in the group were so significant that various countries entered reservations to the agreed text. The major division was between the hardliners, the United States, United Kingdom, West Germany and Japan, who rejected the CF or integrated approach and the accommodationist states led by Canada, the Netherlands and the Nordic countries, who were prepared to accept *dirigiste* attempts at reform. The fragile consensus reached by Group B contained many ideas similar to the G77 text, but there were striking differences. Group B supported improved market access, diversification and multilateral commitments. But indexation was flatly rejected and buffer stocking included as one of a possible range of appropriate measures. A limited role was envisaged for the CF as a residual link between individual buffer stocks.[55] Group D, a peripheral participant in the negotiations gave general support to the plans of the UNCTAD secretariat but in their submission pointedly made no reference to the CF thus indicating opposition to the idea.

Divergent interests among G77 members resurfaced during the conference despite the compromise reached at Manila. Within the G77 there was strong support for indexation from Afghanistan, the Central African Republic, Ecuador, Fiji, Gabon, Iraq, Kenya, Madagascar, Morocco, Niger and Uganda.

On the other hand some countries, such as, Brazil, Papua New Guinea and India, were distinctly cautious about the programme as a whole and therefore unwilling to stress one of its most contentious features. Although the Manila Declaration had listed eighteen products as suitable for inclusion in the IPC those countries with interests in products included in the UNCTAD proposal but excluded by the G77 fought to have their attempted commodities included in any agreed scheme, for example Burma (rice and wool), Lesotho (wheat, rice and wool), and Uruguay (wheat, rice and wool). Another division within the G77 concerned the responsibility of OPEC for world inflation and its proposed contribution to any CF financing. Some developing countries, such as, Chile, India and Pakistan, stressed the harmful effects of the oil price rise and the necessity for remedial action by the oil exporting countries. OPEC strenuously resisted this attempt to attach special responsibility to oil exporters but OPEC ministers meeting in Bali attempted to link cooperation with the West on oil prices to the UNCTAD's success in agreeing a CF[57] and OPEC finance ministers meeting in Paris reputedly established a $300 million fund to support the CF.[58] Those countries satisfied with existing commodity arrangements continued to battle to keep their commodities from inclusion in the IPC. Colombia, for example entered a forceful reservation after the adoption of Resolution 93(IV) and reserved its right to argue the case for the exclusion of coffee from the IPC when the relevant inter-governmental committee was convened.[59]

Within the G77 this conflict of objectives was contained and group unity preserved because of the operation of a number of factors. First, the Manila Declaration which served as the group's negotiating document had been the result of a long and arduous process and most countries insisted that the compromises agreed there were not subject to renegotiation, for example commodity coverage. Secondly, the criticism of OPEC was contained because many non-oil-rich African and Arab states in receipt of substantial economic assistance from OPEC members gave support to OPEC. Moreover, one of the most effective threats that the G77 could use was exercised on its behalf by OPEC, that is the threat to raise oil prices by 10 to 20 cents a barrel and to use the proceeds to finance the CF.[60] Thirdly, the prospect of compromise with Group B was unlikely to occur in the absence of G77 solidarity, and agreement in principle at Nairobi would still leave ample opportunity in the subsequent negotiations to represent specific grievances.

The fragile unity of the G77 was most severely tested not by internal dissension over the Manila Declaration or wrangling over the impact of oil prices but by varying responses to the US proposal to create an International Resources Bank (IRB). The IRB, offered by Henry Kissinger as an alternative to the CF, was a superficially attractive scheme which sought to encourage investment in raw materials. However, it had not been fully thought out and many developing countries were angered by the fact that it was presented as an alternative to the CF. They perceived the IRB as a politically motivated attempt to kill the integrated programme and as a scheme designed more to ensure supplies for the West than to assist the development efforts of the Third World. In the end the

IRB proposal was only narrowly defeated by 33 votes to 31 with 44 abstentions. Seven Latin American countries voted for the proposal, namely Argentina, Bolivia, Chile, Colombia, El Salvador, Nicaragua and Uruguay.

The differences between Group B and the G77 and the differences within the groups resulted in slow and arduous negotiations which in typical UNCTAD fashion were concluded on the penultimate day of the conference. The final agreement enshrined in Resolution 93(IV) was not much more than an agreement to go on talking and the wording left the objectives and follow-up action open to differing interpretations. It was unclear for example whether the negotiating conference on the CF to be convened by the UNCTAD Secretary-General would be concerned with negotiating a CF or discussing the possibility of negotiating a CF. The timetables set in the resolution for the convening of preparatory meetings and negotiations on individual commodities was not a triumph for the G77 since the EEC proposal and various developed countries had mentioned the necessity of a strict timetable. The controversial issue of indexation was dropped and, although given the prime position among the various measures contemplated, buffer stocking was definitely envisaged as one among a variety of measures.

Resolution 93(IV), a product of the organisational framework, could only reflect the lowest common denominator of international consensus. It represented the maximum that the United States, Britain and West Germany were prepared to accept. But it also clearly reflected the cleavages within the G77. First, the commodity coverage suggested by the UNCTAD secretariat had been changed to ensure a coverage which the members of the G77 felt would benefit a larger number of countries and lessen the number on which the proposed measures would have a damaging effect. As has already been pointed out the calculation of gain or loss in this instance is very problematical but the important point is that the 'Nairobi eighteen commodities' reflected the widest measure of consensus in the G77. These commodities were bananas, bauxite, cocoa, coffee, copper, cotton and cotton yarns, hard fibres and products, iron ore, jute and jute products, manganese, meat, phosphates, rubber, sugar, tea, tropical timber, tin and vegetable oils, including olive oil and oilseeds. Importantly the coverage was left open-ended with the provision for the inclusion of other commodities at a later date. Secondly, provision was made for the special interest groups in the G77. Measures were included in the programme which would benefit those countries that did not stand to gain from the operation of international stocks; reference was also made to the special needs of the LDDCs, MSAs and the developing importing countries. Furthermore, specific reference was made to the preservation of the status of existing international arrangements. These wide-ranging measures arose from the necessity to protect the varying and diverse interests of members of the coalition.

With the adoption of Resolution 93(IV) the negotiations entered a different phase. The conclusion of UNCTAD IV produced few firm commitments and plenty of room for backsliding. Progress on the individual commodity negotiations, unless deviating remarkably from historical experience, was bound to be slow and offered an arena for substantial intra-G77 conflict. The CF negotiations presented the only hope for a common G77 position within the forthcoming IPC dialogue.

The Common Fund negotiations

At its fourth session the United Nations Negotiating Conference on a Common Fund adopted the Articles of Agreement of the Common Fund on 27 June 1980.[61] My intention is not to focus in any detail on the long and intense negotiations (see Table 7.1) which led to this agreement but to assess the extent to which the G77's position is understandable in the light of the cleavages examined above and the effect these cleavages had on the group's strategy. Throughout this process once the G77 had attained a common position the group retained a remarkable degree of unity and although internal disputes existed the public face of the group very rarely reflected the inner conflicts. On the other hand, Group B displayed a remarkable degree of incoherence and disunity[62] and the slow pace of progress was mainly attributable to the reluctance of major developed states, especially the United States and West Germany, to accept, first, the principle of a CF and, secondly, the type of fund suggested by the G77.

The UNCTAD environmental context imposed two crucial constraints on the negotiating process. The group system of negotiation made intra-group compromise as important if not more important than inter-group agreement. This constraint was clearly visible at the first negotiating conference where, despite the benefit of preparatory meetings, most of the four-week meeting was spent in intra-group consultation.[63] The second constraint arose from the consensual method of decision making. An exhaustive process of deliberation had to be undertaken in the attempt to reach an agreement acceptable to all parties. This constraint precluded the establishment of a CF between the G77, the like-minded European countries and China. Moreover, the inconclusive nature of the economic analysis provided an additional constraint. The arguments hostile to or sceptical of the UNCTAD secretariat's analysis were used to support the position of the hard-line states and the tentative nature of many findings were used as an excuse to ask for more research to be undertaken. I am not saying that this was a mere intellectual justification or that the economic arguments were used to mask a political decision. No doubt there was an element of this involved; more fundamentally the disputed and uncertain nature of the economic arguments made such behaviour inevitable.

The negotiations for a Common Fund centred around five main issues: (i) objectives and purpose; (ii) financing needs and structure; (iii) source of finance; (iv) modes of operations; (v) decision making and fund management. When the first negotiating conference convened in March 1977 the G77 had been unable to reconcile the conflicting views within the group and therefore was unable to present any outline text on which detailed negotiations could take place. In the absence of a negotiating text the G77 sought a commitment in principle from the

Table 7.1   *Chronology of Common Fund and IPC Meetings, 1976–80*

	1976
22 November 22–6	1st. *Ad Hoc* Intergovernmental Committee for the Integrated Programme for Commodities (Ad Hoc Cttee)
29 November–4 December	1st. Preparatory Meeting for the Negotiation of a Common Fund (Prep. Meet; doc TD/B/IPC/CF/4)
	1977
24 January–8	2nd. Prep. Meet (TD/B/IPC/CF/6)
21 February–1 March	3rd. Prep. Meet (TD/B/IPC/CF/8)
2–3 March	2nd. Ad Hoc Cttee (TD/B/IPC/AC/8)
7 March–2 April	1st. United Nations Negotiating Conference on a Common Fund under the Integrated Programme for Commodities (Neg. Conf on CF; TD/IPC/CF/CONF/8)
11–15 July	3rd. Ad Hoc Cttee (TD/B/IPC/AC/11)
7 November–1 December	2nd. Neg. Conf on CF suspended on 1st. December (TD/IPC/CF/CONF/14, Part I)
12–14 December	4th. Ad Hoc Cttee (TD/B/IPC/AC/15)
	1978
13–17 March	5th. Ad Hoc Cttee (TD/B/IPC/AC/18)
10–15 July	6th. Ad Hoc Cttee (TD/B/IPC/AC/21)
14–30 November	resumed 2nd. session of the Neg. Conf on CF (TD/IPC/CF/CONF/14, Part II)
	1979
12–19 March	3rd. Neg. Conf on CF (TD/B/IPC/CF/19 CONF/19)
22 March	8th. Ad Hoc Cttee (TD/B/IPC/AC/27)
	1979
3–14 September	1st. Interim Committee of the United Nations Negotiating Conference on a Common Fund under the Integrated Programme for Commodities (Interim Cttee; the report of all 5 sessions of the Interim Cttee is published as (TD/IPC/CF/CONF/20)
22 October–2 November	2nd. Interim Cttee
3–14 December	3rd. Interim Cttee
17–18 December	9th. Ad Hoc Cttee (TD/B/IPC/AC/32)
	1980
18 February–5 March	4th. Interim Cttee
8–19 April	5th. Interim Cttee
5–27 June	4th. Neg. Conf on CF (TD/IPC/CF/CONF/ 26)

other groups. Group B countered by arguing that it was impossible to agree in principle to a CF before the precise details of its operations and financing were known. The ensuing stalemate cannot however be attributed to the G77's negotiating strategy[64] and the demand for a political response before technical details were worked out. This is because implicit in the demand for the acceptance of the fund in principle there was a commitment to a particular type of organisation, that is financially independent and interventionist. The hardliners in Group B were unwilling to concede this point. Furthermore the studies prepared by the UNCTAD secretariat for the preparatory meetings were sufficiently technical for a serious debate to be started.[65] It should be noted however that the absence of group consensus also prevented the G77 from responding effectively to Group B's position paper.[66]

When the second session of the negotiating conference convened on 8 November the G77 had an agreed negotiating text.[67] The result of months of intensive discussions in Geneva between the various missions and in the Working Group of 33 on the Common Fund/IPC negotiations the thirteen page text contained no ideas which had not been previously discussed and it replicated many of the ideas produced by the UNCTAD secretariat. The text contained the following proposals: the CF, apart from international commodity stocks, was to finance other measures, for example diversification, productivity improvement, market promotion, research and development and improvements in transport, marketing and distribution. It was also empowered to intervene in markets for which there were no existing international arrangements. Two separate accounts would be opened within the Fund, the first to finance buffer stocking and the second (the so-called Second Window) other measures. It was estimated that the CF would need $6bn.; $3bn. at the outset, consisting of subscribed capital equivalent to $1bn. with the authority to borrow up to $2bn., with a further $3bn. to be raised in similar proportions held as stand-by reserves. The resources of the Fund would come from direct government contributions, voluntary contributions, borrowings and net earnings derived from its operations. The structure of the Fund would consist of a Board of Governors, an Executive Council, a Managing Director and other staff. Decisions in both the Board of Governors and Executive Council would be by simple majority vote. Subsequently the G77 specified that the allocation of votes should be weighted to give them a built-in majority.

Most of these proposals were unpalatable to Group B and their counter-proposals[68] suggested instead (i) a pool fund with finance coming from the individual ICAs and not governments; (ii) activities should be confined to the first window and buffer stock; (iii) other measures should be undertaken by existing financial institutions; (iv) CF management should be undertaken by a small professional secretariat and an executive board; (v) voting procedure should reflect the interests of producers, consumers and the relevant financial and economic interests, that is no built-in majority.

The G77's negotiating strategy in the ensuing negotiations was conditioned by the attempt to satisfy the demands of various sectional interests in the group. In order to maintain internal unity the G77 found it difficult to compromise on certain issues. A Common Fund that did not include provisions other than buffer stocking of the ten core commodities would fail to benefit the African countries. The inclusion of 'other measures' in the G77's November negotiating text was not a surprise and indeed followed from the logic of Resolution 93(IV), the consensus reflected in the Manila Declaration and the submission of the UNCTAD secretariat to the Preparatory Meetings on the Common Fund.[69] The African Group as a whole had an interest in a wider CF and it was in their interest to insist that these measures be an integral part of the CF with guaranteed financial provisions. The African Group was united in its demands and as the largest regional group in the G77 it exercised significant influence in the decision-making process. The rigidity of the African Group on this issue exasperated some Asian and Latin American states. However, it is incorrect to present support for the Second Window as an exclusively African affair. Producers of the non-stockable commodities, for example Central American banana exporters, and other beneficiaries within the G77 also supported a wider CF.[70] Consideration of the distributional impact of the CF was always an important element in a strategy of mixed bargaining. The objectives enshrined in Resolution 93(IV) and its product coverage both supported the concept of other measures. Diversification, research and development, improved marketing, distribution and transport systems were explicitly mentioned as objectives. The coverage of jute, hard fibres, bananas, tropical timber, cotton and vegetable oils surely meant that the CF could not be restricted to stocking activities since some of these products are not stockable.

The distributional impact of the CF created in the developing importing countries a new category of disadvantaged country. These countries, in conjunction with the LDDCs, LLCcs, DICs and MSAs, influenced, as we have shown, the development of the G77 position for Nairobi. In the CF negotiations the crucial political wrangle developed not over whether special provisions should be made for these states but the extent to which other members of the G77, especially OPEC, would provide financial compensation. In an attempt to deflect criticism the OPEC states agreed as early as the first negotiating conference to provide financial assistance to the LDDCs. The key question concerned the extent to which specific measures, in contradistinction to rhetorical support, would be taken to protect the interests of the disadvantaged countries in any agreement. But not all disadvantaged countries took a negative attittude to the CF. Yugoslavia, a potential loser and influential member of the G77, gave positive support to the IPC and was one of the first countries to pledge a specific contribution to the CF.

Countries wary of the CF interfering with ICAs of interest to them supported the idea of a weak fund, favoured Group B's pool proposal and generally gave little support to the G77. Brazil, Colombia, India, Mexico and Pakistan took a very icy approach to the negotiations. Brazil's lack of enthusiasm for the IPC led some members of the G77 to question Brazil's membership of the group. The extent to which important members of the coalition were lukewarm in their support of the group position and willing to accept a conception of the CF nearer to that of Group B undermined the bargaining strength of the G77.

Several crucial factors contributed to coalition maintenance during these negotiations. The institutional framework of the G77 in Geneva helped to contain divisions. The regional groups, contact groups, meetings of the G77 as a whole and the Group of 33 provided fora where conflict could be mediated. Second, the absence of group discipline in the ICA negotiations invested the exhortations to solidarity on the CF with a special importance in the IPC package. Furthermore, the rationale for the existence of the G77 is dependent not on one set of negotiations but on a vulnerability which is experienced over many issues. The over-lapping MTN talks, also taking place in Geneva, provided another issue around which the G77 produced a joint strategy and some leading 'moderates' on the IPC, such as Brazil and India, needed the support of other members of the G77 in the MTNs, which were of greater significance to them. The effort put into opposing various aspects of the CF proposals was consequently relaxed, not out of any conscious trade-off strategy but because time and expertise are limited and in the ordering of priorities the GATT talks took precedence. Finally, the role of personalities should not be discounted. The three leading G77 spokesmen during the negotiations were ambassadors Herbert Walker (Jamaica), Ali Alatas (Indonesia) and Georges Alvares Maciel (Brazil).[71] Both Jamaica and Indonesia were supporters of the IPC and Walker and Alatas worked tirelessly to keep the coalition together.

The protracted negotiations with Group B were often bitter and the search for compromise continued until March 1979.[72] The November 1977 conference was suspended and not resumed until November 1978.[73] It is not necessary to look in any detail at the final agreement reached on the Common Fund. The compromise reached (a) protected the autonomy of existing ICAs, (b) provided special arrangements for the LDDCs, (c) included a second window but one which would be financed almost entirely by voluntary contributions. Directly contributable capital was set at $470m. of which $70m., was earmarked for the second window, and a further $280m. in voluntary contributions was earmarked for the second window.[74] The G77 agreed to this truncated CF because they realised that it was either this or nothing. Like the GSP years had been spent negotiating for a concession of questionable benefit and the final result, dependent as it was on the magnanimity of the developed world, could not conceivably satisfy the initial expectations. While the required number of countries (ninety) had ratified the Agreement establishing the Common Fund for Commodities by January 1986, it was not until July 1988 that the ratifying countries represented the two-thirds of directly contributed capital necessary for the CF to come into force.

The individual commodity negotiations, 1976–80

It would be superfluous to detail the preparatory meetings and individual negotiations that took place in respect of the Nairobi commodities. Conflict was managed and group cohesion maintained through the absence of any serious attempt apart from the rhetorical to impose a group consensus.[76] This was both a necessary and sensible approach because states are unlikely to relinquish perceived vital interests for the sake of rhetorical solidarity. The aim of this section is to explore the impact of the most salient general factors on the attempt to conclude ICAs under the IPC.

The successful conclusion of international commodity negotiations is dependent on the reconciliation of diverse and often conflicting interests. There is no magic formula and the invocation of 'political will' on the part of interested governments is as futile as it is puerile. The UNCTAD secretariat (and by extension the G77) appeared to believe that something called political will would magically transform the negotiating process from an exercise in failure to a shining example of success.[76] As an analytical tool political will is singularly inappropriate being at best a tautology and at worst meaningless. Governments are not autonomous actors and the influence of pressure groups representing traders, fabricators, producer associations and consumer interests is an important determinant of governmental behaviour. Moreover, attempts at market regulation take place in the context of developments in the market and changing market conditions and perceptions of short-term and long-term trends significantly affect behaviour. Producers are reluctant to agree on stabilisation measures when prices are buoyant and consumers hesitate when prices are low. Calculations about security of supply, market share and market access, changing international productivities, differential cost production schedules and the importance of transnational corporations significantly condition the politics of commodity negotiations.[77] Other important variables relate to the complexity of the commodity, the history of intergovernmental consultation on the commodity and the prevailing level of knowledge on the commodity and possible market measures.

Certain factors pertaining to the UNCTAD environmental context had a significant impact on the IPC negotiations. First, the political atmosphere which permeated UNCTAD was not considered favourable by many producers and consumers. The reluctance of the developed capitalist states to grant UNCTAD legitimacy as a negotiating forum has already been discussed. In addition, major developing-country producers of some commodities felt that UNCTAD's usefulness lay in norm creation rather than in the technical negotiations undertaken by ICAs. The mantle of the IPC meant that meetings were open to all states members of UNCTAD and not confined to the major importer and exporter nations, as had been the case in the past. This resulted in a charged ideological and political atmosphere. Secondly, the link between the individual commodity negotiations and the CF created an air of uncertainty, which was generally felt to be inhibiting to the creation of agreements. In a definite manner the two sets of negotiations were linked politically and their respective fates intertwined. It was thus in the interest of those countries that took the minimalist approach (that the size of the CF must be related to the number of commodity agreements and that the CF should be small) to conclude as few agreements as possible at the same time as they were using stalling tactics in the CF talks. On the other hand, countries in favour of both the CF and ICAs had to take the financial implications into account. The early completion of the CF talks was of crucial importance in that these states needed to know what resources would (or would not) be available from the central source and the nature of any provisions made for measures other than buffer stocking. Another link between ICAs and the IPC existed at the level at which governments assessed costs and benefits. The UNCTAD secretariat correctly diagnosed that the 'attitudes of many governments are still dominated by the traditional case-by-case-approach.'[79] My interview material not only confirms this observation but suggests that for members of the G77 these negotiations would not be approached in the integrated manner suggested by the secretariat since self-interest dictated that you kept what you had rather than bargaining it away for some political benefit that would not materialise. Thirdly, regime change in this area could not succeed without the acquiescence of the major importing countries. On the whole, apart from France, none of the major developed states accepted a *dirigiste* approach. They were prepared, nevertheless, to examine each commodity on a case-by-case basis. It is noteworthy that the much vaunted US opposition to commodity agreements on doctrinal grounds did not prevent the Americans in this period from joining the International Sugar Agreement (1977).

The G77 was attempting to develop a coherent strategy for the IPC at a time when developments in the global economy had a dialectical impact on the underlying bases of their solidarity. High oil prices, global inflation and recession in the West combined with fluctuating commodity prices and mounting debt problems underlined the vulnerability of most Third World countries to the vagaries of the global economy. These developments helped to promote the concept of ECDC and intensified efforts to maintain the unity of the G77 in order to effect structural change in the world economy and to increase the impact of the developing countries on international decision making. On the other hand, the economic differentiation within the Third World increased. Some countries embarked on successful policies of industrialisation (the NICs), whilst a new class of global poor was created (the MSAs). These changes in material conditions created competing interests and strains within the coalition.[79] I am not arguing that trends in the world economy removed the rationale for the coalition. The evidence is contradictory and not supportive of any one line of argument. When the IPC was launched, commodity agreements were in existence for cocoa, coffee, olive oil and tin. By 1980 negotiating conferences had only been held for cocoa, natural rubber and sugar. Only three agreements were concluded, the International Sugar Agreement (October 1977) the International Natural Rubber Agreement (October 1979) and a new International Cocoa Agreement (November 1980). The natural rubber agreement was the only new market arrangement to emerge under the programme. Since then the International Wheat Agreement has been renegotiated under the auspices of the International Wheat Council in March 1986. UNCTAD provided the framework for the renegotiation of the International Cocoa Agreement (July 1986), the International Olive Oil Agreement (July 1986), the International Natural Rubber Agreement (March 1987) and the International Sugar Agreement (September 1987). A Tropical Timber Agreement entered into force in April 1985. ICAs also exist for coffee and jute.

Conclusions

The heterogeneity of the G77 and specific cleavages affected the level and nature of group support for the Integrated Programme and the Common Fund. From the first proposals in 1974 to Resolution 93(IV) a process of accommodation between conflicting interests in the coalition was entered into in order to present a united bargaining front. The compromise reached in Manila at the Third Ministerial Meeting was maintained in the ensuing negotiations and all recognised interests were included in the G77's proposals. The G77 represents a conjoining of similar and opposed interests for the purposes of multilateral diplomacy. The IPC negotiations show clearly that the unity of the G77 is not organic but based on the recognition of both similarity and diversity. In pursuit of collective gain individual interests are aggregated. This existence of differing interests does not make the coalition irrational.

The G77 maintained unity in the IPC negotiations through a rational assessment of the nature of the bargaining process. No attempt was made to present a united front in the ICA negotiations. Bargaining on individual commodities not only presented a distributive bargaining process it also confronted G77 members as producers and consumers. A common group position could be sought on the CF first, because a clearer line between the developing and developed states could be drawn and, secondly, this was a process of mixed bargaining. An intensive consultation process on the CF was therefore embarked upon with the object of securing concessions from the developed world. The existence of shared values and the importance of the IPC within the context of the NIEO resulted in the use of persuasion as a favoured method of arriving at group decisions. But the most important reason for the ability of the G77 to maintain unity arose from the institutionalisation of group activity. The existence of regularised contact at regional level, the mushrooming of working groups and committees, the central role of the Working Group of 33 and the importance of the ministerial meetings provided the stable patterns of behaviour and procedures through which interests could be represented and reconciled. Member countries could thus safeguard their interests when they deviated from the majority view. Furthermore the NAM provided both a spur and a challenge to the G77. UNCTAD and the G77 were anxious that results be produced which confirmed their preeminence in the arena of North–South negotiations.

This case study documents the limits to G7 cooperation. The G77 is an instrument for negotiating regime change. It is a coalition of the Third World which presents a united front to the industrialised states. In cases where the simple dichotomy between North and South is replaced by producers and consumers the G77 ceases to have a defined role. The G77 as an institutional mechanism is adept at reconciling divergent interests among its member states. But it cannot perform such a role if the distinctions between group members and non-members are eroded.

Notes

1. For different classificatory schemes see TD/97 — 'Commodity Problems and Policies'; Rangarajan, *Commodity Conflict* (London: Croom Helm, 1978) pp. 56–61; K. Morton & P. Tulloch, *Trade and Developing Countries* (London: Croom Helm, 1977), p.92.
2. The objectives of the IPC were stressed in a number of UNCTAD documents. The original source is to be found in TD/B/498 — 'An Overall Integrated Programme for Commodities' (8 August 1974).
3. J. R. Behrman, *Development, the International Economic Order and Commodity Agreements* (Reading, Mass.: Addison-Wesley, 1978), p.34; M. Radetzki, *International Commodity Market Agreements* (London: Hurst & Co., 1970), pp.5–9.
4. For a more detailed consideration of these issues see Commodities Research Unit Ltd 'A Common Fund — Financial Organisation, Operations and Management' in *Commonwealth Economic Papers No.8 vol.1* (September 1977), pp.3–48; C. P. Brown, *The Political and Social Economy of Commodity Control* (London: Macmillan, 1980), pp.150–5.
5. Rangarajan, op.cit., p.101.
6. Behrman, op.cit., p.58.
7. P. Bairoch, *The Economic Development of the Third World since 1900* (London: Methuen, 1975), chap. 6.
8. TD/B/563 — 'Commodity Trade Indexation' Annex II, p.1. (July 1975).
9. J. Spraos, 'The statistical debate on the net barter terms of trade between primary commodities and manufactures', *Economic Journal*, vol. 90 (1980), p.216.
10. See J. D. Coppock, *International Economic Instability* (New York: McGraw-Hill, 1962).
11. A. I. MacBean, *Export Instability and Economic Development* (London: Allen & Unwin, 1966).
12. See, for example, G. F. Erb & S. Schiavo-Campo, 'Export Instability, Level of development and Economic Size of Less Developed Countries', *Bulletin of the Oxford University Institute of Economics and Statistics* (November 1969), pp.263–83; C. Glezakos, 'Export Instability and Economic Growth: A Statistical Verification', *Economic Development and Cultural Change* (July 1973), pp.670–8; S. Naya, 'Fluctuations in export earnings and Economic Pattern of Asian Countries', *Economic Development and Cultural Change*, 9 July 1973), pp. 629–41; O. Knudsen & A. Parnes, *Trade, Instability and Economic Development* (Lexington, Mass.: D.C. Heath, 1975).
13. J. T. Thoburn, *Primary Commodity Exports and Economic Development* (London: John Wiley, 1977), p.21.
14. See the studies in n.13 and B. Massell, 'Export Concentration and Fluctauations in Export Earnings: A Cross-section Analysis, *American Economic Review* (March 1964), pp.47–63; B. Massell, 'Export Instability and Economic Structure', *American*

Economic Review (September 1970), pp.618–30; N. Khalaf, 'Country Size and Economic Instability', *Journal of Development studies* (July 1976), pp.423–8.

15. For conflicting findings see P. Kenen & C. Voivodas, 'Export Instability and Economic Growth', *Kyklos* vol.4, (1972), pp.791–804 and Glezakos, op.cit.

16. P. Wilson, 'Export Instability and Economic Development. Part I', *Warwick Economic Research Paper No.107* (April 1977), pp.34–6.

17. P. Wilson, 'Export Instability and Economic Development. Part II' – *Warwick Economic Research Paper No.111* (May 1977), pp.28–9.

18. See R. Rothstein, *Global Bargaining* (Princeton, NJ: Princeton University Press, 1979) for a replication of their tables and the original sources.

19. Behrman, op.cit., pp.93–5.

20. Behrman, op.cit., pp.102–5.

21. H. O'Neill, *A Common Interest in a Common Fund* (New York: United Nations, 1977), p.13.

22. W. C. Labys, 'Optional Portfolio Analysis of Multicommodity Stocking Agreements', *Oxford Bulletin of Economics and Statistics'* No.3, vol. 29, pp.219–28; Brown, op.cit., pp 112–15.

23. For a discussion of various estimates see Commonwealth Secretariat — 'Comparative study of the estimates of capital requirements for buffer stock financing', *Commonwealth Economic Papers*, No.8, vol.2 (September, 1977), pp. 49–78.

24. See Rothstein, op.cit., pp.88–9, for these and other estimates.

25. For a more extended discussion see Commonwealth Secretariat, 'The Second Window for Other Measures', *Commonwealth Economic Papers*, No.8, vol.2 (September 1977), pp.15–27.

26. Some UNCTAD economists, for example Dr John Cuddy, did have reservations about the organisation's approach.

27. See Rangarajan, op.cit., for a consideration of different types of market structure.

28. When the programme was first announced the suggested coverage was cocoa, coffee, tea, sugar, copper, tin, rubber, jute, cotton and sisal (core commodities) and bananas, bauxite, iron ore, meats, rice, wheat and wool. Resolution 93(IV) which defined the integrated programme set a list of eighteen commodities which became the basis of the negotiations. These were coffee, cocoa, tea, sugar, copper, tin, rubber, cotton, jute and hard fibres (core commodities) and bananas, bauxite, iron ore, meats, manganese, phosphates, tropical timber, vegetable oils and oilseeds.

29. TD/B/C.1/189 — 'An Integrated Programme for Commodities: 'The Impact on Imports Particularly of Developing Countries' (June 1975).

30. See UNCTAD, 'Impact of Integrated Programme for Commodities' (internal memorandum October 1976) reproduced in O'Neill, op.cit., pp.44–8.

31. It was also a very early analysis. Some countries, for example Pakistan and Venezuela, listed as net exporters claimed to be net importers.

32. See F. G. Adams, J. R. Behrman & M. Lasaga, 'Commodity Exports and NIEO Proposals for Buffer Stocks and Compensatory Finance: Implications for Latin America' in W. A. Baer & M. Gillis (eds.), *Export Diversification and the New Protectionism: The Experience of Latin America* (National Bureau of Economic and Business Research: University of Illinois, 1981), pp.48–76, for an analysis which also shows that Latin American countries stood to gain from the UNCTAD scheme.

33. Behrman, op.cit., p.110. This does not in itself mean that the programme would be beneficial. As the previous section showed economists differ in their judgements. One study calculated that only nine members of the G77 were particularly vulnerable to

the fluctuations of international commodity trade — Barbados, Ivory Coast, Jamaica, Malaysia, Sierra Leone, Zambia and Zimbabwe. *House of Lords Select Committee on Commodity Prices* (London: HMSO, May 1977), vol.1, p.xxx.

34. Behrman, op.cit., p.111.
35. Commonwealth Secretariat, 'The Least Developed Countries and the Common Fund', *Commonwealth Economic Papers*, No.8, vol. 2, (September 1977), p.79–91.
36. Ibid. p.83.
37. In India the conflict between the economic ministries, which argued against Indian support for the IPC, and the foreign ministry, which stressed the political value of the Third World coalition, was won by the foreign ministry.
38. See TD/B/498 — 'An Overall Integrated Programme For Commodities' (8 August 1974).
39. See UNGA Resolution 3202 (S-VI), 'Programme of Action on the Establishment of a New International Economic Order' (1 May 1974).
40. See L. Cerrens, 'An Analysis of the UNCTAD Common Fund' (M A thesis, University of Sussex, 1981), pp.24–9; and Brown, op.cit., pp.78–82, for more extensive treatments of the secretariat and the IPC.
41. TDB Resolution 124(XIV), 'New Approaches to International Commodity Problems and Policies' (13 September 1974).
42. See An Integrated Programme for Commodities (TD/B/C.1/166); An Integrated Programme for Commodities: The Role of International Stocks (TD/B/C.1/166/Supp.1); An Integrated Programme for Commodities: A Common Fund for the Financing of Commodity Stocks (TD/B/C.1/166/ Supp.2); An Integrated Programme for Commodities: The Role of Multilateral Commitments in Commodity Trade (TD/B/C.1/166/Supp.3); An Integrated Programme for Commodities: Compensatory Financing of Export Fluctuations in Commodity Trade (TD/B/C.1/166/Supp.4); An Integrated Programme for Commodities: Trade Measures to Expand Processing of Primary Commodities in Developing Countries (TD/B/C.1/166/Supp.5).
43. See OECD, *Development Cooperation Review Annual* (Paris: OECD, 1977–84).
44. TD/B/SR.390 (26 August 1974). Other states adopting a radical position at this time were Ghana, Iraq and Uganda.
45. Argentina, India and Venezuela see TD/B/SR.391 (26 August 1974).
46. Indian spokesmen were not afraid to give public expression to their disquiet concerning the IPC, for example the Indian delegate to the session of the TDB immediately prior to UNCTAD IV argued that 'the impact of the integrated programme on the imports of the developing countries would have to be carefully studied and appropriate measures for neutralising any adverse effects would have to be incorporated as an essential element of the programme'. (TD/B/SR.432 (7 August 1975).)
47. Sauvant, *The Group of 77*, pp.74–85.
48. See K. P. Sauvant, 'Organizational Infrastructure for Self-Reliance: The Non-Aligned Countries and the Group of 77' in H. Kochler (ed.), *The Principles of Non-alignment* (Vienna & London: International Progress Organisation and Third World Centre, 1982), pp.186–218 for a discussion of increased NAM input.
49. See Fourth Conference of Trade Ministers of OAU Member Countries, 'The African Position on Issues Before the Fourth Session of the United Nations Conference on Trade and Development' 77/MM(III)/5 (24 January 1976).
50. See *Jakarta Declaration* 77/MM(III)/6 (24 January 1976).

50. See *Jakarta Declaration* 77/MM(III)/6 (24 January 1976).
51. Declaration and Action Guidelines Adopted by the Latin American Economic System (SELA). Part B, para (i). See 77/MM(III)/49 (7 February 1976).
52. See Progress Report, as at 22 December 1975, on the Work of the Preparatory Committee and Annexes. 77/MM/III/I/Rev.1 in *Collected Documents* vol.II, pp.337–78.
53. *Manila Declaration and Programme of Action*, Section 1.B. para 9. See 77/MM/(III)/49.7 (7 February 1976).
54. TD/B/C.1/193 — 'An Integrated Programme for Commodities. Specific Proposals for Decision and Action by Governments' (28 October 1975).
55. TD/215 — 'Discussion Paper submitted by Group B as a contribution to the work on commodities'.
56. TD/(IV)GC/1 — 'Ways and means of normalising the development of world commodity markets: position paper of socialist countries.
57. *Sunday Times*, 14 May 1976.
58. *Sunday Times*, 16 May 1976.
59. *Proceedings (1976)*, vol.1, p.50.
60. See *Sunday Times* 23 May 1976, where this was outlined as a possibility at the forthcoming OPEC oil ministers conference in Bali.
61. Draft Agreement Establishing the Common Fund For Commodities. TD/IPC/CF/CONF/L.15. The Final Text is contained in Agreement Establishing the Common Fund For Commodities. TD/IPC/CF/CONF/24 (29 July 1980).
62. See particularly the widely divergent views expressed at the first negotiating conference (7 March–2 April 1977). Norway, Sweden and Finland endorsed the CF but the official Group B position seemed to backtrack on Resolution 93(IV) with the CF being seen as one of several approaches. See the Report of the United Nations Negotiating Conference On A Common Fund Under The Integrated Programme For Commodities. TD/IPC/CONF/8 (26 April 1977). Also see Ursula Wasserman, 'The Common Fund', *Journal of World Trade Law* (July–August 1977), pp.377–9.
63. Brown, op.cit., p.119 calculates that actual negotiations between the groups only lasted for a total of sixteen hours.
64. For an opposed view see Rothstein, op.cit., pp.137–8.
65. Consideration of issues relating to the establishment and operation of a common fund: report by the Secretary-General of UNCTAD (TD/B/IPC//CF.2); Common fund: financial requirements (TD/B/IPC/CF/L.2); Common fund: financing of operations other than stocking (TD/B/IPC/CF/L.3); Common fund: capital subscriptions (TD/B/IPC/CF/L.4); Common fund: mode of operations (TD/B/ IPC/CF/L.5); Common fund: decision-making and management TD/B/IPC/CF/L6); Common fund: borrowing by international organisation (TD/B/IPC/CF/L.9).
66. Public deviations from group policy were made by Malta to stress the needs of net importing countries; Colombia in respect of commodities characterised by structural over-production not being suitable for stocking; and Argentina to argue for a link between the CF and international financial institutions allowing a special contribution to made by the OPEC states. Privately a number of divisions surfaced including Brazil's opposition to other measures; the ACP states' interest in second window activities, particularly since they were under the impression that the EEC would trade-off concessions made under the IPC with those under Lomé; the African countries' insistence on a commodity agreement; and the producers of some commodities, especially the Latin American producers who were unwilling to have their

products associated with the IPC. See Brown, op.cit., pp.121–4.

67. 'Elements of an international agreement on the Common Fund. Position paper submitted by Yugoslavia on behalf of the G77', TD/IPC/CF/CONF/L.4 (7 November 1977).

68. Contained in 'Elements for the basis of a Common Fund. Proposal submitted by countries members of Group B' TD/IPC/CF/CONF/L.5 and Add.1 (7 & 17 November 1977) and 'Other Measures', Paper submitted by Group B TD/IPC/CF/CONF/L.6 (14 November 1977).

69. The impression given by James Mayall, 'The Pressures for a New International Commodity Regime' in Goodwin & Mayall, op.cit., p.24, and Rothstein, op.cit., pp.145–6, is that this was a new demand brought forward in November.

70. See, for example, the reservations expressed by the representative of Ecuador at the conclusion of the March 1979 meeting in 'Report of the United Nations Negotiating Conference on a Common Fund under the Integrated Programme for Commodities on its Third Session', TD/IPC/CONF/19 (28 March 1979), para 18.

71. Also important were Hill (Jamaica) and Brilliantes (Philippines). Similar conclusions were arrived at by Cerrens, op.cit., p.43.

72. These negotiations were mainly informal and as such outside the formal negotiating structure. No record, therefore, exists of these discussions. See Cerrens, op.cit., pp.34–58, for an analysis of the negotiations.

73. For an inside view of these negotiations see Alister McIntyre, 'The Current State of International Commodity Negotiations', in G. Goodwin & J. Mayall, *A New International Commodity Regime* (London: Croom Helm, 1980), pp.63–8.

74. See Resolution on 'Fundamental Elements of the Common Fund' in TD/IPC/CF/CONF/19 Annex 1 (28 March 1979) and Agreement Establishing the Common Fund For Commodities. TD/IPC/CF/CONF/24 (29 July 1980).

76. See, for example, the *Arusha Programme for Collective Self-Reliance and Framework for Negotiations* (77/MM/(IV)/21) where members are urged to 'promote joint action in negotiating . . . individual commodities'.

76. See, for example, TD/228 para 12.

77. It is not possible here to develop the myriad problems faced in negotiating commodity agreements. See Rangarajan, op.cit., C. F. Brown, *Primary Commodity Control* (Oxford: Oxford University Press, 1975).

78. 'Comprehensive Report on Progress under Conference Resolution 93(IV)', Report by the Secretary-General of UNCTAD. TD/B/IPC/AC/20 (15 June 1978) para. 12.

79. It is not possible to give these changing trends the statistical treatment they require. See the IBRD's *World Development Reports* and *Annual Reports* 1976–82 and UNCTAD's *World Economic Outlook* 1978–79; 1979–80 and the *Trade and Development Report*, 1981.

8 Conclusion

Management of the international economic order has been a major preoccupation of state policy since 1945. It has become increasingly understood that in an interdependent world the success of national economic policies is dependent on the global economic environment. Efficiency, stability and economic justice are global as much as national concerns. In the quest for national economic growth and development, states have attempted to coordinate and harmonise their economic policies. The liberal international economic regime established at the end of World War II created a particular set of rules and procedures and enshrined a specific set of norms which have exercised a powerful influence on subsequent global economic management. The liberal bias of the Bretton Woods System appeared natural to some but others questioned its applicability to all parts of the international economic system and to changed economic conditions. From the outset the developing countries have mounted a consistent challenge to the postwar international economic regimes. This attempt to reform existing norms, rules and institutions could only be prosecuted on a collective basis since developing countries lack the necessary power to the institute change on an individual basis.

This book has attempted to explain the dynamics of one particular Third World coalition. The research design addressed three central questions. The first set of questions are concerned with coalition formation. Why did the developing countries form a coalition in the United Nations on economic issues? How did the coalition develop over time? A second set of questions related to the effects of organisational characteristics on group behaviour. How does the UNCTAD environment affect the functioning of the coalition? To what extent does the institutionalisation of group procedures affect the maintenance of unity? A final set of questions addresses the development and management of conflict in the group. What are the stresses and strains in the coalition? What are the limits to cooperation? What importance do members attach to the coalition?

The G77 arose from a convergence of economic circumstances, international decision-making structures and ideological factors. The material conditions faced by the developing countries deteriorated during the 1950s. A shared powerlessness in the face of adverse economic conditions provided a basis for cooperation. Allied to this was the absence of effective structures through which the developing countries could attempt to redress their grievances. The institutional lacunae in world trade and payments presented the developing countries with a concrete issue around which they could coalesce. Moreover, the political process in existing institutions with its emphasis on group politics contributed to the emergence of a grouping of developing countries.

These developments were reinforced by the importance given to economic development at the beginning of the 1960s. The creation of the first UN Development Decade ushered in a set of attitudes and expectations favourable to reform of the international political economy. And the theorisation of international resource allocation in terms of developed and developing countries contributed to a perception of the world which stressed the commonality of interests among the so-called Third World. Economic and institutional factors provided the necessary conditions and theory produced the rationale for action. UNCTAD I in 1964 proved a catalytic event. The confrontational aspect of the conference, the desire to create a new institutional mechanism and the possession of a common ideology produced the conditions which were the immediate factors in the creation of the G77.

The initial causes of coalition formation and the persistence of common traits provide only partial answers to questions concerning coalition maintenance. The UNCTAD framework exerted a number of influences on the G77. These can be categorised under two headings — institutional cooperation and issue saliency. Several distinct but interrelated patterns of institutional cooperation affected the growth and functioning of the G77. First, UNCTAD's division along regional lines accentuates the differences between the G77 and Group B and Group D. Moreover, it reinforces the regional basis of G77 politics. Secondly, the extension of UNCTAD's sphere of activity created both opportunities for increased South–South diplomatic cooperation and North–South discord. Furthermore the dispute over UNCTAD's competence provides a unifying issue for the G77. Thirdly, the development of consensual patterns of decision-making in UNCTAD increased the importance of individual states in their respective regional groups with the result that it becomes relatively easy to mask disagreement in some acceptable form of words rather than accentuate intra-group conflict through the resort to voting. Fourthly, the UNCTAD secretariat, an important actor in the G77's decision-making process, tends to stress cooperative strategies.

The saliency of issues discussed in UNCTAD has a two-fold effect on the G77. UNCTAD has been in the forefront of development diplomacy and global reform efforts. The centrality of the issues discussed in UNCTAD, in the absence of meaningful reform initiatives in other fora, tends to make LDC governments more receptive to intra-group compromise. Failure to reach intra-group agreement on a key issue would most likely weaken the G77's bargaining position on other issues. On the other hand, compromise is inhibited when rejection or acceptance of a particular principle is seemingly tied to quantifiable costs and benefits, for example the individual commodity negotiations under the IPC.

The G77 can be termed an informal, formal coalition. The evidence presented above shows that it has developed a high level of institutionalisation. The group has developed a number of procedures over time which respond creatively to the stresses and strains experienced by the membership. G77 sub-groups and decision-making procedures preserve the continued existence of the group. Indeed, a stable pattern of behaviour developed historically and this deepens the commitment of member states to the organisation and its goals. The reproduction of the regional group, the basic organisational unit of the G77, at all levels of G77 structure and decision-making provides both an element of continuity and a base upon which innovations can be launched. The absence of a secretariat has not in any significant way hindered the growth of cooperation. Its main effect has been a lack of preparedness and lack of focus to G77 negotiating positions. I think that a secretariat would induce an element of rigidty into G77 politics and would therefore be detrimental to the stability of the coalition. The consensus method of decision making in preserving the autonomy of member states provides the sole basis upon which continued support for the organisation's goals can be maintained. Any form of majoritarianism would most likely lead disaffected minorities to withdraw from the coalition.

The case-studies present important evidence and conclusions with respect to the nature and functioning of the G77 in UNCTAD. First, both the GSP and the IPC emerged from the immediate context of North–South relations and seemed the most feasible issues on which to press for change.[1] Promotion of the GSP came on the heels of a GATT discussion of the manufactured exports of the LDCs and in the face of stern opposition to changes in commodity markets. The IPC emerged in the wake of producer power and high hopes for serious negotiations on international commodity policy.[2] Both sets of negotiations developed so that it became impossible to retreat once it had become clear that the hoped for gains would not materialise. To a large extent this is a result of the G77's decision-making process. The cumbersome nature of G77 decision making invests the 'final' group agreement with almost sacrosanct status. No party is willing to unravel the agreement in the hope of finding a better one. And no sectional interest having fought for so long to reach an agreement is prepared to admit that the objective is now of limited appeal. Both case-studies also reveal the mutuality of interest between the G77 and the UNCTAD secretariat in the shaping of G77 demands. A mutuality of interest exists between some members of the G77 and the secretariat but of equal significance are divergencies between the secretariat and other members. It should also be noted that both the GSP and the IPC originated in the UNCTAD secretariat.

It is difficult to assess to what extent the negotiations constituted a learning process for the G77. Undoubtedly the early disagreements over the GSP led to the beginnings of the present organisational structure. On the other hand, it seems that developments have been unplanned and arise to meet specific needs. The CF negotiations were less divisive for group unity than the GSP mainly because the plethora of sub-groups provided avenues through which conflict resolution could be sought. The decision not to attempt to seek group unity with respect to the individual commodity negotiations represented not only a sensible policy in the circumstances but can also be seen as part of a learning process. The

G77 negoitiators, however, seemingly pay very little attention to the political pressures attendant on the governments of the industrialised states. G77 negotiators make only minimal reference to the constraints affecting Group B decision makers. A more sophisticated awareness of the formulation of foreign economic policy in the West would improve the G77's negotiating strategy.

The ability of the G77 to effect regime change is affected by the wider global political economy. NIEO discussions have been effectively shelved since the Cancun summit in 1981. With the advent of the Reagan administration the United States assumed a hardline approach which was even less conducive to the North–South dialogue than any of its predecessors. The importance of the United States in negotiating and implementing change creates a situation where other leading states are unlikely to push ahead with reform efforts when the United States is opposed. The onset of global recession focused attention on the industrialised economies and despite attempts, for example the Brandt Commission reports, to stimulate discussions, North–South issues have been side-stepped. Moreover, the onset of the debt crisis and the favoured solutions to debt problems have tended to marginalise UNCTAD. UNCTAD's approach to trade and development issues fits less easily with the current 'realities' and it lacks the organisational capacity to provide resources to tackle the debt problems of the developing countries. In other words UNCTAD became increasingly marginal to the Third World in the 1980s since it seems to lack both the intellectual and material resources to combat the key economic problems which they face.

The evidence suggests that the G77 is likely to survive the current malaise. Attempts at international regime change by the Third World are likely to become important issues again in the future. The decline of UNCTAD has not been matched by similar declines in other fora in which the G77 is active. And in so far as UNCTAD retains a central role in development diplomacy the G77 is likely once again to play a vital role. The coalition will be maintained as long as international inequality gives rise to collective attempts by the poor to reform the international economic order. It is, however, likely that the demise of UNCTAD, its central organisational focus, would probably lead to the demise of the G77.

In many respects this is a study in international political cooperation. The analysis shows that the G77 represents a diplomatic unity of the developing countries with clearly defined limits. The global political process creates the conditions whereby such an organisation can exist. The G77 as a pressure group is an outgrowth of global institutional politics and fulfils a role within the prevailing structural distribution of power. Access to the sources of power are denied to poor states and global reform initiatives can only be initiated by weak states in so far as they seek strength in numbers. The power of the coalition arises from its ability to set (or at least contribute to the setting of) the agenda rather than an ability to determine outcomes. Majoritarianism in the UN system gives the Third World the opportunity to present demands for change. Given the diversity within the coalition these demands are likely to be all-encompassing ones. Is it surprising that among the plethora of demands, few if any will benefit all states? The key to the coalition lies in its ability to satisfy the demands of a large number of its members, in stressing commonality but accepting diversity.

Our research has shown that an important reason for the continued existence of the coalition resides in the relative costs of remaining a member. First, it has yet to be demonstrated successfully that member states would benefit materially from leaving the G77. Rhetoric on this argument is not the same as convincing argument. Secondly, in respect of both the GSP and IPC we have shown that member governments have not been constrained by coalition membership from pursuing individualistic policies which conflict with the commonly agreed goals and strategy. The effective policing of members is therefore very low. This coupled with the low level of sanctions available for use against deviants means that membership of the G77 need not deter states from pursuing national policies in contexts where these conflict with agreed G77 policy objectives. The resulting lack of importance attached to G77 decisions in a curious way contributes to its continued existence. The G77 is not a coalition founded on individual self-interest, neither is it a group of states characterised by international and domestic weakness seeking power and control in the international system.[3] It is an anti-hegemonic coalition seeking regime change. It is an outgrowth of international politics and the functioning of the postwar international organisational network.

Notes

1. Rothstein R. L., *Global Bargaining* (Princeton, NJ: Princeton University Press, 1979a), persistently and in my view mistakenly criticises the UNCTAD secretariat for pushing the IPC to the centre of the stage. I am not referring to his criticism of the IPC as a negotiating strategy but to the assumption that commodity trade *per se* was the wrong area in which to apply pressure.
2. See J. A. Finlayson & M. W. Zacher, *Managing International Markets* (New York: Columbia University Press, 1988), for an analysis which pays careful attention to the genesis of the demands for reform of commodity markets which culminated in the IPC.
3. See S. D. Krasner, *Structural Conflict* (Berkeley: University of California Press, 1985).

Select bibliography

Primary sources

(a) UNCTAD documents

Proceedings of the United Nations Conference on Trade and Development, First Session, Geneva 1964 (8 vols.).

Proceedings of the United Nations Conference on Trade and Development, Second Session, New Delhi 1968 (5 vols.).

Proceedings of the United Nations Conference on Trade and Development, Third Session, Santiago 1972 (4 vols.).

Proceedings of the United Nations Conference on Trade and Development, Fourth Session, Nairobi 1976 (3 vols.).

Proceedings of the United Nations Conference on Trade and Development, Fifth Session, Manila 1979 (3 vols.).

Proceedings of the United Nations Conference on Trade and Development, Sixth Session, Belgrade 1983 (2 vols.).

Report by the United Nations Conference on Trade and Development on its Seventh Session, Geneva 1987.

Official Records of the Trade and Development Board (1965–88)

Summary Records of the Trade and Development Board (1965–88)

Reports of the Committee on Commodities (1965– 88).

Reports of the Committeee on Manufactures (1965–88).

Reports of the Committee on Invisibles and Financing related to Trade (1965–88).

Reports of the Committee on Shipping (1965–88).

Report of the Group on Preferences on its First Session. TD/B/C.2/15.

Report of the Group on Preferences on its Second Session. TD/B/C.2/38.

Report on the Special Committee on Preferences(SCP). TD/B/C.2/1.

Report of the SCP, First Session. TD/OR/8.Supp.4.

Report of the SCP, Second Session. TD/OR/9.Supp.4.

Report of the SCP, Third Session. TD/B/262.

Report of the SCP, Fourth Session, 1st. Part. TD/B/300.

Report of the SCP, Fourth Session, 2nd. Part. TD/B/329.

Preferences: review of discusions. TD/B/AC.1/1.

The problem of special preferences. TD/16/Supp.1 and Add.1.

Substantive Documentation on the Generalised System of Preferences. TD/B/ AC.5/24; TD/B/AC.5/34.

The Generalised System of Preferences (GSP). TD/124 and Add.1.

Schemes of Generalised System of Preferences implemented by preference giving countries. TD/B/373 Add.1–10; TD/B/378 Add.1–5.

An Overall Integrated Programme for Commodities. TD/B/498.

An Integrated Programme for Commodities (Dec. 1974). TD/B/C.1/166 and Supp.5.

An Integrated Programme for Commodities: A Common Fund for the financing of common stocks: amounts, terms and prospective sources of finance. TD/ B/C.1/184.

An Integrated Programme for Commodities: The impact on imports particularly of developing countries. TD/B/C.1/189.

An Integrated Programme for Commodities: Specific proposals for decision and action by governments. TD/B/C.1/193.

An Integrated Programme for Commodities (Oct. 1975).TD/B/C.1/194-197.

Reports of the Preparatory Meetings for the Negotiation of a Common Fund. TD/B/IPC/4; TD/B/IPC/6; TD/B/IPC/8.

Common Fund: Various Requirements (Dec. 1976). TD/B/IPC/CF/L.2-6 & 9.

Draft Report of the United Nations Negotiating Conference on a Common Fund under the Integrated Programme for Commodities. TD/IPC/CONF/L.7 and Add.2.

Draft Agreement Establishing the Common Fund for Commodities. TD/IPC/ CF/CONF/L.15.

Reports of the United Nations Negotiating Conference on a Common Fund under the Integrated Programme for Commodities. TD/B/IPC/CF/ CONF/8; 14 (Parts I & III); 19; 26.

Agreement Establishing the Common Fund for Commodities. TD/IPC/CF/ CONF/24.

Progress Report under Conference Resolution 93(IV). TD/B/IPC/AC/34 (Sept.1980).

Towards a new trade strategy for development. Report by the Secretary-General of the Conference. E/CONF.46/3. (1964).

Towards a global strategy of development. Report by the Secretary-General. TD/3/Rev.1 (1968).

New directions and new structures for trade and development. Report by the Secretary-General of UNCTAD to the Conference. TD/183 (1976).

Restructuring the international economic framework. Report by the Secretary-General of UNCTAD to the Conference. TD/221 (1979).

Charter of Algiers (TD/38).

Manila Declaration and Programme of Action (TD/195).

Arusha Programmme for Collective Self-Reliance and Framework for Negotiations (TD/236).

(b) Other sources

United Nations — Official Records of the General Assembly (1960–1988).
United Nations — Official Records of the Economic and Social Council (1960–1988).
Sauvant, K. P. (ed.), *The Collected Documents of the Group of 77* (6 vols.) New York: Oceana Publications, 1981.
Sauvant K. P and Miller T. W (eds), *The Collected Documents of the Group of 77* (vols VII–IX) New York: Oceana Publications 1989.

Secondary sources

(a) Books

Adams, F. G., Behrman, J. R. & Lasaga, M, 'Commodity Exports and NIEO Proposals for Buffer Stocks and Compensatory Finance: Implications for Latin America' in W. A. Baer & M. Gillis (eds), *Export Diversification and the New Protectionism: The Experience of Latin America.* National Bureau of Economic and Business Research, University of Illinois, 1981, pp.48–76.
Alger, C. F., 'Personal Contact in Intergovernmental Organizations' in H. G. Kelman (ed.), *International Behaviour.* New York: Holt, Rinehart & Winston, 1965, pp.521–547.
Anell, L. & Nygren, B., *The Developing Countries and the World Economic Order.* London: Frances Pinter, 1980.
Asher, R. E. *et al.*, *The United Nations and the Promotion of the General Welfare.* Washington, DC: The Brookings Institution, 1957.
Bairoch, P., *The Economic Development of the Third World since 1900.* London: Methuen, 1975.
Balassa, B., *Trade Prospects for Developing Countries.* New York: Richard D. Irwin, 1964.
Barry, B. (ed.), *Power and Political Theory.* London: John Wiley, 1976.
Behrman, J. R., *Development, the International Economic Order and Commodity Agreements.* Reading, Mass.: Addison-Wesley, 1978.
Black, E., *The Diplomacy of Economic Development.* Cambridge, Mass.: Harvard University Press, 1960.
Bloch, H. S., *The Challenge of the World Trade Conference.* Columbia University Occasional Paper, 1964–65.
Brown, C. P., *Primary Commodity Control.* London: Oxford University Press, 1975.
   The Political and Social Economy of Commodity Control. London: Macmillan, 1980.
Calleo, D. P, & Rowland, B. M., *America and the World Political Economy.* Bloomington: Indiana University Press, 1974.
Cline, W. R. & Delgado, E. (eds), *Economic Integration in Central America.*

Washington, DC: The Brookings Institution, 1978.

Commonwealth Secretariat, *Commonwealth Economic Papers No.8* London, September 1977.

Coppock, J. D., *International Economic Instability.* New York: McGraw-Hill, 1962.

Cordovez, D., *UNCTAD and Development Diplomacy.* Journal of World Trade Law, 1972.

Cox, R. W. & Jacobson, H. K. (eds.), *The Anatomy of Influence.* New Haven, Conn.: Yale University Press, 1973.

Curzon, G., *Multilateral Commercial Diplomacy.* London: Michael Joseph, 1965.

Cutajar, M. Z. (ed.), *UNCTAD and the North–South Dialogue.* Oxford: Pergamon Press, 1985.

Dam, K., *The Gatt: Law and International Economic Organization.* University of Chicago Press, 1970.

Farley, L. T., *Change Processes in International Organizations.* Cambridge, Mass.: Schenkman, 1981.

Finlayson, J. A. & Zacher, M. W., *Managing International Markets.* New York: Columbia University Press 1988).

Friedeberg, A. S., *The United Nations Conference on Trade and Development of 1964.* Universitaire Pers Rotterdam, 1968.

Friedman, J. R. *et al.* (eds), *Alliance in International Politics.* Boston: Allyn & Bacon, 1970.

Gardner, R. N., *Sterling–Dollar Diplomacy.* London: Oxford University Press, 1958.

GATT, *Trends in International Trade. Report by a Panel of Experts* Geneva, 1958.

GATT, *The Role of GATT in Relation to Trade and Develpoment.* Geneva, 1964.

Gauhar, A. (ed.), *Regional Integration: The Latin American Experience.* London: The Third World Foundation, 1985.

Goodwin, G. & Mayall, J. (eds), *A New International Commodity Regime.* London: Croom Helm, 1980.

Gosovic, B., *UNCTAD: Conflict and Compromise.* Leyden: A. W. Sitjhoff, 1971.

Haas, E. B., Beyond the Nation-State. Palo Alto Calif.: Stanford University Press, 1964.

Hadwen, J. G. & Kaufmann, J., *How United Nations Decisions Are Made.* Leyden: A. W. Sitjhoff, 1960.

Hall, K. 'Technical Assistance and Organisational Support for Developing Countries in International Economic Negotiations: A Report' in *The Group of 77: Strengthening Its Negotiating Capacity* (Nyon: Third World Forum, 1979).

Hansen, R. D. *Beyond the North–South Stalemate.* New York: McGraw-Hill, 1979.

Hill, M., *The United Nations System.* Cambridge: Cambridge University Press, 1978.

Hovet, T., *Bloc Politics in the United Nations.* Cambridge, Mass.: Harvard University Press, 1960.

Howard, M., *War and the Liberal Conscience.* London: Maurice Temple Smith, 1978.

IBRD, *Commodity Trade and Price Trends.* Washington, DC, 1975.

IBRD, *World Development Reports, 1976–84.* Washington, DC, 1976–84.

Isaacs, J. C., *Power and Marxist Theory.* Ithaca, NY: Cornell University Press, 1987.

Johnson, H. G., *Economic Policies Towards Less Developed Countries* London: George allen & Unwin, 1967.

Jütte, R. & Grosse-Jütte, A. (eds), *The Future of International Organization.* London: Frances Pinter, 1981.

Kaufmann, J., *Conference Diplomacy.* Leyden: A. W. Sitjhoff, 1968.

Kenwood, A. G. & Lougheed, A. L., *The Growth of the International Economy.* London: George Allen & Unwin, 1971.

Kim, S., *China, the United Nations and World Order.* Princeton, NJ: Princeton University Press, 1979.

Kirdar, U., *The Structure of United Nations Economic Aid to Underdeveloped Countries.* The Hague: Martinus Nijhoff, 1966.

Knudsen, O. & Parnes, A., *Trade Instability and Economic Development.* Lexington, Mass.: D.C. Heath, 1975.

Kochler, H., (ed.), *The Principles of Non-Alignment.* Vienna &London: International Progress Organisation and Third World Centre, 1982.

Kolko, G., *The Politics of War.* New York: Vintage Books, 1970.

Koul, A. K., *The Legal Framework of UNCTAD in World Trade.* Leyden: A. W. Sitjhoff, 1977.

Krasner, S. D. (ed.), *International Regimes.* Ithaca, NY: Cornell University Press, 1983.

Little, I. M. D., *Economic Development.* New York: Basic Books, 1982.

Lukes, S., *Power: A Radical View,* London: Macmillan, 1974.

MacBean, A., *Export Instability and Economic Development.* London: George Allen & Unwin, 1966.

Milenky, E. S., *The Politics of Regional Organization in Latin America.* New York: Praeger, 1973.

Mitchell, C. R., *The Structure of International Conflict.* London: Macmillan, 1981.

Mortimer, R. A. *The Third World Coalition in World Politics.* NewYork: Praeger, 1980.

Morton, K. & Tulloch, T. *Trade and Developing Countries.* London: Croom Helm, 1977.

Murray, T., *Trade Preferences for Developing Countries.* London: Macmillan, 1977.

Nicholson, M., *Conflict Analysis.* London: The English Universities Press, 1968.

Ogley, R. C., *The United Nations and East–West Relations 1945–1971.* ISIO Monograph, University of Sussex, 1972.

Olson, M., *The Logic of Collective Action.* New York: Schoken, 1968.

O'Neill, H., *A Common Interest in a Common Fund.* New York: United Nations, 1977.

Patterson, G., *Discrimination in International Trade.* Princeton, NJ: Princeton University Press, 1966.

Pincus, J., *Trade, Aid and Development.* New York: McGraw-Hill, 1967.

Rae, D. W. & Taylor, M., *The Analysis of Political Cleavages*. New Haven, Conn.: Yale University Press, 1970.

Rangarajan, L. N., *Commodity Conflict*. London: Croom Helm, 1978.

Riker, W., *The Theory of Political Coalitions*. New Haven, Conn.: Yale University Press, 1962.

Robertson, C. L., 'The Creation of UNCTAD' in R. W. Cox (ed.), *International Organisation: World Politics*. London: Macmillan, 1969, pp.258–74.

Rothstein, R. L. *Global Bargaining*. Princeton, NJ: Princeton University Press, 1979.

Sauvant, K. P., *The Group of 77*. New York: Oceana Publications, 1981.
    (ed.), *Changing Priorities on the International Agenda*. Oxford: Pergamon, 1981.

Sewell, J. P., *UNESCO and World Politics*. Princeton, NJ: Princeton University Press, 1975.

Thoburn, J. T., *Primary Commodity Exports and Economic Development*. London: John Wiley, 1977.

Thomas, J. M. & Bennis, W. G. (eds), *Management of Change and Conflict*. Harmondsworth: Penguin Books, 1972.

Tulloch, P., *The Politics of Preferences*. London: Croom Helm, 1975.

Ul Haq, M., *The Poverty Curtain*. New York: Columbia University Press, 1973.

Walton, R. E. & McKersie, R. B., *A Behavioural Theory of Labor Negotiations*. New York: McGraw-Hill, 1965.

Warr, P., *Psychology and Collective Bargaining*. London: Hutchinson, 1973.

Weintraub, S., *Trade Preferences for Less Developed Countries*. New York: Praeger, 1967.

Weiss, T. G., *Multilateral Development Diplomacy in UNCTAD*. London: Macmillan, 1986.
    & Jennings, A., *More for the Least? Prospects for Poorest Countries in the Eighties*. Lexington, Mass.: D. C. Heath, 1983.

Wilcox, C., *A Charter for World Trade*. New York: Macmillan, 1949.

Wilgress, E. D., *A New Attempt at Internationalism. The International Trade Conferences and the Charter. A study of ends and means*. Paris: Société d'édition d'enseigment supérieur, 1949.

Williams, G., *Third World Political Organizations*. London: Frances Pinter, 1981.

Wilson, P., *Export Instability and Economic Development*. Warwick Economic Research Papers Nos. 107 & 111, 1977.

(b) Articles

Agor, W. A. 'Latin American Inter-State Politics: Patterns of Cooperation and Conflict', *Inter-American Economic Affairs* (Autumn 1972), pp.19–33.

Baldwin, R. E. & Murray, T. 'MFN Tariff Reductions and Developing Country Trade Benefits Under the GSP', *Economic Journal* (March 1977), pp.30–46.

Bhattacharya, A. K., 'The Influence of the International Secretariat: UNCTAD and

Generalised Tariff Preferences', *International Organization* (Winter 1976), pp.75–90.

Colson, J-P. 'Le Groupe des 77 et le probleme de l'unité des pays du tiers monde', *Revue Tiers Monde* (October–December 1972), pp.813–30.

Cordovez, D. 'The Making of UNCTAD', *Journal of World Trade Law* (May:June 1967), pp.243–328.

Erb, G. F. & Schiavo-Campo, S. 'Export Instability, Levels of Development and Economic Size of Less Developed Countries', *Bulletin, Oxford University Institute of Economics and Statistics* (November, 1969), pp.263–83.

Fawcett, J., 'International Trade Organisation', *British Yearbook of International Law* (1947), pp.376–82.

Flanders, M. J. 'Prebisch on Protectionism: An Evaluation', *Economic Journal* (June 1964), pp.305–26.

Frank, I. 'Aid, Trade and Economic Development: Issues Before the U.N. Conference', *Foreign Affairs* (January 1964), pp.210– 26.

Gardner, R. N. 'The United Nations Conference on Trade and Development', *International Organization* (Winter 1968), pp.99–130.

Geldart, C. & Lyons, P. 'The Group of 77: A Perspective View', *International Affairs* (Winter 1980–81), pp.79–101.

Glezakos, C., 'Export Instability and Economic Growth: A Statistical Verification', *Economic Development and Cultural Change* (July 1973), pp.670–8.

Goodwin, G. L. 'The United Nations Conference on Trade and Development', *Yearbook of World Affairs* (1965), pp.1–25.

Gosovic, B., 'UNCTAD: North–South Encounter', *International Conciliation* (May 1968), pp.1–80.

Head, J. G., 'Public Goods and Public Policy', *Public Finance* (1962), pp. 197–219.

Hindley, B., 'The UNCTAD Agreement on Preferences', *Journal of World Trade Law* (November–December 1971), pp.694–702.

Howell, D., 'Failure at UNCTAD II — Divided Rich and Embittered Poor', *Round Table* (July 1968).

Iida, K., 'Third World Solidarity: The Group of 77 in the UN General Assembly', *International Organization* (Spring 1988), pp. 375–95.

Iqbal, Z., 'The GSP Examined', *Finance and Development* (September 1975), pp.34–39.

Kenen, P. & Voivodos, C. 'Export Instability and Economic Growth', *Kyklos* (1972), pp.791–804.

Keohane, R. O. 'Reciprocity in International Relations', *International Organization* (Winter 1986), pp.1–27.

Khalaf, N., 'Country Size and Economic Instability', *Journal of Development Studies* (July 1976), pp.423–8.

Kratochwil, F. & Ruggie, J. G. 'International Organization: A State of the Art on the Art of the State', *International Organization* (Autumn 1986), pp.753–75.

Krishnamurti, R., 'The Agreement on Preferences: A Generalised System in Favour of Developing Countries', *Journal of World Trade Law* (January–

February 1971), pp.45–60.

Lamond, A., 'UNCTAD's Twenty Years of Pioneering Efforts in Trade and Development', *IDS Bulletin* (July 1984), pp.4–6.

Lavichenko, M. & Ornatsky, I., 'World Trade Conference: Barometer of Inter-state Relations', *International Affairs* (Moscow) (January 1964), pp.62–8.

Lijphart, A., 'The Analysis of Bloc Voting in the General Assembly: a critique and a proposal', *American Political Science Review* (December 1963), pp.902–17.

Massell, B. F. 'Export Concentration and Fluctuations in Export Earnings', *American Economic Review* (March 1964), pp.47–63.
   'Export Instability and Economic Structure' *American Economic Review* (September 1970), pp.618–30.

Metzer, S.D., 'Developments in the Law and Institutions of International Economic Relations. UNCTAD.' *American Journal of International Law* (July 1967), pp.756–75.

Miles, C., 'Trade and Aid: the second UNCTAD', *World Today* (July 1968), pp.64–71.

Naya, S., 'Fluctuations in Export Earnings and Economic Pattern of Asian Countries', *Economic Development and Cultural Change* (July 1973), pp.629–41.

Ogley, R. C. 'Towards a General Theory of International Organisation', *International Relations* (1969), pp.599–619.

Olson, M. & Zeckhauser, R., 'An Economic Theory of Alliances', *Review of Economics and Statistics* (August 1966), pp.266–79.

Pinegin, B., 'Unsolved Problems of World Trade', *International Affairs* (Moscow) (January 1964), pp.69–73.

Prebisch, R., 'The Role of Commercial Policies in Underdeveloped Countries', *American Economic Review, Papers and Proceedings* (May 1959), pp.215–73.

Ruggie, J. G. 'International Regimes, Transactions and Change: Embedded Liberalism in the Post War Economic Order', *International Organization* (Winter 1982), pp.379–415.

Schmitter, P., 'Three Neo-Functional Hypotheses About International Integration,, *International Organization* (Winter 1969), pp.161–6.

Singer, H. W., 'The Distribution of Gains Between Investing and Borrowing Countries', *American Economic Review, Papers and Proceedings* (May 1950), pp.473–85.

Smyth, D. C., 'The Global Economy and the Third World: Coalition or Cleavage?', *World Politics* (July 1977), pp.584–610.

Spraos, J., 'The Statistical Debate on the Net Barter Terms of Trade between Primary Commodities and Manufactures', *Economic Journal* (1980), pp.107–28.

Subhan, M., 'The Confrontation between Developed and Developing Countries in the UNCTAD', *Revue du Sud-est Asiatique* (1966), pp.219–36.

Sundar Rajan, K.S., 'Tariff Preferences and Developing Countries' *Proceedings of the American Society of International Law* (1966), pp.86–93.

Weintraub, S., 'After the U.N. Trade Conference: Lessons and Portents',

Foreign Affairs (October 1964), pp.37–50.

Williams, M. A. 'The Group of 77, UNCTAD V and the North–South Dialogue', *IDS Bulletin* (January 1980), pp.5–8.

(c) Unpublished dissertations

Ansari, J. A., 'UNCTAD: Objectives and Performance, 1964–1976' (D.Phil, University of Sussex, 1983).

Cerrens, L., 'An Analysis of the UNCTAD Common Fund' (M.A., University of Sussex 1981).

Lancaster, C. J. 'The Politics of the Powerless: Pressures In The United Nations For Economic Development, 1945–1965, (Ph.D University of London, 1972).

(d) Newspapers and annual publications

The Economist (London)
Far Eastern Economic Review (Hong Kong), vols. XLV–LVIII.
The Guardian (London)
The Observer (London)
The Sunday Times (London)
The Times (London)
UN Yearbook of International Trade Statistics (New York)
UN Statistical Yearbook (New York)
UNCTAD Monthly Bulletin (Geneva)

Index